NINJA FOODI

Smart XL Grill

Cookbook for Beginners

Simple, Delicious, and Low-Budget Ninja Foodi Smart XL Grill Recipes to

Grill, Air Crisp, Roast, Bake, Broil and Dehydrate

D1567643

Sona Boissonneault

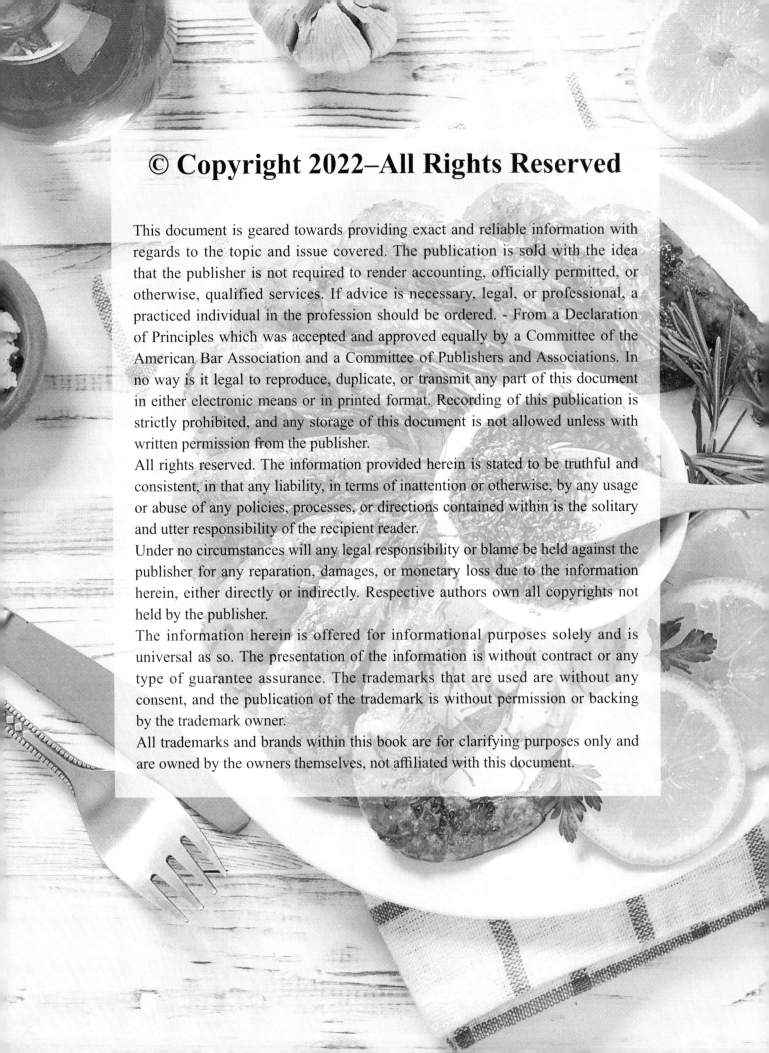

TABLE OF CONTENTS

Introduction

The Ninja Foodi Smart XL Grill is a unique product that allows you to grill your food indoors. It has a smokeless grill system which means you can enjoy the flavor of grilled food without the smoke. The grill also has a sear function that allows you to sear your food to lock in the flavor. The grill is also large enough to cook for a family or a group of friends. The Ninja Foodi Smart XL Grill is one of the most popular appliances on the market. And for good reason! This grill is amazing! It can cook food to perfection and it is so versatile. You can use it to grill, bake, roast, and even air fry! The Ninja Foodi Smart XL Grill Cookbook is the perfect guide to help you get the most out of your grill. This cookbook is packed with recipes that are easy to follow and will have you grilling like a pro in no time! So, whether you are a beginner or a seasoned pro, the Ninja Foodi Smart XL Grill Cookbook is a must-have for anyone who owns a Ninja Foodi Smart XL Grill. We need the Ninja Foodi Smart XL Grill because it is a 6-in-1 indoor grill. It also has a 6-quart capacity, making it large enough to feed a family of four. Plus, the Ninja Foodi Smart XL Grill is smart enough to know how to cook your food to perfection, thanks to its temperature probe.

One of the best things about the Ninja Foodi Smart XL Grill is its versatility. Not only can you use it as a traditional grill, but you can also use it as a smoker, roaster, and even oven. This means that you can cook just about anything you want on this grill, and you don't have to worry about having multiple grills or smokers taking up space in your backyard. Another great thing about the Ninja Foodi Smart XL Grill is its size. This grill is big enough to accommodate a family of four, but it's still compact enough to fit on most patios or decks. This makes it the perfect grill for those who want to be able to cook for a large group but don't have the space for a full-sized grill. If you're looking for a grill that is both versatile and easy to use, then you need to check out the Ninja Foodi Smart XL Grill. If you're a fan of the Ninja Foodi Grill, then you'll love the new Ninja Foodi Smart XL Grill Cookbook. This cookbook is packed with recipes specifically designed for the Ninja Foodi Grill, so you can get the most out of your grill.

What is Ninja Foodi Smart XL Grill?

The Ninja Foodi Smart XL grill is a high-tech indoor grill that allows you to cook your food to perfection. This grill features a smart cooking system that monitors and adjusts the temperature of the grill to ensure that your food is cooked evenly.

When it comes to grilling, the Ninja Foodi Smart XL Grill is in a league of its own. This grill is packed with features that make it the perfect choice for those who love to entertain. The Smart XL Grill has five stainless steel burners that provide even heat across the

entire grilling surface. The grill also has a sear zone that gets hot enough to sear meats and vegetables. The Ninja Foodi Smart XL Grill also has a smart temperature control system that allows you to set the perfect temperature for your food. The grill will then automatically adjust the flame to maintain that temperature. The grill also has a LED control panel that makes it easy to see what temperature the grill is at. The control panel also has a timer so you can keep track of your food. The Ninja Foodi Smart XL Grill also comes with a side burner that is perfect for cooking sides or sauces. The side burner has temperature control so you can cook easily.

If you're looking for a top-of-the-line indoor grill that can do it all, the Ninja Foodi Smart XL Grill is the one for you. This grill has incredible features that make it a must-have for any home cook.

Here are just a few of the reasons why we love the Ninja Foodi Smart XL Grill:

- It's a true multi-user. The Ninja Foodi Smart XL Grill can do it all. Whether you want to grill, air fry, bake, or roast, this grill can do it all. It's the perfect grill for those who want to make the most of their indoor cooking space. Also, it's big enough to feed a crowd. With its large cooking surface, you can easily cook for a group of people.
- The Ninja Foodi Smart XL Grill is a versatile indoor grill that can do it all. With its innovative Smart Cook

System, the Ninja Foodi Smart XL Grill can grill, sear, bake, roast, and air fry all your favorite foods. The secret to the Ninja Foodi Smart XL Grill's success is its unique Cyclonic Grilling Technology. This technology uses a powerful airflow system to circulate heat evenly across the grill's cooking surface, resulting in perfectly cooked food every time.

- In addition to its incredible cooking performance, the Ninja Foodi Smart XL Grill also comes with a host of other features that make it the perfect choice for any grilling enthusiast. For example, the grill's digital display makes it easy to keep track of cooking times and temperatures. And if that wasn't enough, the Ninja Foodi Smart XL Grill also comes with a built-in temperature probe.

- In short, this grill has plenty of features that make it a standout option, including its ability to sear, its six-in-one cooking capabilities, and its Ninja Foodi Smart Cook System. Whether you're grilling up a steak or making a delicious pizza, the Ninja Foodi Smart XL Grill is up to the task.

Benefits of Using Ninja Foodi Smart XL Grill:

When it comes to grilling, many people think that they need to go out and buy a separate grill. However, with the Ninja Foodi Smart XL Grill, you can do it all in one appliance. The Ninja Foodi Smart XL Grill is a 6-in-1 indoor grill that allows you to grill, air crisp, roast, bake, broil and dehydrate all in one appliance. It also has a smart temperature control that allows you to set the grill to your desired temperature and the grill will do the rest. The grill also has a sear function that allows you to get that perfect sear on your food. The Ninja Foodi Smart XL Grill is a great appliance for those who love to grill but don't want to deal with the hassle of a separate grill.

While grilling, you need good weather, good company, and of course, a great grill. If you're looking for a grill that will make your cookouts the talk of the town, then you need the Ninja Foodi Smart XL Grill. This grill is perfect for those who love to entertain, as it can accommodate a large amount of food. It also has a ton of features that make grilling easier than ever, such as temperature control and a self-cleaning function.

One of the best things about the Ninja Foodi Smart XL Grill is that it comes with a searing function. This means that you can get those perfect grill marks on your food, without having to worry about overcooking it. Another great feature of this grill is the even heat distribution. This ensures that your food will be cooked evenly. As the name suggests, the Ninja Foodi Smart XL Grill is a smart grill that has been designed to make your grilling experience easier and more enjoyable.

If you're looking for a high-quality, durable, and versatile grill, the Ninja Foodi Smart XL Grill is a great option. Here are some of the benefits of using this grill

- This grill is very durable. It is made from high-quality materials, so it's built to last and it can withstand the wear and tear of grilling.

- This grill is versatile and can be used to cook a variety of foods. You can use it to grill meats, vegetables, and even pizzas

- The grill is very easy to clean. You can just wipe it down with a damp cloth after each use.

- The Ninja Foodi Smart XL Grill is easy to use, so you can get started grilling right away. You just need to plug it in and it will be ready to use.

- This grill is a great option for those who want to save space, as

it's compact and easy to store.
- The Ninja Foodi Smart XL Grill is a great value for the money, as it's a high-quality grill that's affordable.

Step by Step Using Ninja Foodi Smart XL Grill

The Smart XL Grill also comes with a recipe book, so you can get started cooking right away.

Grilling

Grilling is a great way to cook food and Ninja Foodi Smart XL Grill makes it even better. This grill is super easy to use and comes with some great features. For one, it has a built-in temperature gauge so you can grill your food to perfection. And if you're worried about flare-ups, don't be. This grill has a special flare-up prevention feature. So go ahead and fire up the grill. Your food will thank you.
- Choose your protein. Whether you're grilling chicken, steak, fish, or vegetables, make sure to pick a high-quality option.
- Preheat your grill. Turn on the Ninja Foodi grill and set it to the appropriate temperature for your protein.
- Season your protein. Before placing it on the grill, make sure to season your protein with salt, pepper, and any other desired spices.
- Grill your protein. Place your protein on the grill and cook it for the recommended amount of time, flipping it over halfway through.
- Remove from grill and enjoy. Once your protein is cooked through, remove it from the grill and enjoy!

Air Crisping

Air crisping is a popular way to cook food, and the Ninja Foodi Smart XL Grill is a great option for those who want to try it. This grill has a built-in air fryer that can be used to cook a variety of foods. Air frying is a healthier alternative to traditional frying methods, as it uses less oil and produces less grease. The Ninja Foodi Smart XL Grill is also equipped with a dehydrator, so you can make your own dried snacks or ingredients.
- Preheat your grill by selecting the Air Crisp function and setting the temperature up to 400°F.
- Cut your food into small pieces so that it cooks evenly.
- Place your food in the grill basket and lower it into the grill.
- Cook for the recommended time, flipping halfway through.
- Enjoy your delicious, healthy, and easy-to-make air-fried food!

Baking

Baking in the Ninja Foodi Smart XL Grill is really easy and a great way to make delicious and healthy meals for your family. The grill comes with a baking tray that can be used to cook a variety of food items. You can use the grill to bake chicken, fish, steak, pork chops, and even pizzas. The possibilities are endless when it comes to baking in the Ninja Foodi Smart XL Grill.
- Preheat your grill by pressing the "Power" button, then selecting the "Bake" function. Use the "+" and "-" buttons to set the desired temperature.
- Place your food on the grill grates, close the lid, and let it cook! Depending on what you're baking, you may need to flip or rotate your food halfway through cooking.
- When your food is cooked through, press the "Power" button to turn off the grill. Carefully remove your food from the grill grates and enjoy!

Roasting

Roasting is a great way to cook food in the Ninja Foodi Smart XL Grill. It allows you to cook food evenly and quickly, and it also gives your food a nice flavor. There are a few things to keep in mind when you are roasting in the Ninja Foodi Smart XL Grill. First, make sure that you preheat the grill to the correct temperature. Second, use a roasting rack to help ensure even cooking. Third, cook the food for the recommended time.
- Preheat your grill to the desired temperature. For a medium-rare roast,

we recommend preheating to 425°F.

- Season your roast with your favorite spices or herbs.
- Place the roast on the grill and cook for the recommended time. For a medium-rare roast, we recommend cooking for about 10 minutes.
- Remove the roast from the grill and let it rest for a few minutes before slicing and serving. Enjoy!

Dehydrating

Dehydrating is a great way to preserve food and make it last longer. And with the Ninja Foodi Smart XL Grill, it's easy to dehydrate your favorite foods.

- Preheat the grill to the dehydrating setting.
- Place the food to be dehydrated on the grill grates.
- Close the lid and let the grill work its magic.
- Check on the food periodically to make sure it is dehydrating evenly.
- Once the food is dehydrated to your desired level, remove it from the grill and enjoy!

Broiling

- Add the crispy finishing touch to meals or melt cheese on sandwiches. And with the Ninja Foodi Smart XL Grill, it's easier than ever to broil your food to perfection.
- Place cooking pot in the unit with the indent on the pot aligned with the bump on the main unit. Place ingredients in the pot. Ensure the splatter shield is in place, then close the hood.
- Press the BROIL button. The default temperature setting will display. Use the set of arrows to the left of the display to adjust the temperature up to 500°F.
- Use the set of arrows to the right of the display to adjust the cook time, in 1-minute increments up to 30 minutes, or, if using the thermometer, refer to the Using the Food Smart Thermometer section.
- Press START/STOP to begin. (The unit does not preheat in Broil mode.).
- When cook time is complete, the unit will beep and END will appear on the display.

Functions

One of the best things about the Ninja Foodi Smart XL Grill is its versatility. Not only can you use it as a grill, but you can also use it as an oven, a slow cooker, or a steamer. This means that you can cook just about anything you want on this appliance. Another great thing about the Ninja Foodi Smart XL Grill is its size. This grill is large enough to cook for a crowd, but it's also compact enough to fit on most countertops. Finally, the Ninja Foodi Smart XL Grill is very easy to use. There are no complicated controls or settings to worry about. Just set the temperature and timer and you're good to go.

If you're a fan of grilling, you know that there's nothing quite like the taste of food cooked over an open flame. But if you're new to grilling, or just looking for a way to step up your game, the Ninja Foodi Smart XL Grill is a great option. This grill is designed to make grilling easier and more versatile, and it comes with a built-in thermometer to help you cook your food to perfection. This grill is packed with features that make it a great option for both beginner and experienced grilles. Grilling is a great way to cook food and the Ninja Foodi Smart XL Grill is a great grill to use. This grill is very easy to use and it cooks food very well. Here is a step-by-step guide to using the Ninja Foodi Smart XL Grill.

- Before you begin, make sure that the grill is properly assembled. All of the parts should be in their proper place and the grill should be level.
- Choose your fuel. The Ninja Foodi Smart XL Grill can be used with charcoal, wood, or gas.
- Now, you need to preheat the grill. To do this, you need to press the power button and then press the preheat button. The grill will preheat to 400°F. Depending on what fuel you're using, this step will vary. For charcoal, light the coals and let them burn until they're covered in gray ash. For wood, use a chimney starter to light the wood and let it burn until it's reduced to embers.
- Next, you need to add your food to the grill. You can either grill your food directly on the grill or you can use a grill pan. If you are using a grill pan, you need to place it on the grill before you add your food.

- Be sure to leave enough space between each piece of food so that it can cook evenly.
- Close the lid of the grill and let the food cook for the recommended amount of time.
- The last step of the Ninja Foodi Smart XL Grill guide is to clean the grill. It is important to clean the grill after each use to prevent the build-up of food and grease. To clean the grill, simply remove the grates and wipe them down with a damp cloth. Be sure to also clean the splatter shield and the outside of the grill.

Now that you've made the perfect meal with your Ninja Foodi Smart XL Grill, what's next?

Here are a few ideas to keep the party going:

- Make some S'mores! The grill is still hot, so why not make use of it? Break out the marshmallows, chocolate, and graham crackers, and, get toasting.
- Have a water balloon fight. If you're feeling playful, fill up some water balloons and have a blast! Just be sure to clean up afterward.
- Sit back and relax. You've earned it! Now is the time to sit back and enjoy the fruits of your labor. Whether you're enjoying your meal or the company of those around you, take a moment to savor the moment.

How to Use the Thermometer?

If you're like most people, you probably don't give much thought to how you use a thermometer when grilling. But if you want to get the most out of your grilled food, it's important to understand how to use a thermometer correctly. Here are a few tips to help you get the best results:

- Place the thermometer in the thickest part of the food. This will help ensure that the temperature is accurate.
- Avoid placing the thermometer in direct contact with the heat source. This can cause the thermometer to give a false reading.
- Preheat the grill before cooking. This will help the food cook evenly.
- Use the thermometer to check the temperature of the grill, not the food. The temperature of the grill can fluctuate, so it's important to check it regularly.
- Don't rely on the thermometer alone. Use your judgment to determine when the food is cooked.

Accessories

When it comes to the Ninja Foodi Smart XL Grill, there are a few essential accessories that you'll need to make the most of your grilling experience. Here are a few things to consider picking up:

- A set of grill brushes: You'll need something to help clean the grates before and after cooking. A good set of grill brushes will make the job a whole lot easier.
- A set of tongs: Tongs are essential for flipping and removing food from the grill. Make sure to get a good set that won't let you down.
- A grill cover: A cover is important for keeping your grill clean and protected when not in use. Make sure to get one that fits your grill model perfectly.

With these essential accessories in hand, you'll be ready to grill up a storm on your Ninja Foodi Smart XL Grill. Happy grilling!

Straight from the Store

If you're looking for a top-of-the-line indoor grill that can do it all, look no further than the Ninja Foodi Smart XL Grill. This grill is perfect for those who want to be able to cook all of their favorite foods indoors, without having to deal with the hassle and mess of a traditional grill. The Ninja Foodi Smart XL Grill comes with six smart cooking functions that make it easy to grill, air crisp, roast, bake, dehydrate, and broil. It also comes with a temperature probe for perfect results every time. So if you're looking for an indoor grill that can do it all, the Ninja Foodi Smart XL Grill is a perfect choice.

Cleaning and Caring for Ninja Foodi Smart XL Grill

Cleaning:

Cleaning the grill is simple. The cooking plates are removable and dishwasher-safe. You can also wipe them down with a damp cloth. The splatter shield and grease cup are also dishwasher-safe. To clean the outside of the grill, use a damp cloth or sponge. Avoid using harsh chemicals or cleaners. Cleaning your grill is important to ensure that your food tastes great and doesn't stick to the grill. Here are a few tips on how to clean your Ninja Foodi Smart XL Grill:

- Use a grill brush to scrape off any food that is stuck to the grill.
- Soak a cloth in soapy water and wipe down the grill to remove any grease or dirt.
- Rinse the grill with water to remove any soap residue.
- Dry the grill with a clean cloth to prevent rusting.
- Apply a light layer of cooking oil to the grill to prevent sticking.

Following these simple tips will help keep your grill clean and in good condition. There are many reasons to clean your Ninja Foodi Smart XL Grill, but here are just a few:

- To keep it looking nice. Just like any other appliance in your home, you want your grill to look its best. A clean grill will be much more visually appealing than one that is covered in grease and grime.
- To prevent rust. If you don't clean your grill regularly, the rust can start to form. Not only does this look unsightly, but it can also cause your grill to function less effectively.
- To improve flavor. When you cook on a dirty grill, the food can pick up unwanted flavors from the grime that is on the surface. A clean grill will help ensure that your food tastes its best.
- To extend the life of your grill. With proper care and cleaning, your grill will last longer. This is an investment that you will want to protect.

Caring:

Caring for the grill is also relatively easy. Be sure to keep the grill covered when not in use. Store it in a cool, dry place. If you plan on storing it for an extended per period sure to clean it thoroughly first. Like any grill, your Ninja Foodi will need some care and maintenance to keep it running like new. Here are a few tips to help you keep your grill in tip-top shape. Before each use, check the grill grates to make sure they're clean and free of debris. A good scrub with a wire brush will

do the trick. After each use, give the grill a good wipe-down water. Be sure to get in all the nooks and crannies, including the splatter shield. Rinse the soap off and dry the grill before storing. Every few months, it's a good idea to give your grill a deep clean. Start by removing the grates and giving them a good scrub. Then, clean out the splatter shield.

We should care about the Ninja Foodi Smart XL Grill because it is a great product that can help us cook our food more evenly and quickly. It also has a lot of features that can help us clean it easily and keep it looking new for longer.

Grilling Tips

The Ninja Foodi Smart XL Grill is one of the best grills on the market, and we've got some tips to help you get the most out of it.

- Preheat your grill. This may seem like a no-brainer, but it's worth mentioning. The last thing you want is to put your food on the grill only to realize it's not hot enough. Preheating will help ensure that your food cooks evenly.
- Use the right tools. For the best results, you need to use the right tools. That means using a grill brush to clean the grates before you cook and tongs to flip your food.
- Be patient. One of the biggest mistakes people make when grilling is flipping the food too often.
- Make sure your grill is clean before you begin. A clean grill will help ensure your food cooks evenly and doesn't stick.
- Use a brush or spatula to oil your grill before cooking. This will help prevent your food from sticking.
- Make sure your food is cooked evenly by flipping it regularly.
- Use a thermometer to check the internal temperature of your food to ensure it is cooked properly.
- Remove your food from the grill when it is finished cooking and let it rest for a few minutes before serving.
- Be careful not to overcook your food. grilled food can quickly become dry and tough if it is overcooked.
- When in doubt, undercook your food slightly. It is better to err on the side of undercooked than overcooked food.

Frequently Asked Questions

If you're like most people, you probably have a few questions about the Ninja Foodi Smart XL Grill Cookbook. Here are a few of the most frequently asked questions:

Q: What is the Ninja Foodi Smart XL Grill?

A: The Ninja Foodi Smart XL Grill is a countertop grill that can cook food indoors or outdoors. It has a built-in smart temperature probe that monitors the internal temperature of the food, so you can cook it to perfection every time.

Q: What is the Ninja Foodi Smart XL Grill Cookbook?

A: The Ninja Foodi Smart XL Grill Cookbook is a comprehensive guide to grilling with the Ninja Foodi Smart XL Grill. It includes over 100 recipes specifically designed for grilling with the Ninja Foodi, as well as tips and techniques for getting the most out of your grill.

Q: How does the Ninja Foodi Smart XL Grill work?

A: The Ninja Foodi Smart XL Grill uses Cyclonic Grilling Technology to cook food evenly and quickly. The smart temperature probe monitors the internal temperature of the food, so you can cook it to perfection every time.

Q: Who is the Ninja Foodi Smart XL Grill Cookbook for?

A: The Ninja Foodi Smart XL Grill Cookbook is for anyone who owns a Ninja Foodi Smart XL Grill or is considering purchasing one. It's also for anyone who loves to grill!

Q: What are the benefits of the Ninja Foodi Smart XL Grill?

A: The Ninja Foodi Smart XL Grill is a versatile cooking appliance that can be used indoors or outdoors. It has a built-in smart temperature probe that monitors the internal temperature of the food, so you can cook it to perfection every time. Additionally, the Ninja Foodi Smart XL Grill is easy to clean

Q: What type of recipes are included in the Ninja Foodi Smart XL Grill Cookbook?

A: It includes recipes for everything from chicken and fish to burgers and steaks. And, of course, there are recipes for sides and desserts, too. Whether you're looking for a quick and easy meal or something a little more elaborate, the Ninja Foodi Smart XL Grill has you covered.

Notes

If you're like me, you love your Ninja Foodi Smart XL grill. And, you also love finding new and interesting recipes to try out on it. Well, I've got some good news for you – there's a new cookbook out that is specifically tailored for cooking with the Ninja Foodi Smart XL grill.

The Ninja Foodi Smart XL grill cookbook is a great guide for those who want to learn how to cook with a Ninja Foodi Smart XL grill. This cookbook includes recipes for both beginner and experienced grilles alike. Whether you're looking to make a simple meal or something more complicated, this cookbook has you covered. One of the best things about the Ninja Foodi Smart XL grill is that it's very versatile. You can use it to cook a variety of different foods, including meats, vegetables, and even desserts. The cookbook includes recipes for all of these different types of foods.

The Ninja Foodi Smart XL grill cookbook is packed with over 100 recipes that are specifically designed for the grill. Whether you're looking for something new to make for breakfast, lunch, or dinner, there's sure to be a recipe in here that you'll love. And, best of all, each recipe comes with easy-to-follow instructions that make grilling a breeze. So, what are you waiting for? Pick up a copy of the Ninja Foodi Smart XL grill cookbook and start grilling!

4-Week Meal Plan

Week 1

Day 1:
Breakfast: Breakfast Frittata
Lunch: Lemony Zucchini
Snack: Grilled Corn
Dinner: Simple Filet Mignon
Dessert: Brownies Muffins

Day 2:
Breakfast: Scrambled Eggs
Lunch: Hasselback Sweet Potatoes with Rosemary
Snack: Air Fried Pizza, Egg rolls
Dinner: Spiced Lamb Chops
Dessert: Apple Bread Pudding

Day 3:
Breakfast: Breakfast Sausages
Lunch: Sugar Snap Peas
Snack: Jacket Potatoes
Dinner: Orange Glazed Pork Chops
Dessert: Air Fryer S'mores

Day 4:
Breakfast: Ham Spinach Ballet
Lunch: Cheesy Cabbage
Snack: Falafel with Yogurt and Cucumber Dip
Dinner: Herbed Beef Tenderloin
Dessert: Maple Baked Pears

Day 5:
Breakfast: Cheesy Beans Sandwich
Lunch: Chicken Lettuce Wraps
Snack: Steamed and Crisped Asparagus
Dinner: Garlic Lamb Loin Chops
Dessert: Milky Donuts

Day 6:
Breakfast: Crustless Spinach Quiche
Lunch: Vegetable Skewers
Snack: Chicken Tenders
Dinner: BBQ Pork Ribs
Dessert: Stuffed Apples

Day 7:
Breakfast: Raspberry Stuffed French Toast
Lunch: Hasselback Potatoes with Garlic
Snack: Dehydrated Apple Crisps
Dinner: Beef Kebabs Skewers
Dessert: Chocolate Mug cake

Week 2

Day 1:
Breakfast: Zucchini Omelet
Lunch: Tofu with Mushrooms
Snack: Air Fryer Hush Puppies
Dinner: Buttered Strip Steaks
Dessert: Vanilla Donuts

Day 2:
Breakfast: Cheesy Avocado Sandwich
Lunch: Grilled Broccolini with Sauce
Snack: Meatballs
Dinner: Spiced Pork Ribs
Dessert: Pumpkin Streusel Pie Bars

Day 3:
Breakfast: French Toasts
Lunch: Sweet Potato & Chickpea Pitas
Snack: Crispy Prawns
Dinner: Glazed Beef Kabobs
Dessert: Peach Cobbler

Day 4:
Breakfast: Trout Frittata
Lunch: Radicchio with Blue Cheese
Snack: Banana Chips
Dinner: Glazed Ham
Dessert: Candied Pecans

Day 5:
Breakfast: French Toast
Lunch: Zucchini and Yellow Squash
Snack: Tortilla Chips
Dinner: Nut Crusted Rack of Lamb
Dessert: Chocolate Souffle

Day 6:
Breakfast: Supreme Breakfast Burrito
Lunch: Cheesy Beef Burger Balls with Tomatoes
Snack: Chili-Lime Pineapple
Dinner: Spiced Rib-Eye Steak
Dessert: Lava Cake

Day 7:
Breakfast: Crispy Bread Rolls
Lunch: Sausage-Stuffed Zucchini
Snack: Air Fry Scallops
Dinner: Citrus Pork Chops
Dessert: Fruity Crumble

Week 3

Day 1:
Breakfast: Egg in a Bread Basket
Lunch: Portobello Mushrooms Florentine
Snack: Rice Bites
Dinner: Beef with Onion
Dessert: Grilled Pineapple Dessert

Day 2:
Breakfast: French Toast Sticks
Lunch: Sesame Green Beans
Snack: Cheesy & Creamy Corn
Dinner: Lemony Pork Kabobs
Dessert: Maple Baked Pears

Day 3:
Breakfast: Salmon Ricotta Toast
Lunch: Coconut Sweet Potatoes
Snack: Tofu Burgers
Dinner: Minty Lamb Loin Chops
Dessert: Brownies

Day 4:
Breakfast: Breakfast Pancakes
Lunch: Chicken Stuffed Mini Peppers
Snack: Glazed Tofu Kabobs
Dinner: Marinated Rib-Eye Steak
Dessert: Stuffed Apples

Day 5:
Breakfast: Zucchini Fritters
Lunch: Stuffed Zucchini Rolls
Snack: Grilled Corn
Dinner: Spiced Pork Tenderloin
Dessert:

Day 6:
Breakfast: Savory French Toasts
Lunch: Parmesan Asparagus
Snack: Falafel Balls with Yogurt and Cucumber Dip
Dinner: Herbed Rack of Lamb
Dessert: Shortbread Fingers

Day 7:
Breakfast: Spanish Style Frittata
Lunch: Beans & Oat Burgers
Snack: Crispy Prawns
Dinner: Lemony Flank Steak
Dessert: Raisin Bread Pudding

Week 4

Day 1:
Breakfast: Broccoli Cheese Scrambled Eggs
Lunch: Spinach and Feta Pita
Snack: Dehydrated Apple Crisps
Dinner: Brined Pork Chops
Dessert: Mini Apple Pies

Day 2:
Breakfast: Bacon Cups
Lunch: Marinated Mushrooms
Snack: Air Fryer Hush Puppies
Dinner: Garlicky Lamb Chops
Dessert: Sweet Plantains

Day 3:
Breakfast: Green Courgette Fritters
Lunch: Baked Beet Chips
Snack: Banana Chips
Dinner: Mignon Steak
Dessert: Air Fried Oreos

Day 4:
Breakfast: Strawberry Stuffed French Toast
Lunch: Seasoned Artichokes
Snack: Jacket Potatoes
Dinner: Lamb Chops with Apple Sauce
Dessert: Brownies Muffins

Day 5:
Breakfast: Cheese Sandwich
Lunch: Herbed Eggplant
Snack: Steamed and Crisped Asparagus
Dinner: Oregano Sirloin Steak
Dessert: Lemon Bars

Day 6:
Breakfast: Salmon Ricotta Toast
Lunch: Zucchini with Italian Dressing
Snack: Air Fried Pizza, Egg Rolls
Dinner: Honey Roasted Pork Ribs
Dessert: Chocolate Souffle

Day 7:
Breakfast: French Toast Skewers
Lunch: Veggie Kabobs
Snack: Chicken Tenders
Dinner: Herbed Leg of Lamb
Dessert: Strawberry Cupcakes

Chapter 1 Breakfast Recipes

Tuna Sandwich

Prep Time: 15 minutes | Cook Time: 5 minutes | Servings: 4

Ingredients:

6 ounces white tuna, drained
¼ cup bell pepper, seeded and finely chopped
¼ cup celery, finely chopped
2 tablespoons red onion, finely chopped
¼ cup mayonnaise
4 bread slices
4 teaspoons unsalted butter, softened
3 ounces Swiss cheese

Preparation:

1. In a bowl, place the tuna and with a fork, break up clumps. 2. Add the bell pepper, celery, onion, and mayonnaise and stir to combine. 3. Spread one teaspoons butter on one side of each bread slice. 4. Place 2 bread slices onto a work surface, buttered side down. 5. Place tuna mixture over bread slices evenly and top with the cheese. 6. Cover with remaining bread slices, buttered side up. 7. Arrange the lightly greased "Grill Grate" in the crisper basket in the cooking pot of Ninja Foodi Smart XL Grill. 8. Close the Grill with lid and press "Power" button. 9. Select "Grill" and then use the set of arrows to the left of the display to adjust the temperature to "MED". 10. Use the set of arrows to the right of the display to adjust the cook time to 5 minutes. 11. Press "Start/Stop" to begin preheating. When the display shows "Add Food", open the lid and place the sandwiches onto the "Grill Grate". 12. With your hands, gently press down each sandwich. Close the Grill with lid. 13. After 3 minutes of cooking, flip the sandwiches. 14. When the cooking time is completed, open the lid and place the sandwiches onto a platter. 15. Cut 2 halves of each sandwich and serve warm.

Serving Suggestions: Serve with tomato ketchup.
Variation Tip: Feel free to use cheese of your choice.
Nutritional Information per Serving: Calories: 310 | Fat: 18.1g | Sat Fat: 7.6g | Carbohydrates: 17.2g | Fiber: 0.9g | Sugar: 2.5g | Protein: 19.7g

Avocado Toast

Prep Time: 15 minutes | Cook Time: 5 minutes | Servings: 4

Ingredients:

2 avocados
2 teaspoons lemon juice
Salt and black pepper, to taste
4 slices of bread
½ cup feta cheese
1 cup cherry tomatoes, halved
¼ cup basil
1 tablespoon balsamic vinegar

Preparation:

1. Cut the avocado in half and scoop the flesh into a small bowl. Combine the lemon juice, salt, and pepper in a mixing bowl. Crush the ingredients together using a fork. 2. Cover the bread with the mixture. 3. Feta cheese, tomatoes, and basil go on top. 4. Season with salt and pepper to taste. 5. Select the "Air Crisp" button on the Ninja Foodi Smart XL Grill and regulate the time for 3 minutes at 320°F. 6. Place the toast in the Ninja Foodi when it displays "Add Food." 7. Air crisp for 3 minutes. 8. Drizzle a little amount of balsamic vinaigrette over the top.

Serving Suggestions: Garnish with parmesan cheese.
Variation Tip: You can use white wine instead of balsamic vinegar.
Nutritional Information per Serving: Calories: 294 | Fat: 20g | Sat Fat: 5g | Carbohydrates: 25g | Fiber: 8g | Sugar: 4g | Protein: 8g

Chocolate Chip Pancake Bites

Prep Time: 10 minutes | Cook Time: 5 minutes | Servings: 4

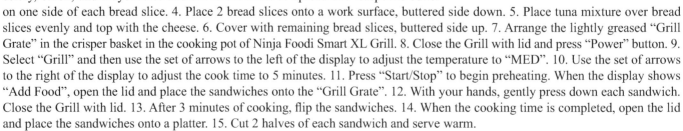

Ingredients:

1 cup pancake mix
1 cup water
½ cup mini chocolate chips

Preparation:

1. Select the "Bake" button on the Ninja Foodi Smart XL Grill and regulate the settings at 320°F for 5 minutes. 2. In a large bowl, merge the pancake mix, water, and mini chocolate chips. 3. Drop the mixture in small balls in the Ninja Foodi when it displays "Add Food". 4. Bake for about 5 minutes, tossing once in between. 5. Dole out in a plate and serve warm.

Serving Suggestions: Serve topped with the sour cream and smoked salmon slices.
Variation Tip: You can use red potatoes too.
Nutritional Information per Serving: Calories: 67 | Fat: 1.3g | Sat Fat: 0.5g | Carbohydrates: 12.1g | Fiber: 0.4g | Sugar: 0.9g | Protein: 6.8g

Tofu Burgers

Prep Time: 15 minutes | Cook Time: 12 minutes | Servings: 8

Ingredients:

1 pound extra-firm tofu, pressed, drained and sliced	1 tablespoon Dijon mustard
2 large eggs	1 tablespoon low-sodium soy sauce
½ cup sunflower seeds	1 teaspoon ground cumin
½ cup cashews	1 teaspoon smoked paprika
½ cup dried breadcrumbs	½ teaspoon cayenne powder
½ cup fresh mushrooms, sliced	¼ teaspoon salt
	1 tablespoon extra-virgin olive oil

Preparation:

1. Place the tofu and remaining ingredients except for the olive oil in a food processor and pulse until well combined. 2. Make 8 equal-sized patties from the mixture. 3. Set the patties aside for 10 minutes. 4. Gently coat each patty with olive oil. 5. Arrange the lightly greased "Grill Grate" in the crisper basket in the cooking pot of Ninja Foodi Smart XL Grill. 6. Close the Grill with lid and press "Power" button. 7. Select "Grill" and then use the set of arrows to the left of the display to adjust the temperature to "MED". 8. Use the set of arrows to the right of the display to adjust the cook time to 12 minutes. Press "Start/Stop" to begin preheating. 9. When the display shows "Add Food", open the lid and place the patties onto the "Grill Grate". 10. With your hands, gently press down each patty. Close the Grill with lid. 11. After 7 minutes of cooking, flip the patties. 12. When the cooking time is completed, open the lid and serve hot.

Serving Suggestions: Serve with lemon wedges.

Variation Tip: Make sure to use dried breadcrumbs.

Nutritional Information per Serving: Calories: 182 | Fat: 12.3g | Sat Fat: 2g | Carbohydrates: 10.2g | Fiber: 1.3g | Sugar: 1.6g | Protein: 10.5g

Crispy Bread Rolls

Prep Time: 20 minutes | Cook Time: 19 minutes | Servings: 4

Ingredients:

5 large potatoes, boiled and mashed	8 bread slices, trimmed
2 small onions, chopped finely	2 tablespoons olive oil, divided
2 green chilies, seeded and chopped finely	½ teaspoon ground turmeric
2 tablespoons fresh cilantro, chopped finely	½ teaspoon mustard seeds
	1 teaspoon curry powder
	Salt, to taste

Preparation:

1. In a large skillet, merge 1 tablespoon of olive oil and mustard seeds on medium heat. 2. Sauté for about 30 seconds and add onions. 3. Sauté for about 5 minutes and add curry powder and turmeric. 4. Sauté for about 30 seconds and add the mashed potatoes and salt. 5. Mix thoroughly and eliminate from the heat. 6. Dish out into a bowl and keep aside to cool. 7. Stir in the chilies and cilantro and form 8 oval-shaped patties from this mixture. 8. Moisten the bread slices, then use your hands to press the moisture out. 9. Center one burger on each slice of bread, then fold the bread up around the patty. 10. After sealing the sides to keep the filling in place, equally drizzle the rolls with the remaining olive oil. 11. Select the "Air Crisp" button on the Ninja Foodi Smart XL Grill and regulate the time for 13 minutes at 390°F. 12. Place the bread rolls in a Ninja Foodi when it displays "Add Food". 13. Air Crisp for about 13 minutes and shift into a platter to serve warm.

Serving Suggestions: Serve with your favorite sauce.

Variation Tip: You can also add red chili flakes for added spiciness.

Nutritional Information per Serving: Calories: 446 | Fat: 8.3g | Sat Fat: 1.3g | Carbohydrates: 85.6g | Fiber: 12.6g | Sugar: 7.7g | Protein: 9.7g

Breakfast Frittata

Prep Time: 10 minutes | Cook Time: 10 minutes | Servings: 3

Ingredients:

2 tablespoons butter
3 cups cornbread and sausage stuffing
6 large eggs

¼ cup heavy cream
½ teaspoon sea salt, finely ground
1 tablespoon green onions, chopped

Preparation:

1. Select the "Grill" button on the Ninja Foodi Smart XL Grill and regulate the time for 10 minutes at MED. 2. Whip eggs with sea salt, cream, and green onions in a bowl. 3. Brush the butter on the Grill Grate. 4. Place the cornbread and sausage stuffing in the Ninja Foodi when it 5. displays "Add Food" and top with the egg mixture. 6. Grill for 10 minutes, flipping once in between. 7. Dole out in a platter and serve warm.

Serving Suggestions: You can enjoy this Breakfast Frittata with the toasted bread slices.
Variation Tip: You can add tomatoes and parsley in the frittata.
Nutritional Information per Serving: Calories: 367 | Fat: 29.3g | Sat Fat: 13.7g | Carbohydrates: 7.5g | Fiber: 0.1g | Sugar: 0.9g | Protein: 18.8g

Scrambled Eggs

Prep Time: 10 minutes | Cook Time: 8 minutes | Servings: 2

Ingredients:

½ tablespoon butter
4 large eggs

Salt and black pepper, to taste
4 tablespoons milk

Preparation:

1. Select the "Grill" button on the Ninja Foodi Smart XL Grill and regulate the time for 8 minutes at MED. 2. Whip eggs with milk, salt, and black pepper in a bowl. 3. Place the egg mixture in the Ninja Foodi when it displays "Add Food" and top with butter. 4. Grill for 8 minutes, flipping once in between. 5. Dole out in a platter and serve warm.

Serving Suggestions: Serve with toasted bagels
Variation Tip: You can also use olive oil instead of butter.
Nutritional Information per Serving: Calories: 184 | Fat: 13.4g | Sat Fat: 5.3g | Carbohydrates: 2.3g | Fiber: 0g | Sugar: 2.1g | Protein: 13.6g

Cheesy Beans Sandwich

Prep Time: 15 minutes | Cook Time: 12 minutes | Servings: 6

Ingredients:

3 poblano peppers, stemmed, cut lengthwise and seeded
3 tablespoons salsa
1 (14-ounces) can pinto beans, rinsed and drained
⅛ teaspoon salt

3 scallions, sliced thinly
2 tablespoons plain yogurt
⅓ cup Monterey Jack cheese, shredded
2 tablespoons fresh cilantro, chopped
6 sourdough bread slices

Preparation:

1. In a small microwave-safe bowl, place poblano peppers and cover it with a plastic wrap. 2. Microwave on high for about 3-4 minutes. 3. Remove the bowl of poblano peppers from microwave and set aside to cool slightly. 4. In a small bowl, mix together the salsa, pinto beans, and salt and with a potato masher, mash until a paste forms. 5. In a second bowl, mix together the scallions, yogurt, Monterey jack cheese, and cilantro. 6. Place the pinto beans mixture over 4 bread slices and top with cheese mixture, followed by 2 pieces of poblano peppers. 7. Cover with the remaining bread slices. 8. Arrange the lightly greased "Grill Grate" in the crisper basket in the cooking pot of Ninja Foodi Smart XL Grill. 9. Close the Grill with lid and press "Power" button. 10. Select "Grill" and then use the set of arrows to the left of the display to adjust the temperature to "MED". 11. Use the set of arrows to the right of the display to adjust the cook time to 8 minutes. 12. Press "Start/Stop" to begin preheating. When the display shows "Add Food", open the lid and place the sandwiches onto the "Grill Grate". 13. With your hands, gently press down each sandwich. Close the Grill with lid. 14. After 4 minutes of cooking, flip the sandwiches. 15. When the cooking time is completed, open the lid and place the sandwiches onto a platter. 16. Cut 2 halves of each sandwich and serve warm.

Serving Suggestions: Serve with ketchup.
Variation Tip: Monterey Jack cheese can be replaced with cheddar cheese.
Nutritional Information per Serving: Calories: 189 | Fat: 2.5g | Sat Fat: 1.3g | Carbohydrates: 32.2g | Fiber: 7.2g | Sugar: 2.8g | Protein: 10.9g

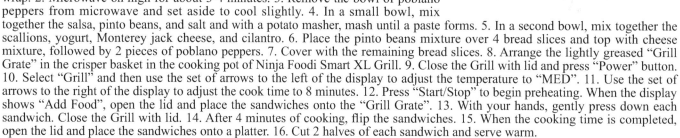

Ham Spinach Ballet

Prep Time: 5 minutes | Cook Time: 11 minutes | Servings: 8

Ingredients:

3 pounds fresh baby spinach
½ cup cream
28-ounce ham, sliced

4 tablespoons butter, melted
Salt and black pepper, to taste

Preparation:

1. Select the "Bake" button on the Ninja Foodi Smart XL Grill and regulate the time for 8 minutes at 350°F. 2. Put butter and spinach in a pan and sauté for 3 minutes. 3. Top with cream, ham slices, salt, and black pepper. 4. Place the ham and spinach mixture in the Ninja Foodi when it displays "Add Food". 5. Bake for about 8 minutes and shift into a platter to serve warm.

Serving Suggestions: Serve with toasted bagels.
Variation Tip: You can also use baby kale instead of baby spinach.
Nutritional Information per Serving: Calories: 261 | Fat: 15.8g | Sat Fat: 7.2g | Carbohydrates: 10.5g | Fiber: 5g | Sugar: 1g | Protein: 21.5g

Broccoli Cheese Scrambled Eggs

Prep Time: 10 minutes | Cook Time: 13 minutes | Servings: 6

Ingredients:

2 tablespoons butter
12 ounces broccoli florets
Salt and black pepper, to taste
¼ cup water

¾ cup cheddar cheese, shredded
8 eggs
2 tablespoons milk

Preparation:

1. Select the "Air Crisp" button on the Ninja Foodi Smart XL Grill and regulate the time for 3 minutes at 320°F. 2. Put butter and broccoli in a pot and sauté for 3 minutes. 3. Add water, salt, and black pepper, and cook for 10 minutes after covering with lid on medium-low heat. 4. Whip eggs with milk, cheddar cheese, salt, and black pepper in a bowl. 5. Place the broccoli mixture in the Ninja Foodi when it displays "Add Food" and top with whipped eggs. 6. Air Crisp for 3 minutes, flipping once in between. 7. Dole out in a platter and serve warm.

Serving Suggestions: Serve with browned toast slices.
Variation Tip: You can also add mozzarella cheese.
Nutritional Information per Serving: Calories: 197 | Fat: 14.6g | Sat Fat: 7.3g | Carbohydrates: 4.7g | Fiber: 1.5g | Sugar: 1.7g | Protein: 12.7g

Chocolate Stuffed French Toast

Prep Time: 10 minutes | Cook Time: 8 minutes | Servings: 4

Ingredients:

⅓ cup whole milk
2 eggs
1 teaspoon sugar
½ teaspoon vanilla extract

Pinch of salt
4 bread slices
1 (1½-ounce) chocolate bar, halved

Preparation:

1. In a bowl, whisk together the milk, eggs, sugar, vanilla extract, and salt. 2. Place 1 chocolate piece over 2 bread slices. 3. Cover with remaining bread slices. 4. Dip both sides of sandwiches into beaten eggs evenly. 5. Arrange the lightly greased "Grill Grate" in the crisper basket in the cooking pot of Ninja Foodi Smart XL Grill. 6. Close the Grill with lid and press "Power" button. 7. Select "Grill" and then use the set of arrows to the left of the display to adjust the temperature to "MED". 8. Use the set of arrows to the right of the display to adjust the cook time to 8 minutes. 9. Press "Start/Stop" to begin preheating. When the display shows "Add Food", open the lid and place the sandwiches onto the "Grill Grate". 10. With your hands, gently press down each sandwich. Close the Grill with lid. 11. After 4 minutes of cooking, flip the sandwiches. 12. When the cooking time is completed, open the lid and place the sandwiches onto a platter. 13. Cut 2 halves of each sandwich and serve warm.

Serving Suggestions: Serve alongside the fresh berries.
Variation Tip: Use a high-quality chocolate bar.
Nutritional Information per Serving: Calories: 130 | Fat: 5.3g | Sat Fat: 3.3g | Carbohydrates: 13g | Fiber: 0.6g | Sugar: 8.2g | Protein: 4.9g

Zucchini Omelet

Prep Time: 15 minutes | Cook Time: 0 minutes | Servings: 2

Ingredients:

1 teaspoon butter
1 zucchini, julienned
4 eggs
¼ teaspoon fresh basil, chopped
¼ teaspoon red pepper flakes, crushed
Salt and black pepper, as required

Preparation:

1. Choose the "Air Crisp" button on the Ninja Foodi Smart XL Grill and regulate the settings at 350°F for 8 minutes. 2. In a skillet, put the butter and zucchini and cook for about 4 minutes over medium heat. 3. Meanwhile, in a bowl, merge together the basil, eggs, red pepper flakes, salt, and black pepper. 4. Add the cooked zucchini and gently, stir to combine. 5. Transfer the mixture into the Ninja Foodi when it displays "Add Food". 6. Air crisp for about 8 minutes, tossing the omelet in between. 7. Dish out the omelet in a platter and serve warm.

Serving Suggestions: Serve it with toasted white slices.

Variation Tip: You can use olive oil instead of butter.

Nutritional Information per Serving: Calories: 159 | Fat: 10.9g | Sat Fat: 4g | Carbohydrates: 4.1g | Fiber: 1.2g | Sugar: 2.4g | Protein: 12.3g

French Toasts

Prep Time: 10 minutes | Cook Time: 5 minutes | Servings: 2

Ingredients:

2 eggs
¼ cup evaporated milk
3 tablespoons sugar
2 teaspoons olive oil
⅛ teaspoon vanilla extract
4 bread slices

Preparation:

1. Select the "Grill" button on the Ninja Foodi Smart XL Grill and regulate the settings at MED for 5 minutes. 2. In a large bowl, mingle all the ingredients except bread slices. 3. Coat the bread slices evenly with the egg mixture. 4. Arrange the bread slices in the Ninja Foodi when it displays "Add Food". 5. Grill for 5 minutes, stirring once in between. 6. Dole out in a plate when grilled completely and serve warm.

Serving Suggestions: You can serve it with maple syrup.

Variation Tip: You can also drizzle some cinnamon for added flavor.

Nutritional Information per Serving: Calories: 261 | Fat: 12g | Sat Fat: 3.6g | Carbohydrates: 30.6g | Fiber: 0.4g | Sugar: 22.3g | Protein: 9.1g

Zucchini Fritters

Prep Time: 5 minutes | Cook Time: 11 minutes | Servings: 8

Ingredients:

10½ ounces zucchini, grated and squeezed
7 ounces Halloumi cheese
¼ cup all-purpose flour
2 eggs
1 teaspoon fresh dill, minced
Salt and black pepper, to taste

Preparation:

1. Select the "Air Crisp" button on the Ninja Foodi Smart XL Grill and regulate the time for 7 minutes at 360°F. 2. Merge together all the ingredients in a large bowl. 3. Make small fritters from this mixture and place them in the Ninja Foodi when it displays "Add Food". 4. Air Crisp for about 7 minutes and shift into a platter to serve warm.

Serving Suggestions: Serve with tomato ketchup.

Variation Tip: You can also use almond flour instead of all-purpose flour.

Nutritional Information per Serving: Calories: 127 | Fat: 8.6g | Sat Fat: 5.5g | Carbohydrates: 5g | Fiber: 0.5g | Sugar: 1.4g | Protein: 7.6g

Trout Frittata

Prep Time: 15 minutes | Cook Time: 20 minutes | Servings: 4

Ingredients:

2 tablespoons olive oil
1 onion, sliced
6 eggs
½ tablespoon horseradish sauce

2 tablespoons crème Fraiche
2 hot-smoked trout fillets, chopped
¼ cup fresh dill, chopped

Preparation:

1. Select the "Grill" button on the Ninja Foodi Smart XL Grill and regulate the time for 15 minutes at Medium. 2. Take a skillet, put the oil and onion and sauté for about 5 minutes over medium heat. 3. Meanwhile, in a bowl, mingle together the eggs, horseradish sauce, trout fillets, dill, and crème Fraiche. 4. Now, transfer the onion mixture into the Ninja Foodi when it displays "Add Food" and top with the egg mixture. 5. Grill for 15 minutes, flipping once in between. 6. Dole out in a platter and serve warm.

Serving Suggestions: Serve with toasted bagels.
Variation Tip: You can also use butter instead of olive oil.
Nutritional Information per Serving: Calories: 250 | Fat: 18.6g | Sat Fat: 4.1g | Carbohydrates: 4.9g | Fiber: 1g | Sugar: 1.7g | Protein: 16.3g

Spanish Style Frittata

Prep Time: 20 minutes | Cook Time: 14 minutes | Servings: 4

Ingredients:

½ cup frozen corn
½ of chorizo sausage, sliced
1 potato, boiled, peeled and cubed
2 tablespoons feta cheese, crumbled

3 jumbo eggs
1 tablespoon olive oil
Salt and black pepper, to taste

Preparation:

1. Select the "Grill" button on the Ninja Foodi Smart XL Grill and regulate the time for 8 minutes at MED. 2. Add chorizo sausage, corn, and potato and cook for about 6 minutes. 3. Whisk together eggs, salt, and black pepper in a small bowl. 4. Place the sausage mixture into the Ninja Foodi when it displays "Add Food" and top with the egg mixture and feta cheese. 5. Grill for 8 minutes, flipping once in between. 6. Dole out in a platter and serve warm.

Serving Suggestions: Serve with toasted bagels.
Variation Tip: You can also use baby kale instead of baby spinach.
Nutritional Information per Serving: Calories: 144 | Fat: 8.5g | Sat Fat: 2.4g | Carbohydrates: 11.5g | Fiber: 1.5g | Sugar: 1.4g | Protein: 6.6g

Supreme Breakfast Burrito

Prep Time: 15 minutes | Cook Time: 8 minutes | Servings: 2

Ingredients:

2 eggs
2 whole-wheat tortillas
4-ounces chicken breast slices, cooked
¼ of avocado, peeled, pitted and sliced

2 tablespoons mozzarella cheese, grated
2 tablespoons salsa
Salt and black pepper, to taste

Preparation:

1. Select the "Air Crisp" button on the Ninja Foodi Smart XL Grill and regulate the time for 3 minutes at 355°F. 2. Whisk together eggs in a bowl and dust with salt and black pepper. 3. Transfer into a non-stick pan. 4. Sauté for about 5 minutes and remove eggs from the pan. 5. Divide the eggs in each tortilla, followed by chicken slice, avocado, salsa and mozzarella cheese. 6. Roll up each tortilla tightly and transfer in the Ninja Foodi when it displays "Add Food". 7. Air Crisp for 3 minutes and dish out in a platter to serve.

Serving Suggestions: Serve with lime and coriander rice.
Variation Tip: You can also make these burritos with corn tortillas.
Nutritional Information per Serving: Calories: 313 | Fat: 15.9g | Sat Fat: 5.8g | Carbohydrates: 15.2g | Fiber: 3.5g | Sugar: 1.2g | Protein: 29.4g

Egg in a Bread Basket

Prep Time: 10 minutes | Cook Time: 10 minutes | Servings: 2

Ingredients:

2 bread slices
2 eggs

½ tablespoon olive oil
Salt and black pepper, to taste

Preparation:

1. Select the "Bake" button on the Ninja Foodi Smart XL Grill and regulate the time for 10 minutes at 320°F. 2. Cut a piece from the center of bread slices through a cookie cutter. 3. Place the bread slices on the Ninja Foodi baking tray after greasing them with olive oil and crack eggs in them. 4. Dust the egg in a bread hole with salt and black pepper. 5. Place the baking tray in the Ninja Foodi when it displays "Add Food". 6. Bake for 10 minutes and dole out in a platter to serve warm.

Serving Suggestions: Serve alongside bacon.

Variation Tip: You can use both the white or bran bread.

Nutritional Information per Serving: Calories: 117 | Fat: 8.2g | Sat Fat: 1.9g | Carbohydrates: 4.9g | Fiber: 0.2g | Sugar: 0.7g | Protein: 6.2g

French Toast Sticks

Prep Time: 10 minutes | Cook Time: 5 minutes | Servings: 4

Ingredients:

2 tablespoons soft butter
4 bread, sliced into sticks
2 eggs, gently beaten
1 pinch cinnamon

1 pinch ground cloves
Salt, to taste
1 pinch nutmeg

Preparation:

1. Select the "Air Crisp" button on the Ninja Foodi Smart XL Grill and regulate the time for 5 minutes at 365°F. 2. In a large bowl, mingle eggs with salt, butter, cinnamon, nutmeg, and ground cloves. 3. Dip the breadsticks in the egg mixture and transfer in the Ninja Foodi when it displays "Add Food". 4. Air Crisp for 5 minutes, stirring once in between. 5. Dole out in a plate and serve warm.

Serving Suggestions: You can serve it with maple syrup.

Variation Tip: You can also add margarine instead of butter.

Nutritional Information per Serving: Calories: 150 | Fat: 8.8g | Sat Fat: 4.5g | Carbohydrates: 13g | Fiber: 0.7g | Sugar: 1.3g | Protein: 4.7g

Salmon Ricotta Toast

Prep Time: 10 minutes | Cook Time: 5 minutes | Servings: 4

Ingredients:

4 bread slices
8 ounces ricotta cheese
4 ounces smoked salmon
1 shallot, sliced

1 cup arugula
1 garlic clove, minced
1 teaspoon lemon zest
¼ teaspoon black pepper

Preparation:

1. Choose the "Air Crisp" button on the Ninja Foodi Smart XL Grill and regulate the settings at 355°F for 5 minutes. 2. Place the bread slices in the Ninja Foodi when it displays "Add Food". 3. Air crisp for about 5 minutes, tossing in between and dish out. 4. In a food processor, merge garlic, ricotta cheese, and lemon zest and pulse until smooth. 5. Spread this mixture over each bread slice and top with salmon, arugula, and shallot. 6. Dust with black pepper and serve warm.

Serving Suggestions: Serve topped with tomato slices if you desire.

Variation Tip: You can also use whole-wheat bread slices.

Nutritional Information per Serving: Calories: 144 | Fat: 6g | Sat Fat: 3.1g | Carbohydrates: 9.3g | Fiber: 0.4g | Sugar: 0.7g | Protein: 12.7g

Cheesy Avocado Sandwich

Prep Time: 15 minutes | Cook Time: 5 minutes | Servings: 4

Ingredients:

4 sourdough bread slices
2 teaspoons olive oil
2 ounces cheddar cheese, sliced
½ of medium avocado, peeled, pitted and sliced

1 plum tomato, cut into ¼-inch slices
Salt and ground black pepper, as required
2 teaspoons mayonnaise

Preparation:

1. Brush one side of each bread slice with the oil. 2. Place 2 bread slices on a work surface, oiled side down. 3. Divide ½ cheese over both slices, followed by, avocado and tomato. 4. Sprinkle with salt and black pepper and top with remaining cheese. 5. Spread the mayonnaise on the inside of the remaining bread slices. 6. Place the mayonnaise coated bread slices on top of the sandwiches, oiled side up. 7. Arrange the lightly greased "Grill Grate" in the crisper basket in the cooking pot of Ninja Foodi Smart XL Grill. 8. Close the Grill with lid and press "Power" button. 9. Select "Grill" and then use the set of arrows to the left of the display to adjust the temperature to "MED". 10. Use the set of arrows to the right of the display to adjust the cook time to 5 minutes. 11. Press "Start/Stop" to begin preheating. When the display shows "Add Food", open the lid and place the sandwiches onto the "Grill Grate". 12. With your hands, gently press down each sandwich. Close the Grill with lid. 13. When the cooking time is completed, open the lid and place the sandwiches onto a platter. 14. Cut 2 halves of each sandwich and serve warm.

Serving Suggestions: Serve with ketchup.
Variation Tip: Use real mayonnaise.
Nutritional Information per Serving: Calories: 194 | Fat: 12.8g | Sat Fat: 4.5g | Carbohydrates: 14.8g | Fiber: 2.5g | Sugar: 1.4g | Protein: 6.6g

Breakfast Pancakes

Prep Time: 15 minutes | Cook Time: 20 minutes | Servings: 8

Ingredients:

1½ teaspoons baking powder
1½ cups all-purpose flour
3 teaspoons sugar, granulated
1 large egg

2 tablespoons unsalted butter, melted
¼ teaspoon kosher salt
1½ cups buttermilk

Preparation:

1. Select the "Grill" button on the Ninja Foodi Smart XL Grill and regulate the time for 8 minutes at MED. 2. Merge flour, baking powder, sugar, and salt in a bowl. 3. Mingle egg, buttermilk, and butter in another bowl. 4. Fold the egg mixture thoroughly in the flour mixture. 5. Place the pancake mixture in the Ninja Foodi when it displays "Add Food". 6. Grill for 8 minutes, flipping once in between and dole out in a platter to serve warm.

Serving Suggestions: Serve drizzled with maple syrup.
Variation Tip: You can also use coconut flour instead of all-purpose flour.
Nutritional Information per Serving: Calories: 145 | Fat: 4.1g | Sat Fat: 2.3g | Carbohydrates: 22.1g | Fiber: 0.7g | Sugar: 3.8g | Protein: 4.8g

Breakfast Bacon

Prep Time: 1 minutes | Cook Time: 9 minutes | Servings: 6

Ingredients:

6 bacon strips
½ tablespoon olive oil

Preparation:

1. Choose the "Air Crisp" button on the Ninja Foodi Smart XL Grill and regulate the settings at 350°F for 9 minutes. 2. Place the bacon into the Ninja Foodi when it displays "Add Food" and drizzle with olive oil. 3. Air crisp for about 9 minutes, tossing in between. 4. Dish out the bacon in a platter and serve warm.

Serving Suggestions: Serve it with half fried egg.
Variation Tip: You can use butter instead of olive oil.
Nutritional Information per Serving: Calories: 110 | Fat: 10.2g | Sat Fat: 3.2g | Carbohydrates: 0g | Fiber: 0g | Sugar: 0g | Protein: 4g

Bacon Cups

Prep Time: 10 minutes | Cook Time: 15 minutes | Servings: 6

Ingredients:

6 bread slices
6 bacon slices
1 scallion, chopped
6 eggs

3 tablespoons green bell pepper, seeded and chopped
2 tablespoons low-fat mayonnaise

Preparation:

1. Select the "Bake" button on the Ninja Foodi Smart XL Grill and regulate the time for 15 minutes at 375°F. 2. Place each bacon slice in a prepared muffin cup. 3. Cut the round bread slices with a cookie cutter and place over the bacon slices. 4. Top evenly with bell pepper, scallion, and mayonnaise and crack 1 egg in each muffin cup. 5. Place these cups in the Ninja Foodi when it displays "Add Food". 6. Bake for 15 minutes and dish out to serve.

Serving Suggestions: Serve topped with cherry tomatoes
Variation Tip: You can also use red or yellow bell pepper.
Nutritional Information per Serving: Calories: 229 | Fat: 14.4g | Sat Fat: 4.3g | Carbohydrates: 11g | Fiber: 1.1g | Sugar: 4.1g | Protein: 14g

Savory French Toasts

Prep Time: 10 minutes | Cook Time: 7 minutes | Servings: 2

Ingredients:

¼ cup chickpea flour
3 tablespoons onion, finely chopped
2 teaspoons green chili, seeded and finely chopped
Water, as required

4 bread slices
½ teaspoon red chili powder
¼ teaspoon ground turmeric
¼ teaspoon ground cumin
Salt, to taste

Preparation:

1. Select the "Grill" button on the Ninja Foodi Smart XL Grill and regulate the settings at MED for 7 minutes. 2. In a large bowl, mingle all the ingredients except bread slices. 3. Coat the bread slices evenly with egg mixture. 4. Arrange the bread slices in the Ninja Foodi when it displays "Add Food". 5. Grill for 7 minutes, flipping once in between. 6. Dole out in a plate when grilled completely and serve warm.

Serving Suggestions: Serve with green mint dip.
Variation Tip: You can increase or decrease spices as per your taste.

Nutritional Information per Serving: Calories: 151 | Fat: 2.3g | Sat Fat: 0.3g | Carbohydrates: 26.7g | Fiber: 5.4g | Sugar: 4.3g | Protein: 6.5g

Chicken Omelet

Prep Time: 10 minutes | Cook Time: 13 minutes | Servings: 2

Ingredients:

1 teaspoon butter
1 onion, chopped
½ jalapeño pepper, seeded and chopped

3 eggs
¼ cup chicken, cooked and shredded

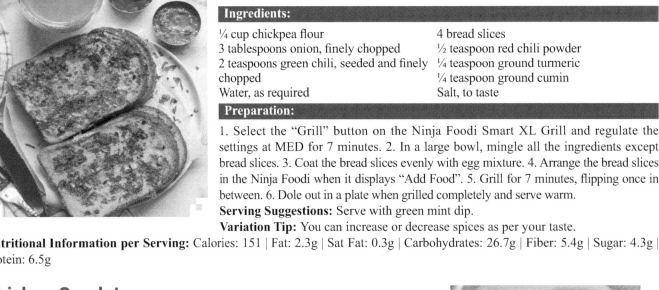

Preparation:

1. Select the "Bake" button on the Ninja Foodi Smart XL Grill and regulate the time for 10 minutes at 350°F. 2. In a skillet, put butter and onions and sauté for 5 minutes over medium heat. 3. Add jalapeño pepper and sauté for 1 minute. 4. Stir in the chicken and dish it out in a plate. 5. Meanwhile, whisk together the eggs, salt, and black pepper in a bowl. 6. Place the chicken mixture in the Ninja Foodi when it displays "Add Food" and top with whisked eggs. 7. Air Crisp for 10 minutes, flipping once in between. 8. Dole out in a platter and serve warm.

Serving Suggestions: Serve with browned toast slices.
Variation Tip: You can also add mozzarella and cheddar cheese.
Nutritional Information per Serving: Calories: 161 | Fat: 9.1g | Sat Fat: 3.4g | Carbohydrates: 5.9g | Fiber: 1.3g | Sugar: 3g | Protein: 19g

Beans & Quinoa Burgers

Prep Time: 20 minutes | Cook Time: 10 minutes | Servings: 6

Ingredients:

For Burgers:

1 tablespoon extra-virgin olive oil
½ of red onion, chopped
1 garlic clove, minced
1 cup fresh kale, tough ribs removed
1 cup carrots, peeled and chopped roughly

⅓ cup fresh parsley
15 ounces cooked cannellini beans
1 cup cooked quinoa
1 cup gluten-free oats

For Seasoning Mixture:

½ cup BBQ sauce
1 teaspoon dried oregano
1 teaspoon chili powder

1 teaspoon ground cumin
Salt and ground black pepper, as required

Preparation:

1. For burgers: in a medium-sized pan, heat the oil over medium heat and sauté the onion and garlic for about 5 minutes. 2. With a slotted spoon, transfer the onion mixture into a large-sized owl. 3. In a food processor, add kale, carrots, and parsley and pulse until grated. 4. Transfer the kale mixture into the bowl of onion mixture. 5. In the food processor, add white beans to and pulse until mashed slightly. 6. Transfer the mashed beans into the bowl of kale mixture. 7. For seasoning mixture: in a small-sized mixing bowl, add all ingredients and mix well. 8. Add the cooked quinoa, oats, and seasoning mixture in the bowl of kale mixture and mix until well combined. 9. Make 6 equal-sized patties from the mixture. 10. Arrange the lightly greased "Grill Grate" in the crisper basket in the cooking pot of Ninja Foodi Smart XL Grill. 11. Close the Grill with lid and press "Power" button. 12. Select "Grill" and then use the set of arrows to the left of the display to adjust the temperature to "MED". 13. Use the set of arrows to the right of the display to adjust the cook time to 10 minutes. 14. Press "Start/Stop" to begin preheating. When the display shows "Add Food", open the lid and place the patties onto the "Grill Grate". 15. With your hands, gently press down each patty. Close the Grill with lid. 16. After 5 minutes of cooking, flip the patties. 17. When the cooking time is completed, open the lid and serve hot.

Serving Suggestions: Serve alongside the green sauce.

Variation Tip: You can use canned beans.

Nutritional Information per Serving: Calories: 268 | Fat: 5g | Sat Fat: 0.6g | Carbohydrates: 47.4g | Fiber: 8.4g | Sugar: 8.9g | Protein: 9.5g

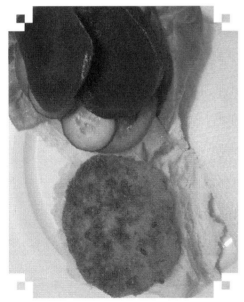

Beans & Oat Burgers

Prep Time: 15 minutes | Cook Time: 10 minutes | Servings: 8

Ingredients:

1 tablespoon olive oil
1 large onion, finely chopped
4 garlic cloves, minced
1 medium carrot, peeled and shredded
2 teaspoons red chili powder
1 teaspoon ground cumin
Ground black pepper, as required
1 (15-ounce) can pinto beans, rinsed and

drained
1 (15-ounce) can black beans, rinsed and drained
1½ cups quick-cooking oats
2 tablespoons low-sodium soy sauce
2 tablespoons Dijon mustard
1 tablespoon ketchup

Preparation:

1. In a large non-stick skillet, heat oil over medium-high heat and sauté the onion for about 2 minutes. 2. Add the garlic and sauté for about 1 minute. 3. Stir in carrot and spices and cook for about 2-3 minutes, stirring frequently. 4. Remove from heat and set aside. 5. In a large bowl, add both cans of beans and with a potato masher, mash slightly. 6. Add the carrot mixture, oats, soy sauce, mustard and ketchup and mix until well combined. 7. Make 8 (3½-inch) patties from the mixture. 8. Arrange the lightly greased "Grill Grate" in the crisper basket in the cooking pot of Ninja Foodi Smart XL Grill. 9. Close the Grill with lid and press "Power" button. 10. Select "Grill" and then use the set of arrows to the left of the display to adjust the temperature to "MED". 11. Use the set of arrows to the right of the display to adjust the cook time to 10 minutes. 12. Press "Start/Stop" to begin preheating. When the display shows "Add Food", open the lid and place the patties onto the "Grill Grate". 13. With your hands, gently press down the patties. Close the Grill with lid. 14. After 5 minutes of cooking, flip the patties. 15. When the cooking time is completed, open the lid and serve hot.

Serving Suggestions: Serve alongside the fresh salad.

Variation Tip: You can use beans of your choice.

Nutritional Information per Serving: Calories: 241 | Fat: 3.8g | Sat Fat: 0.6g | Carbohydrates: 41.4g | Fiber: 12g | Sugar: 2.3g | Protein: 12.5g

Spicy Tofu Slices

Prep Time: 15 minutes | Cook Time: 7 minutes | Servings: 6

Ingredients:

1 teaspoon paprika

½ teaspoon cayenne powder

½ teaspoon ground coriander

½ teaspoon ground cumin

¼ teaspoon ground turmeric

3 tablespoons olive oil

1 tablespoon fresh lime juice

1 tablespoon garlic, minced

2 (14-ounce) packages extra-firm tofu, drained, pressed, cut into 12 slices crosswise and pat dried

Preparation:

1. In a clean bowl, blend together the spices. 2. In a small pan, heat the olive oil over medium heat and sauté the spice mixture, lime juice, and garlic for about 1 minute. 3. Immediately, remove from the heat. 4. In the pan, add the tofu slices and coat with the spiced oil evenly. 5. Arrange the lightly greased "Grill Grate" in the crisper basket in the cooking pot of Ninja Foodi Smart XL Grill. 6. Close the Grill with lid and press "Power" button. 7. Select "Grill" and then use the set of arrows to adjust the temperature to "MED". 8. Use the set of arrows to the right of the display to adjust the cook time to 6 minutes. 9. Press "Start/Stop" to begin preheating. When the display shows "Add Food", open the lid and place the tofu slices onto the "Grill Grate". 10. With your hands, gently press down each tofu slice. Close the Grill with lid. 11. After 3 minutes of cooking, flip the tofu slices. 12. When the cooking time is completed, open the lid and serve hot.

Serving Suggestions: Serve with the garnishing of lime zest.

Variation Tip: Make sure to pat dry the tofu slices before seasoning.

Nutritional Information per Serving: Calories: 185 | Fat: 14.9g | Sat Fat: 1.7g | Carbohydrates: 3.6g | Fiber: 0.8g | Sugar: 0.7g | Protein: 13.3g

Strawberry Stuffed French Toast

Prep Time: 15 minutes | Cook Time: 8 minutes | Servings: 4

Ingredients:

¼ cup creamy peanut butter

4 (½-inch thick) challah bread slices

3 tablespoons seedless strawberry jam

½ teaspoon ground cinnamon

3 large eggs

⅓ cup 2% milk

3 tablespoons maple syrup, divided

⅓ teaspoon vanilla extract

4 fresh strawberries, hulled and halved

Preparation:

1. Spread peanut butter over 2 bread slices. 2. Spread jam over remaining 2 bread slices evenly and top each with strawberry slices. 3. Then sprinkle with cinnamon and cover with peanut butter-coated slices. 4. In a shallow dish, whisk together the eggs, milk, 3 tablespoons of maple syrup and vanilla extract. 5. Dip the sandwiches in egg mixture evenly. 6. Arrange the lightly greased "Grill Grate" in the crisper basket in the cooking pot of Ninja Foodi Smart XL Grill. 7. Close the Grill with lid and press "Power" button. 8. Select "Grill" and then use the set of arrows to the left of the display to adjust the temperature to "MED". 9. Use the set of arrows to the right of the display to adjust the cook time to 8 minutes. 10. Press "Start/Stop" to begin preheating. When the display shows "Add Food", open the lid and place the sandwiches onto the "Grill Grate". 11. With your hands, gently press down each sandwich. Close the Grill with lid. 12. After 4 minutes of cooking, flip the sandwiches. 13. When the cooking time is completed, open the lid and place the sandwiches onto a platter. 14. Brush each with remaining maple syrup. 15. Cut 2 halves of each sandwich and serve warm.

Serving Suggestions: Serve with Sliced Cheese

Variation Tip: Use unsalted peanut butter.

Nutritional Information per Serving: Calories: 307 | Fat: 13g | Sat Fat: 3.2g | Carbohydrates: 39.3g | Fiber: 5g | Sugar: 12g | Protein: 10.8g

French Toast Skewers

Prep Time: 15 minutes | Cook Time: 8 minutes | Servings: 4

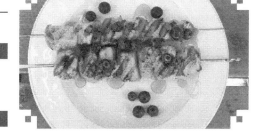

Ingredients:

3 eggs
½ cup milk
1 teaspoon vanilla extract
½ teaspoon ground cinnamon
5 cups crusty bread cubes

Preparation:

1. Whisk together the eggs, milk, vanilla extract, and cinnamon in a bowl. 2. Coat the bread cubes with egg mixture evenly. 3. Thread the bread cubes onto pre-soaked wooden skewers. 4. Arrange the lightly greased "Grill Grate" in the crisper basket in the cooking pot of Ninja Foodi Smart XL Grill. 5. Close the Grill with lid and press "Power" button. 6. Select "Grill" and then use the set of arrows to the left of the display to adjust the temperature to "MED". 7. Use the set of arrows to the right of the display to adjust the cook time to 8 minutes. 8. Press "Start/Stop" to begin preheating. When the display shows "Add Food", open the lid and place the skewers onto the "Grill Grate". 9. With your hands, gently press down each skewer. Close the Grill with lid. 10. After 4 minutes of cooking, flip the skewers. 11. When the cooking time is completed, open the lid and serve.
Serving Suggestions: Serve with the drizzling of maple syrup.
Variation Tip: Cut the bread into equal-sized cubes.
Nutritional Information per Serving: Calories: 139 | Fat: 3.6g | Sat Fat: 1.1g | Carbohydrates: 20.6g | Fiber: 0.8g | Sugar: 6.4g | Protein: 5.7g

French Toast

Prep Time: 15 minutes | Cook Time: 4 minutes | Servings: 4

Ingredients:

¼ cup milk
4 eggs
2 tablespoons sugar
½ teaspoon vanilla extract
1 teaspoon ground cinnamon
¼ teaspoon ground nutmeg
4 thick-cut bread slices
¼ cup fresh strawberries, hulled and sliced
¼ cup fresh blueberries

Preparation:

1. In a shallow baking dish, add milk, eggs, sugar, vanilla extract, cinnamon, and nutmeg and beat until well combined. 2. Dip each bread slice in milk mixture for about 5-10 seconds per side. 3. Arrange the lightly greased "Grill Grate" in the crisper basket in the cooking pot of Ninja Foodi Smart XL Grill. 4. Close the Grill with lid and press "Power" button. 5. Select "Grill" and then use the set of arrows to the left of the display to adjust the temperature to "MED". 6. Use the set of arrows to the right of the display to adjust the cook time to 4 minutes. 7. Press "Start/Stop" to begin preheating. When the display shows "Add Food", open the lid and place the bread slices onto the "Grill Grate". 8. With your hands, gently press down each bread slice. Close the Grill with lid. 9. After 2 minutes of cooking, flip the bread slices. 10. When the cooking time is completed, open the lid and serve warm with the topping of berries.
Serving Suggestions: Serve with the topping of maple syrup.
Variation Tip: Use one-day-old bread.
Nutritional Information per Serving: Calories: 158 | Fat: 4.8g | Sat Fat: 1.6g | Carbohydrates: 21g | Fiber: 1.3g | Sugar: 9.1g | Protein: 8.6g

Green Courgette Fritters

Prep Time: 15 minutes | Cook Time: 33 minutes | Servings: 2

Ingredients:

½ teaspoon sea salt
½ teaspoon baking powder
4½ oz. courgette, coarsely grated
1 large free-range egg
3 tablespoons plain flour
2 ounces frozen peas, thawed
Black pepper, to taste
1½ teaspoons ground cumin

Preparation:

1. Select the "Air Crisp" button on the Ninja Foodi Smart XL Grill and regulate the time for 7 minutes at 360°F. 2. Merge together all the ingredients in a large bowl. 3. Make small fritters from this mixture and place them in the Ninja Foodi when it displays "Add Food". 4. Air Crisp for about 7 minutes and shift into a platter to serve warm.
Serving Suggestions: Serve with mango yogurt chutney.
Variation Tip: You can also add use zucchini in this recipe.
Nutritional Information per Serving: Calories: 143 | Fat: 2g | Sat Fat: 0.2g | Carbohydrates: 26g | Fiber: 5.7g | Sugar: 6.6g | Protein: 9g

Raspberry Stuffed French Toast

Prep Time: 10 minutes | Cook Time: 8 minutes | Servings: 4

Ingredients:

4 bread slices
¼ cup cream cheese, softened
2 tablespoons raspberry jelly

2 eggs
2 tablespoons butter

Preparation:

1. Arrange 2 bread slices onto a plate. 2. Spread 2 tablespoons of cream cheese onto 1 bread slice. 3. Spread 1 tablespoon of jelly onto the other slice. 4. Place the jelly side-down over the cream cheese. 5. Repeat with the remaining slices, cream cheese and jelly. 6. In a shallow dish, whisk the eggs. Dip both sides of sandwiches into beaten eggs evenly. 7. Arrange the lightly greased "Grill Grate" in the crisper basket in the cooking pot of Ninja Foodi Smart XL Grill. 8. Close the Grill with lid and press "Power" button. 9. Select "Grill" and then use the set of arrows to the left of the display to adjust the temperature to "MED". 10. Use the set of arrows to the right of the display to adjust the cook time to 5 minutes. 11. Press "Start/Stop" to begin preheating. When the display shows "Add Food", open the lid and place the sandwiches onto the "Grill Grate". 12. With your hands, gently press down each sandwich. Close the Grill with lid. 13. After 3 minutes of cooking, flip the sandwiches. 14. When the cooking time is completed, open the lid and place the sandwiches onto a platter. 15. Cut 2 halves of each sandwich and serve warm.

Serving Suggestions: Serve with a dusting of powdered sugar.
Variation Tip: You can use any kind of fruit jelly.
Nutritional Information per Serving: Calories: 268 | Fat: 13.5g | Sat Fat: 7.5g | Carbohydrates: 12.7g | Fiber: 0.4g | Sugar: 5.5g | Protein: 7.5g

Cheese Sandwich

Prep Time: 10 minutes | Cook Time: 5 minutes | Servings: 4

Ingredients:

4 bread slices
4 tablespoons butter, softened

4 ounces cheddar cheese, shredded

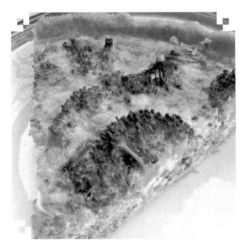

Preparation:

1. Arrange the bread slices onto a smooth surface. 2. Spread the butter on one side of each bread slice. 3. Place 2 bread slices onto the platter, buttered side down, and sprinkle with cheese. 4. Top each with the 1 of remaining bread slices, buttered side up. 5. Arrange the lightly greased "Grill Grate" in the crisper basket in the cooking pot of Ninja Foodi Smart XL Grill. 6. Close the Grill with lid and press "Power" button. 7. Select "Grill" and then use the set of arrows to the left of the display to adjust the temperature to "MED". 8. Use the set of arrows to the right of the display to adjust the cook time to 5 minutes. 9. Press "Start/Stop" to begin preheating. When the display shows "Add Food", open the lid and place the sandwiches onto the "Grill Grate". 10. With your hands, gently press down each sandwich. Close the Grill with lid. 11. After 3 minutes of cooking, flip the sandwiches. 12. When the cooking time is completed, open the lid and place the sandwiches onto a platter. 13. Cut 2 halves of each sandwich and serve warm.

Serving Suggestions: Serve with the drizzling of butter.
Variation Tip: Use unsalted butter.
Nutritional Information per Serving: Calories: 270 | Fat: 20.9g | Sat Fat: 13.3g | Carbohydrates: 11.7g | Fiber: 0.6g | Sugar: 0.8g | Protein: 9.6g

Chicken Broccoli Quiche

Prep Time: 10 minutes | Cook Time: 12 minutes | Servings: 8

Ingredients:

1 frozen ready-made pie crust
1 egg
⅓ cup cheddar cheese, grated
¼ cup boiled broccoli, chopped
¼ cup cooked chicken, chopped

½ tablespoon olive oil
3 tablespoons whipping cream
Salt to taste
Pepper to taste

Preparation:

1. Select the "Grill" button on Ninja Foodi Smart XL Grill and regulate the time for 10 minutes at MED. 2. Take a bowl and add egg with whipping cream, cheese, salt, and black pepper. Whisk well. 3. Arrange pie in a greased pan and press in the bottom and sides gently and pour the egg mixture over pie crust. 4. Top with chicken and broccoli. 5. Place the pie pan in Ninja Foodi when it displays "Add Food". 6. Grill for 12 minutes. 7. Serve warm and enjoy.

Serving Suggestions: Served with chopped cilantro on top.
Variation Tip: You can use simple cream instead of whipping cream.
Nutritional Information per Serving: Calories: 140 | Fat: 10g | Sat Fat: 3.2g | Carbohydrates: 8.3g | Fiber: 0.2g | Sugar: 0.8g | Protein: 4g

Chocolate Cherry Sandwich

Prep Time: 10 minutes | Cook Time: 8 minutes | Servings: 6

Ingredients:

6 (½-inch-thick) bread slices
2 tablespoons cherry preserves
1 (4-ounce) bittersweet chocolate bar, cut
into thirds
3 tablespoons unsalted butter, melted

Preparation:

1. Arrange the bread slices onto a smooth surface. 2. Spread the cherry preserves onto 6 bread slices. 3. Top each slice with 1 piece of chocolate. 4. Cover with the remaining bread slices. 5. Brush both sides of each sandwich the melted butter. 6. Arrange the lightly greased "Grill Grate" in the crisper basket in the cooking pot of Ninja Foodi Smart XL Grill. 7. Close the Grill with lid and press "Power" button. 8. Select "Grill" and then use the set of arrows to the left of the display to adjust the temperature to "MED". 9. Use the set of arrows to the right of the display to adjust the cook time to 8 minutes. 10. Press "Start/Stop" to begin preheating. When the display shows "Add Food", open the lid and place the sandwiches onto the "Grill Grate". 11. With your hands, gently press down each sandwich. Close the Grill with lid. 12. After 4 minutes of cooking, flip the sandwiches. 13. When the cooking time is completed, open the lid and place the sandwiches onto a platter. 14. Cut 2 halves of each sandwich and serve warm.

Serving Suggestions: Serve with a sprinkling of cinnamon.

Variation Tip: You can also use semi-sweet chocolate.

Nutritional Information per Serving: Calories: 197 | Fat: 13.5g | Sat Fat: 8.6g | Carbohydrates: 18.1g | Fiber: 1.7g | Sugar: 9.6g | Protein: 2.3g

---

Breakfast Sausages

Prep Time: 5 minutes | Cook Time: 10 minutes | Servings: 3

Ingredients:

1 tablespoon brown sugar
2 teaspoons dried sage
2 teaspoons salt
1 teaspoon ground black pepper
¼ teaspoon dried marjoram
⅛ teaspoon crushed red pepper flakes
1 pinch ground cloves
2 pounds ground pork

Preparation:

1. Select the "Grill" button on the Ninja Foodi Smart XL Grill and regulate the time for 10 minutes at MED. 2. Mingle brown sugar, sage, salt, black pepper, marjoram, red pepper flakes, and cloves in a bowl. 3. Combine ground pork with the spice mixture and make sausage-shaped patties from this mixture. 4. Place the patties in the Ninja Foodi when it displays "Add Food". 5. Grill for 10 minutes, flipping once in between. 6. Dole out in a platter and serve warm.

Serving Suggestions: Serve these Breakfast Sausages inside the buns.

Variation Tip: You can use pork, chicken, or beef sausages as required.

Nutritional Information per Serving: Calories: 447 | Fat: 10.7g | Sat Fat: 3.7g | Carbohydrates: 3.8g | Fiber: 0.4g | Sugar: 2.9g | Protein: 79.3g

---

Crustless Spinach Quiche

Prep Time: 15 minutes | Cook Time: 33 minutes | Servings: 4

Ingredients:

1 tablespoon butter, melted
1 (10-ounce) package frozen spinach, thawed
5 organic eggs, beaten
Salt and black pepper, to taste
3 cups Monterey Jack cheese, shredded

Preparation:

1. Select the "Bake" button on the Ninja Foodi Smart XL Grill and regulate the time for 30 minutes at 360°F. 2. Put butter and spinach in a pan and sauté for 3 minutes. 3. Top with eggs, Monterey Jack cheese, salt, and black pepper. 4. Move this mixture in a greased quiche mold and place inside the Ninja Foodi when it displays "Add Food". 5. Bake for about 30 minutes and shift into a platter to serve warm.

Serving Suggestions: Serve with your favorite salad.

Variation Tip: You can also add some cheddar cheese.

Nutritional Information per Serving: Calories: 437 | Fat: 34.3g | Sat Fat: 19.7g | Carbohydrates: 3.6g | Fiber: 1.6g | Sugar: 1.1g | Protein: 29.7g

Chapter 2 Snack and Appetizer Recipes

Grilled Corn

Prep Time: 5 minutes | Cook Time: 20 minutes | Servings: 2

Ingredients:

4 ears of corn
4 tablespoons of butter
1 teaspoon chili powder
½ teaspoon kosher salt
½ of a lime juiced

½ teaspoon black pepper
½ cup of grated parmesan cheese
Avocado spray oil
Cilantro, for garnishing

Preparation:

1. Select the "Grill" button on the Ninja Foodi Smart XL Grill and regulate the time for 10 minutes at MED. 2. Spray oil on the Grill Grate. 3. Place the corn in the Ninja Foodi when it displays "Add Food." 4. Grill for 15-20 minutes, flipping after every 5 minutes. 5. Melt the butter, chili powder, pepper, salt, and lime juice in a small bowl. Mix well once melted. 6. Once the corn is done and charred from the outside, take it out and brush it with the butter mixture. 7. Then roll it in parmesan cheese. 8. Garnish with cilantro, and enjoy.

Serving Suggestions: You can enjoy this with mayonnaise or cream as well.

Variation Tip: You can add herb mix instead of red chili.

Nutritional Information per Serving: Calories: 340 | Fat: 19.2g | Sat Fat: 10.8g | Carbohydrates: 41.3g | Fiber: 6.4g | Sugar: 7g | Protein: 8.7g

Air Fried Pizza, Egg rolls

Prep Time: 5 minutes | Cook Time: 20 minutes | Servings: 3

Ingredients:

12 egg roll wrappers
12 pepperoni
12 mozzarella cheese slices
6 Italian sausages, chopped

1 jar pizza sauce
1 egg
¼ teaspoon avocado oil

Preparation:

1. Cook Italian sausages and half of the pizza sauce in a pan. 2. Place the egg roll sheet in the diamond length. 3. On the wrap, place the cheese, spoonful of the sausage mixture, and pepperoni towards the side of the diamond. 4. Roll the first corner tightly over the filling. 5. Fold the wrapper and finish the roll. Damp the last point of the roll with the egg wash. 6. Select the "Air Crisp" button on the Ninja Foodi Smart XL Grill to 400°Fahrenheit. 7. Place the rolls in the Ninja Foodi Crisper Basket when it displays "Add Food ."Spray with the avocado oil and air fry the rolls for 15-20 minutes, flipping once between the cooking time. 8. Remove from the Ninja Foodi and serve with extra pizza sauce. Enjoy!!

Serving Suggestions: Add extra cheese on top of the rolls

Variation Tip: You can use chicken meat or beef instead of sausages.

Nutritional Information per Serving: Calories: 59 Fat: 3.1g | Sat Fat: 1.4g | Carbohydrates: 4.3g | Fiber: 0.3g | Sugar: o.4g | Protein: 3.4g

Crispy Prawns

Prep Time: 15 minutes | Cook Time: 8 minutes | Servings: 4

Ingredients:

1 egg
½ pound nacho chips, crushed

18 prawns, peeled and deveined

Preparation:

1. In a shallow dish, crack the egg, and beat well. 2. Crush nacho chips in another dish and set aside. 3. Dip the prawn into a beaten egg and then coat it with the nacho chips. 4. Select "Air Crisp" mode onNinja Foodi Smart XL Grill and regulate the temperature to 355°F. 5. Place the prawns in the crisper basket in a single layer. 6. Air crisp for 8 minutes, flipping in the middle. 7. Serve hot!

Serving Suggestions: Serve with ketchup or tartar sauce.

Variation Tip: You can add seasoned breadcrumbs instead of nachos for coating.

Nutritional Information per Serving: Calories: 425 | Fat: 17.6g | Sat Fat: 3.1g | Carbohydrates: 36.6g | Fiber: 2.6g | Sugar: 2.2g | Protein: 28.6g

Scotch Eggs

Prep Time: 20 minutes | Cook Time: 5 minutes | Servings: 4

Ingredients:

8 ounces sausage

4 large eggs

Breading:

½ cup breadcrumbs

⅛ teaspoon chipotle pepper, ground

½ tablespoon maple sugar

Egg Mixture:

1 large egg

1 teaspoon mustard paste

1 tablespoon maple syrup

1 teaspoon hot sauce

Dipping Sauce:

1 teaspoon maple sugar

2 tablespoons sour cream

Preparation:

1. Boil eggs in a separate saucepan and set aside. 2. Mix the breading mixture by combining bread crumbs, sugar, and ground pepper. Set it aside. 3. Mix egg with maple syrup, hot sauce, and mustard. 4. Press around 2 ounces of sausage on the palm to ⅛-¼" thick. Place the egg in the center and wrap the ground sausage around the egg. 5. Dip the coated egg into the egg mixture and then breading mixture and coat thoroughly. Repeat this step for a second coating. 6. Select "air crisp" on Ninja Foodi smart XL Grill and preheat for 10 minutes. Then, regulate the temperature at 375°F for 7 minutes. 7. When Ninja Foodi displays "Add Food," place the scotch eggs in the basket and spray oil on the eggs. Flip the eggs after the first 4 minutes. 8. Prepare dip sauce by combining sour cream with maple sugar. 9. Slice the Scotch eggs in half, and serve. Enjoy!

Serving Suggestions: Serve with fresh salad.

Variation Tip: You can use chili garlic sauce as a dipping sauce.

Nutritional Information per Serving: Calories: 346 | Fat: 23.5g | Sat Fat: 7.7g | Carbohydrates: 13.4g | Fiber: 1.2g | Sugar: 3g | Protein: 19.8g

Chicken Tenders

Prep Time: 20 minutes | Cook Time: 10 minutes | Servings: 4

Ingredients:

1½ pounds chicken tenders

Oil for spritzing about 2 teaspoons

Dry Breading

1 cup plain breadcrumbs

1 teaspoon fine grind sea salt

Wet Batter

1 large egg

½ cup cold water

2 tablespoons hot sauce

¾ cup all-purpose flour sifted

Preparation:

1. Combine bread crumbs with salt and set aside. 2. Prepare wet batter by combining all the ingredients well and mixing until there are no lumps. 3. Coat chicken tenders in the wet batter and then with crumbs. 4. Select the "air crisp" button on the Ninja Foodi Smart XL Grill and regulate the time for 10 minutes at MED. Then, place chicken tenders in the Ninja Foodi when it displays "Add Food." 5. Place chicken tenders in the Ninja Foodi when it displays "Add Food." Cook for 5 minutes. 6. Serve and enjoy!

Serving Suggestions: You can serve it with French fries.

Variation Tip: You can also serve it with tartar sauce.

Nutritional Information per Serving: Calories: 480 | Fat: 21g | Sat Fat: 5g | Carbohydrates: 28g | Fiber: 2g | Sugar: 2g | Protein: 41g

Dehydrated Apple Crisps

Prep Time: 10 minutes | Cook Time: 7 hours | Servings: 4

Ingredients:

1-pound Honey Crisp Apples

4 cups water

2 tablespoons lemon juice

Preparation:

1. In a bowl, mix water and lemon juice. 2. Slice apples with the slicer with skin on. (you can remove the skin if you prefer. 3. Put apple slices in the lemon water to prevent from browning. 4. Once all the apples are sliced, take them out of the water and place them over the kitchen towel and pat dry them. 5. Select the "Dehydrate" button on the Ninja Foodi Smart XL Grill and regulate on 135°F for 7 hours. 6. Make sure to place slices in a single layer on the bottom tray and air crisp basket. 7. Line them both in the Ninja Foodi and start. 8. Check the apples halfway through and toss them with a spoon. 9. You can store these in a ziplock bag for a week 10. Serve and Enjoy!!

Serving Suggestions: Serve them on the cheese platter with nuts

Variation Tip: You can add cinnamon powder to the crisps to add a different flavor.

Nutritional Information per Serving: Calories: 104 | Fat: 0.2g | Sat Fat: 0g | Carbohydrates: 28.1g | Fiber: 3.7g | Sugar: 24.3g | Protein: 0.4g

Falafel with Yogurt and Cucumber Dip

Prep Time: 10 minutes | Cook Time: 12 minutes | Servings: 3

Ingredients:

1 cup overnight presoaked chickpeas
1 cup packed fresh parsley
1 cup fresh chopped cilantro
1 green onion
2 cloves of garlic
Dipping sauce:
½ cup Greek yogurt
2 tablespoons cucumber, shredded and squeezed
½ teaspoon fine grind sea salt

1½ tablespoons olive oil
½ teaspoon salt
¼ teaspoon black pepper
¼ teaspoon cumin
¼ teaspoon onion powder

½ tablespoon parsley, finely chopped
½ tablespoon cilantro, finely chopped
1 teaspoon lemon zest
2 teaspoons lemon juice

Preparation:

1. Combine chickpeas, parsley, cilantro, garlic, onion, and spices in a food processor. 2. Pulse till everything is well combined. Scrape down the sides of the processor bowl as and when required. 3. Select the "Air Crisp" button on the Ninja Foodi Smart XL Grill and regulate the time for 12 minutes at 350°F. 4. Spray the basket with oil and place falafel balls in the Ninja Foodi when it displays "Add Food." 5. Air Crisp for 12 minutes, flipping in between. 6. Remove the falafel on a cooling rack until ready to serve. Yogurt Dip: Finely grate cucumber and squeeze out all liquid. Add to the yogurt and the rest of the ingredients. Mix well and serve with falafel balls.

Serving Suggestions: Drizzle sauce on the top, along with cilantro.
Variation Tip: You can also serve it with hummus.
Nutritional Information per Serving: Calories: 235 Fat: 14.9g | Sat Fat: 2g | Carbohydrates: 21g | Fiber: 6g | Sugar: 3.7g | Protein: 6.6g

Banana Chips

Prep Time: 5 minutes | Cook Time: 10 minutes | Servings: 2

Ingredients:

4 bananas, barely ripe
2 teaspoons avocado oil

¼ teaspoon kosher salt

Preparation:

1. Select "Air Crisp" mode and preheat Ninja Foodi Smart XL Grill to 350°F. 2. Slice the bananas into ¼-inch thick slices. 3. Mix the oil in the banana slices until well coated. 4. Place a single layer of banana slices in the crisper basket when it displays "Add Food." 5. Sprinkle the banana slices with kosher salt. 6. Air fry for 8-10 minutes at 350°F, flipping halfwaythrough, until bananas are lightly brown and crispy. 7. Remove from the grill and let cool on a baking sheet or cooling rack. Repeat with remaining bananas.

Serving Suggestions: Serve with ketchup.
Variation Tip: Add in some paprika powder for taste variation.
Nutritional Information per Serving: Calories: 216 | Fat: 1.4g | Sat Fat: 0.4g | Carbohydrates: 54.2g | Fiber: 6.3g | Sugar: 28.9g | Protein: 2.6g

Tortilla Chips

Prep Time: 5 minutes | Cook Time: 7 minutes | Servings: 2

Ingredients:

6 corn tortillas
Salt, as required

Oil, for spraying

Preparation:

1. Stack tortillas on one another and cut them in triangles. 2. Spray tortilla triangles with oil. 3. Select "Air Crisp" mode on Ninja Foodi Smart XL Grill and regulate temperature at MED for 10 minutes. 4. Once it displays "Add Food", place tortilla triangles in the crisper basket and air fry for 7 minutes. Shake mid-way through the cooking time. 5. Serve and enjoy!

Serving Suggestions: You can serve it with salsa and sour cream.
Variation Tip: You can also garnish with parmesan cheese.
Nutritional Information per Serving: Calories: 85 | Fat: 1g | Sat Fat: 1g | Carbohydrates: 17g | Fiber: 2g | Sugar: 1g | Protein: 2g

Air Fryer Hush Puppies

Prep Time: 10 minutes | Cook Time: 10 minutes | Servings: 10

Ingredients:

1 large egg
½ cup half & half
1 tablespoon white vinegar
1 tablespoon sugar
½ tablespoon onion powder
1 teaspoon sea salt, fine grind

¼ teaspoon chipotle
1 teaspoon baking powder
1 cup cornmeal
1 cup flour all-purpose
½ cup corn frozen or canned, drained
¼ cup white sugar, for coating

Preparation:

1. Select "Air Crisp" mode on Ninja Foodi Smart XL Grill. Regulate the heat to 400°For 10 minutes. 2. Preheat the Ninja Foodi 400°F/204°C for at least 10 minutes. 3. Mix egg, half and half, and vinegar in a medium-sized bowl. Whisk until well combined and set it aside. 4. Combine sugar, salt, onion powder, chipotle, cornmeal, and baking powder in the egg mixture. 5. Add flour to the mixture and combine well. 6. Add corn and fold in the batter. 7. Take a tablespoon full of the batter and shape it into a ball. 8. Place sugar in a shallow dish and roll the balls in the sugar. 9. When the Ninja Foodi displays "Add Food," take out the basket and spray with the oil. Place the hush puppies in one layer on the basket and Air Crisp at 400°F/204°C for about 4-5 minutes. Flip halfway through the cooking time and then air crisp for another 3-5 minutes or until the outside is golden brown. 10. Cool hush puppies on the cooling rack. 11. Serve and enjoy!!

Serving Suggestions: Serve with sour cream and garnish with chopped Parsley and lemon wedges.
Variation Tip: You can add smoked paprika to the mixture.
Nutritional Information per Serving: Calories: 164 | Fat: 3g | Sat Fat: 1g | Carbohydrates: 30g | Fiber: 2g | Sugar: 7g | Protein: 4g

Meatballs

Prep Time: 10 minutes | Cook Time: 10 minutes | Servings: 6

Ingredients:

1 lb. ground beef
1½ tablespoons Worcestershire sauce
¾ teaspoon sea salt
¾ teaspoon basil
¾ teaspoon onion powder

1 large egg
⅓ cup bread crumbs
¼ teaspoon black pepper
¾ teaspoon garlic powder

Preparation:

1. Select "Broil" mode on the Ninja Foodi Smart XL Grill and regulate the cook time for 10 minutes. 2. Combine the ground beef with all the seasonings and ingredients in a mixing bowl. Mix well to combine. 3. Shape 2 tbsps of the mixture into a ball. 4. When the Ninja Foodi is preheated and displays "Add Food," spray the crisper basket with oil and meatballs on the bottom of the basket. 5. Broil at 375°F/190°C for 5 minutes. After 5 minutes, flip the meatballs and cook another 3-5 minutes. The internal temp should be 165°F/75°C. 6. Remove and Serve!

Serving Suggestions: Serve with fresh thyme on top.
Variation Tip: You can add white pepper for taste variation.
Nutritional Information per Serving: Calories: 253.9 | Fat: 1.1g | Sat Fat: 0.3g | Carbohydrates: 21g | Fiber: 2.6g | Sugar: 0g | Protein: 25g

Rice Bites

Prep Time: 15 minutes | Cook Time: 18 minutes | Servings: 4

Ingredients:

3 cups cooked risotto
⅓ cup Parmesan cheese, grated
1 egg, beaten

3 ounces mozzarella cheese, cubed
¾ cup breadcrumbs

Preparation:

1. In a bowl, mix together the risotto, Parmesan cheese, and egg. 2. Make 20 equal-sized balls from the mixture. 3. Insert a mozzarella cube in the center of each ball, and smooth the risotto mixture to cover the mozzarella. 4. Coat the balls evenly with breadcrumbs. 5. Select "Air Crisp" mode on Ninja Foodi Smart XL Grill and regulate the temperature to 390°F for preheating. 6. Place the balls in a single layer on crisper basket and air crisp at 390°F for 10 minutes or until they are golden brown. 7. Serve!

Serving Suggestions: Serve it with your favorite dip and garnish with chives.
Variation Tip: You can add any other cheese.
Nutritional Information per Serving: Calories: 279 | Fat: 7.3g | Sat Fat: 7g | Carbohydrates: 50.7g | Fiber: 1.2g | Sugar: 0.6g | Protein: 9.4g

Cheesy & Creamy Corn

Prep Time: 15 minutes | Cook Time: 12 minutes | Servings: 4

Ingredients:

4 ears corn, husks removed
2 tablespoons olive oil, divided
Salt and ground black pepper, as required
1 cup Cotija cheese, crumbled
¼ cup sour cream

¼ cup mayonnaise
3-4 tablespoons fresh lime juice
1 teaspoon onion powder
1 teaspoon garlic powder
¼ cup fresh cilantro, chopped

Preparation:

1. Rub each ear of corn with oil evenly and season with salt and black pepper. 2. Arrange the lightly greased "Grill Grate" in the crisper basket in the cooking pot of Ninja Foodi Smart XL Grill. 3. Close the Grill with lid and press "Power" button. 4. Select "Grill" and then use the set of arrows to the left of the display to adjust the temperature to "MAX". 5. Use the set of arrows to the right of thr display to adjust the cook time to 12 minutes. 6. Press "Start/Stop" to begin preheating. When the display shows "Add Food", open the lid and place the ears of corn onto the "Grill Grate". 7. Close the Grill with lid. 8. After 6 minutes, flip the ears of corn. 9. Meanwhile, in a bowl, place the remaining ingredients except for cilantro and mix well. 10. Transfer the ears of corn onto a platter and top with the cheese mixture evenly. 11. Garnish with cilantro and serve.
Serving Suggestions: Serve alongside lime wedges.
Variation Tip: Use fresh ears of corn.
Nutritional Information per Serving: Calories: 291 | Fat: 17.1g | Sat Fat: 4.2g | Carbohydrates: 34.3g | Fiber: 4.3g | Sugar: 6.4g | Protein: 6.3g

Glazed Tofu Kabobs

Prep Time: 20 minutes | Cook Time: 11 minutes | Servings: 4

Ingredients:

1 (14-ounce) package extra-firm tofu, pressed, drained and cut into cubes
⅓ cup miso
2 egg yolks

2 tablespoons sake
2 tablespoons mirin
2 tablespoons sugar
3 tablespoons water

Preparation:

1. Arrange a heatproof bowl over a pan of simmering water. 2. In the bowl, add miso, egg yolks, sake, mirin, and sugar and stir to combine. 3. Slowly, add the water, stirring continuously or until a thick mixture forms. 4. Remove the bowl of glaze from heat and set aside. 5. Thread the tofu cubes onto the skewers. 6. Arrange the lightly greased "Grill Grate" in the crisper basket in the cooking pot of Ninja Foodi Smart XL Grill. 7. Close the Grill with lid and press "Power" button. 8. Select "Grill" and then use the set of arrows to the left of the display to adjust the temperature to "MED". 9. Use the set of arrows to the right of the display to adjust the cook time to 9 minutes. 10. Press "Start/Stop" to begin preheating. When the display shows "Add Food", open the lid and place the skewers onto the "Grill Grate". 11. With your hands, gently press down each skewers. Close the Grill with lid. 12. After 3 minutes of cooking, flip the skewers. 13. After 6 minutes of cooking, flip the skewers and coat with miso mixture generously. 14. When the cooking time is completed, open the lid and serve hot.
Serving Suggestions: Serve with peanut sauce.
Variation Tip: You can substitute the mirin with dry sherry.
Nutritional Information per Serving: Calories: 223 | Fat: 9.4g | Sat Fat: 1.6g | Carbohydrates: 23.4g | Fiber: 1.6g | Sugar: 12.5g | Protein: 3.8g

Chicken Satay

Prep Time: 10 minutes | Cook Time: 6 minutes | Servings: 6

Ingredients:

1½ lbs chicken breast boneless, skinless
½ cup coconut milk
2 cloves garlic, minced (about 1 teaspoon)
2" piece ginger, grated (about 2 teaspoons)
2 teaspoons of turmeric

1 teaspoon sea salt fine grind
1 tablespoon lemongrass paste
1 tablespoon chili garlic sauce
2 teaspoons lemon juice

Preparation:

1. Merge all the ingredients in a medium-sized bowl. 2. Cut chicken into ½» strips and place in the marinade for 20 minutes. 3. Select the "Grill" button on the Ninja Foodi Smart XL Grill and preheat for minutes at LO. 4. Weave the chicken strip into the skewers and place them inside the Ninja Foodi when it displays "Add Food." 5. Grill for about 6 minutes and shift into a platter to serve warm.
Serving Suggestions: Serve with mayonnaise or any favorite dip.
Variation Tip: You can also garnish it with chopped peanuts or cilantro.
Nutritional Information per Serving: Calories: 185 | Fat: 7.7g | Sat Fat: 4.3g | Carbohydrates: 3.1g | Fiber: 0.6g | Sugar: 1.2g | Protein: 24.6g

Chili-Lime Pineapple

Prep Time: 5 minutes | Cook Time: 15 minutes | Servings: 6

Ingredients:

1 fresh pineapple
3 tablespoons brown sugar
1 tablespoon lime juice
1 tablespoon olive oil

1 tablespoon honey
1½ teaspoons chili powder
Dash salt

Preparation:

1. Remove any eyeballs from the pineapple before peeling it. Remove the core and cut lengthwise into six wedges. 2. Mix the remaining ingredients to make the glaze. Brush the pineapple with half of the glaze. 3. Select the "Grill" button on Ninja Foodi Smart XL Grill and regulate the setting at MED for 6 minutes. 4. Arrange them in the Ninja Foodi when it displays "Add Food" and shower with olive oil. 5. Grill for about 6 minutes, turning them occasionally. 6. Serve and enjoy!

Serving Suggestions: Serve with steak.

Variation Tip: You can use agave nectar instead of honey.

Nutritional Information per Serving: Calories: 97 | Fat: 2g | Sat Fat: 0g | Carbohydrates: 50g | Fiber: 1g | Sugar: 13g | Protein: 1g

Candied Pecans

Prep Time: 10 minutes | Cook Time: 1 hour | Servings: 8

Ingredients:

1 lb. pecan halves
1 cup sugar, granulated
1 teaspoon ground cinnamon

1 teaspoon salt
1 egg white
1 tablespoon water

Preparation:

1. Select "Bake" on the Ninja Foodi Smart XL Grill. Preheat the grill and regulate the temperature at 250°Fahrenheit for 1 hour. 2. Beat egg white and water with the hand whisker until frothy. 3. Mix sugar, cinnamon, and salt together. 4. In a large mixing bowl, dump pecans and mix egg white in. 5. Afterward, slowly add the sugar mixture and toss the pecans. 6. When the grill displays "Add Food," line the cooking pot of Ninja Foodi Smart XL Grill with parchment paper. Place sugar-coated pecans and spread in a single layer. 7. Bake for 1 hour and shake the basket halfway through the cooking time. 8. Cool them down on a cooling tray. Serve and enjoy.

Serving Suggestions: You can serve them cream cheese or mascarpone cheese

Variation Tip: You can use cocoa powder to have variation in taste.

Nutritional Information per Serving: Calories: 504 | Fat: 41.8g | Sat Fat: 4.4g | Carbohydrates: 33.3g | Fiber: 6.2g | Sugar: 27g | Protein: 6.8g

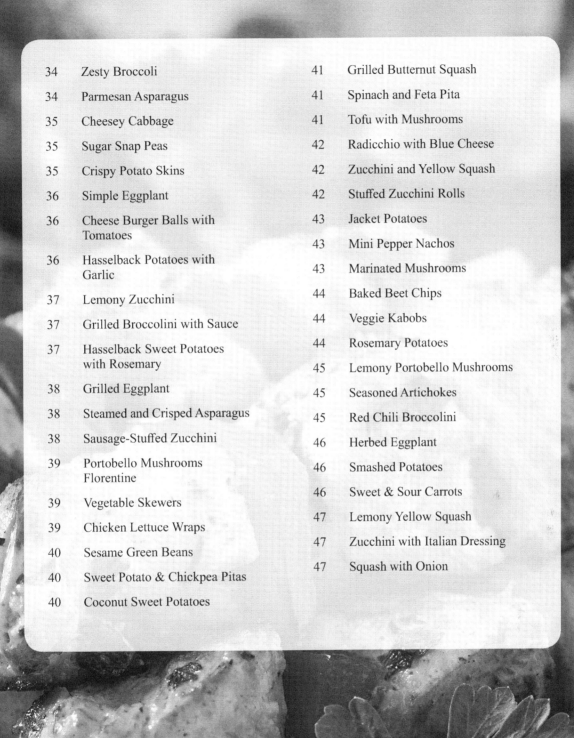

Chapter 3 Vegetable and Sides Recipes

Zesty Broccoli

Prep Time: 15 minutes | Cook Time: 10 minutes | Servings: 4

Ingredients:

4 tablespoons balsamic vinegar
4 tablespoons soy sauce
2 tablespoons canola oil

2 teaspoons maple syrup
2 broccoli heads, cut into florets
1 teaspoon sesame seeds

Preparation:

1. In a large-sized bowl, whisk together the vinegar, soy sauce, oil, and maple syrup. 2. Add the broccoli florets and toss to coat well. 3. Arrange the lightly greased "Grill Grate" in the crisper basket in the cooking pot of Ninja Foodi Smart XL Grill. 4. Close the Grill with lid and press "Power" button. 5. Select "Grill" and then use the set of arrows to the left of the display to adjust the temperature to "MAX". 6. Use the set of arrows to the right of the display to adjust the cook time to 10 minutes. 7. Press "Start/Stop" to begin preheating. When the display shows "Add Food", open the lid and place the broccoli florets onto the "Grill Grate". 8. With your hands, gently press down each broccoli floret. Close the Grill with lid. 9. When the cooking time is completed, open the lid and place the broccoli onto a large-sized serving platter. 10. Sprinkle with sesame seeds serve immediately.

Serving Suggestions: Serve with a sprinkling of red pepper flakes.

Variation Tip: Choose broccoli heads with tight, green florets and firm stalks.

Nutritional Information per Serving: Calories: 131 | Fat: 7.9g | Sat Fat: 0.6g | Carbohydrates: 12.5g | Fiber: 3.7g | Sugar: 4.5g | Protein: 4.8g

Parmesan Asparagus

Prep Time: 15 minutes | Cook Time: 35 minutes | Servings: 4

Ingredients:

1 cup balsamic vinegar
½ cup heavy cream
3 tablespoons Parmesan cheese, grated and divided
1 pound fresh asparagus, tough ends

removed
2 tablespoons vegetable oil
1 teaspoon salt
1 tablespoon fresh lemon juice

Preparation:

1. For balsamic reduction: in a small-sized pan, add balsamic vinegar over high heat and bring to a boil. 2. Reduce the heat to low and simmer for about 20 minutes. 3. Meanwhile, for Parmesan sauce: in a small-sized pan, add the heavy cream and 2 tablespoons of Parmesan cheese over low heat and cook for about 10-12 minutes, stirring frequently. 4. In a bowl, add asparagus, oil, and salt and toss to coat well. 5. Arrange the lightly greased "Grill Grate" in the crisper basket in the cooking pot of Ninja Foodi Smart XL Grill. 6. Close the Grill with lid and press "Power" button. 7. Select "Grill" and then use the set of arrows to the left of the display to adjust the temperature to "MED". 8. Use the set of arrows to the right of the display to adjust the cook time to 10 minutes. 9. Press "Start/Stop" to begin preheating. When the display shows "Add Food", open the lid and place the asparagus onto the "Grill Grate". 10. With your hands, gently press down the asparagus. Close the Grill with lid. 11. After 5 minutes of cooking, flip the asparagus. 12. When the cooking time is completed, open the lid and place the cooked asparagus into a bowl. 13. Drizzle with balsamic reduction. 14. Garnish with remaining Parmesan cheese and serve alongside the sauce.

Serving Suggestions: Serve alongside any entrée meat dish.

Variation Tip: Use high-quality balsamic vinegar.

Nutritional Information per Serving: Calories: 193 | Fat: 15.5g | Sat Fat: 6.7g | Carbohydrates: 6.2g | Fiber: 2.4g | Sugar: 2.5g | Protein: 7.3g

Cheesey Cabbage

Prep Time: 10 minutes | Cook Time: 30 minutes | Servings: 4

Ingredients:

4 ounces of crumbled blue cheese
½ cup mayonnaise
½ cup sour cream
1 tablespoon juice from 1 lemon

salt and ground black pepper, to taste
1 medium head green cabbage, cut into
6 wedges
2 tablespoons extra-virgin olive oil

Preparation:

1. Mash blue cheese with a fork. Whisk in the mayonnaise, sour cream, and lemon juice. Set aside and season with salt and pepper to taste. 2. Select the "Grill" button on Ninja Foodi Smart XL Grill and regulate the setting at MED for 6 minutes. 3. Arrange them in the Ninja Foodi when it displays "Add Food" and shower with olive oil. 4. Grill for about 6 minutes, turning them occasionally. 5. Cook until the cabbage is browned on the second side, about 2 minutes more. 6. Toss cabbage with olive oil, salt, and pepper in a large mixing basin. Place on a serving plate. Pour on the sauce. 7. Serve and enjoy!

Serving Suggestions: Garnish with scallion.
Variation Tip: You can also add cherry tomatoes.
Nutritional Information per Serving: Calories: 320 | Fat: 28g | Sat Fat: 8g | Carbohydrates: 13g | Fiber: 4g | Sugar: 7g | Protein: 7g

Sugar Snap Peas

Prep Time: 10 minutes | Cook Time: 10 minutes | Servings: 4

Ingredients:

½ cup buttermilk
1 tablespoon Dijon mustard
1 tablespoon apple cider vinegar
½ teaspoon sugar
For the Snap Peas:
1 pound of sugar snap peas, trimmed

1 garlic clove, minced
½ cup finely chopped fresh dill
¼ cup thinly sliced fresh chives
salt and black pepper, to taste

2 teaspoons vegetable oil

Preparation:

1. To make the dressing: In a medium mixing bowl, add buttermilk, mustard, vinegar, sugar, and garlic. 2. Sprinkle salt and pepper after adding the dill and chives. 3. Toss snap peas with oil until evenly coated in a large mixing bowl. Season with salt and pepper to taste. 4. Select the "Bake" button on Ninja Foodi Smart XL Grill and regulate the settings at 325°F for 8 minutes. 5. Arrange them in the Ninja Foodi when it displays "Add Food." 6. Bake for about 8 minutes. 7. Cook until the peas are barely browned on the second side, about 15 seconds. Place on a platter. 8. Serve and enjoy!

Serving Suggestions: Sprinkle sesame seeds on top.
Variation Tip: You can also drizzle with black vinegar.
Nutritional Information per Serving: Calories: 94 | Fat: 6g | Sat Fat: 1g | Carbohydrates: 8g | Fiber: 2g | Sugar: 5g | Protein: 4g

Crispy Potato Skins

Prep Time: 5 minutes | Cook Time: 20 minutes | Servings: 2

Ingredients:

2 medium russet potatoes
cooking spray

1 tablespoon minced fresh rosemary
⅛ teaspoon freshly ground black pepper

Preparation:

1. Pierce the potatoes with a fork. 2. Choose the "Air Crisp" button on the Ninja Foodi Smart XL Grill and regulate the settings at 375°F for 4 minutes. 3. Arrange them in the Ninja Foodi when it displays "Add Food." 4. Air crisp for about 10 minutes, tossing them in between. 5. Halve the potatoes and scrape the pulp, leaving some potato flesh attached to the skin. Save the pulp. 6. Using cooking spray, coat each potato skin. 7. In a small bowl, combine the rosemary and pepper. Put the skins back and cook for 5 to 10 minutes. Serve right away. 8. Serve and enjoy!

Serving Suggestions: Serve with sauce.
Variation Tip: You can also add chili flakes on top.
Nutritional Information per Serving: Calories: 50 | Fat: 2g | Sat Fat: 2g | Carbohydrates: 10g | Fiber: 4g | Sugar: 1g | Protein:2g

Simple Eggplant

Prep Time: 15 minutes | Cook Time: 6 minutes | Servings: 4

Ingredients:

2 large eggplants, cut into ⅛-inch thick slices lengthwise

Salt, as required

Preparation:

1. Arrange the eggplant slices onto a smooth surface in a single layer and sprinkle with salt. 2. Set aside for about 10 minutes. 3. With a paper towel, pat dry the eggplant slices to remove the excess moisture and salt. 4. Arrange the lightly greased "Grill Grate" in the crisper basket in the cooking pot of Ninja Foodi Smart XL Grill. 5. Close the Grill with lid and press "Power" button. 6. Select "Grill" and then use the set of arrows to the left of the display to adjust the temperature to "MED". 7. Use the set of arrows to the right of the display to adjust the cook time to 6 minutes. 8. Press "Start/Stop" to begin preheating. When the display shows "Add Food", open the lid and place the eggplant slices onto the "Grill Grate". 9. With your hands, gently press down each eggplant slice. Close the Grill with lid. 10. After 3 minutes of cooking, flip the eggplant slices. 11. When the cooking time is completed, open the lid and serve hot.

Serving Suggestions: Serve with a drizzling of olive oil.

Variation Tip: Pat dry the eggplant slices thoroughly.

Nutritional Information per Serving: Calories: 69 | Fat: 0.5g | Sat Fat: 0g | Carbohydrates: 16.1g | Fiber: 9.7g | Sugar: 8.2g | Protein: 2.7g

Cheese Burger Balls with Tomatoes

Prep Time: 10 minutes | Servings: 4

Ingredients:

1 lb. lean ground beef
¼ cup onion, finely chopped
1 clove garlic, minced
1 tablespoon mustard
½ teaspoon salt

4 slices of cheddar cheese, chopped
24 dill pickle chips
4 large green lettuce leaves, torn into small pieces
12 cherry tomatoes

Preparation:

1. Add beef, onion, garlic, mustard sauce, and salt in a bowl and mix. Make small balls from this mixture. 2. Select the "Bake" button on the Ninja Foodi Smart XL Grill and regulate the settings at 350°F for 15 minutes. 3. Arrange them in the Ninja Foodi when it displays "Add Food." 4. Bake for about 15 minutes. 5. Top cheese and bake for more 3 minutes until cheese melts. 6. Layer pickle chip, lettuce, and tomato on a toothpick and place on each meatball. Serve.

Serving Suggestions: Top with cream cheese.

Variation Tip: You can also add spring onions.

Nutritional Information per Serving: Calories: 307 | Fat:.19.9g | Sat Fat: 7.2g | Carbohydrates: 20.3g | Fiber: 4.5g | Sugar: 7.8g | Protein: 30.1g

Hasselback Potatoes with Garlic

Prep Time: 15 minutes | Cook Time: 15 minutes | Servings: 4

Ingredients:

4 medium russet potatoes, scrubbed
4 large cloves garlic, thinly sliced
4 ounces Parmesan cheese, 2 ounces thinly sliced, 2 ounces grated

2 tablespoons olive oil
Kosher salt
Freshly ground black pepper

Preparation:

1. Select the "Roast" button on the Ninja Foodi Smart XL Grill and regulate the settings at MED for 10 minutes. 2. Take a tiny slice of each potato and cut it lengthwise. Next, remove the ends of each potato. 3. Place each potato between two chopsticks or wooden spoons to function as a stop for the knife, and carefully make vertical slices every ⅛ inch. 4. Under running water, rinse the potato. 5. Place potatoes on a platter and microwave for 5 minutes on high. Microwave the potatoes for another 5 minutes on the other side. 6. Insert garlic and Parmesan slices into slits in the potatoes. 7. Brush olive oil over potatoes and sprinkle salt and pepper to taste. Top with grated Parmesan cheese. 8. Arrange them in the Ninja Foodi when it displays "Add Food." 9. Roast for about 10 minutes, tossing once in between. 10. Dole out on a plate when roasted and serve topped with mirin mixture. 11. Serve and enjoy!

Serving Suggestions: Serve with ketchup.

Variation Tip: You can use any cheese.

Nutritional Information per Serving: Calories: 352 | Fat: 15g | Sat Fat: 5g | Carbohydrates: 42g | Fiber: 4g | Sugar: 2g | Protein: 13g

Lemony Zucchini

Prep Time: 15 minutes | Cook Time: 7 minutes | Servings: 6

Ingredients:

4 large zucchinis, sliced
2 tablespoons fresh lemon juice
2 teaspoons fresh mint leaves, minced

2 tablespoons canola oil
2 garlic cloves, minced
Fresh ground black pepper to taste

Preparation:

1. Select the "Air Crisp" button on Ninja Foodi Smart XL Grill and regulate the settings at 375°F for 4 minutes. 2. Arrange the zucchini slices in the Ninja Foodi when it displays "Add Food." 3. Brush oil on top. 4. Air crisp for about 10 minutes, tossing them in between. 5. Add lemon juice, garlic, and black pepper and stir fry for about two minutes. 6. Stir in mint and cook for about one to two minutes. 7. Serve hot.

Serving Suggestions: Serve with goat or feta cheese on top.

Variation Tip: You can also use a small amount of garlic powder.

Nutritional Information per Serving: Calories: 79 | Fat: 5.1g | Sat Fat: 0.5g | Carbohydrates: 7.7g | Fiber: 2.5g | Sugar: 3.9g | Protein: 2.7g

Grilled Broccolini with Sauce

Prep Time: 10 minutes | Cook Time: 15 minutes | Servings: 4

Ingredients:

1 pound broccolini, trimmed
2 teaspoons vegetable oil

salt and black pepper, to taste
¼ cup chili sauce

Preparation:

1. Toss broccolini with oil in a large mixing bowl. Season with salt and pepper to taste. 2. Select the "Bake" button on the Ninja Foodi Smart XL Grill and regulate the settings at 325°F for 8 minutes. 3. Arrange them in the Ninja Foodi when it displays "Add Food." 4. Bake for about 8 minutes. 5. Dollop spoonfuls of chili sauce over the broccolini when ready to serve. 6. Serve and enjoy!

Serving Suggestions: Sprinkle sesame seeds on top.

Variation Tip: You can also drizzle with black vinegar.

Nutritional Information per Serving: Calories: 64 | Fat: 3g | Sat Fat: 0g | Carbohydrates: 8g | Fiber: 4g | Sugar: 2g | Protein: 2g

Hasselback Sweet Potatoes with Rosemary

Prep Time: 10 minutes | Cook Time: 35 minutes | Servings: 4

Ingredients:

6 medium cloves garlic, minced
2 teaspoons fresh rosemary, chopped
1 ½ tablespoons of olive oil

4 medium sweet potatoes, scrubbed
Kosher salt, to taste
Freshly ground black pepper, to taste

Preparation:

1. Combine garlic, rosemary, and 1 teaspoon olive oil in a small bowl. Place aside. 2. Cut a thin slice of each sweet potato lengthwise to make an even base for the sweet potato to rest on. Next, remove the ends of each sweet potato. 3. Place each sweet potato between two chopsticks, and carefully make vertical slices every ⅛ inch. 4. Place sweet potatoes on a platter and microwave for 4 minutes on high. Microwave the sweet potatoes for another 4 minutes on the other side. 5. Select the "Grill" button on Ninja Foodi Smart XL Grill and regulate the setting at MED for 6 minutes. 6. Arrange them in the Ninja Foodi when it displays "Add Food" and shower with olive oil. 7. Grill for about 6 minutes, turning them occasionally. 8. Dole on a platter. 9. Brush sweet potatoes with remaining olive oil and sprinkle salt and pepper. Cook for more than 15 minutes on the grill. 10. Spread the garlic and rosemary mixture on top of the sweet potatoes, and cook for another 10 minutes, or until the sweet potatoes are soft in the center and crisp around the edges. 11. Remove and set aside for 5 minutes before serving. 12. Serve and enjoy!

Serving Suggestions: Sprinkle parsley on top.

Variation Tip: You can also sprinkle shredded cheese.

Nutritional Information per Serving: Calories: 125 | Fat: 2g | Sat Fat: 0g | Carbohydrates: 26g | Fiber: 4g | Sugar: 7g | Protein: 3g

Grilled Eggplant

Prep Time: 30 minutes | Cook Time: 10 minutes | Servings: 4

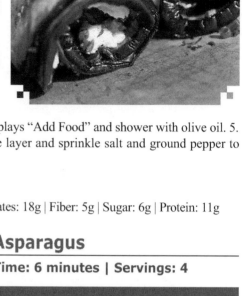

Ingredients:

1 eggplant	Salt and pepper, to taste
Olive oil for brushing	Parsley to sprinkle

Preparation:

1. Cut the eggplant lengthwise into ¼-inch thick slices. Gently season with salt. Allow to stand for about 20 minutes. 2. Select the "Grill" button on Ninja Foodi Smart XL Grill and regulate the setting at MED for 6 minutes. 3. Brush the eggplant slices gently with olive oil on one side. 4. Arrange them in the Ninja Foodi when it displays "Add Food" and shower with olive oil. 5. Grill for about 6 minutes, turning them occasionally. 6. Dole on a platter in a single layer and sprinkle salt and ground pepper to taste. Sprinkle parsley on top. 7. Serve and enjoy!

Serving Suggestions: Serve with mint yogurt.

Variation Tip: You can also add cheese.

Nutritional Information per Serving: Calories: 224 | Fat: 13g | Sat Fat: 8g | Carbohydrates: 18g | Fiber: 5g | Sugar: 6g | Protein: 11g

Steamed and Crisped Asparagus

Prep Time: 5 minutes | Cook Time: 6 minutes | Servings: 4

Ingredients:

1 pound medium-sized asparagus, about 16 spears	¼ teaspoon black pepper
1 tablespoon olive oil	½ ounce parmesan cheese
½ teaspoon fine grind sea salt	1 lemon

Preparation:

1. Rinse the asparagus and break off the ends. Lightly spray the asparagus with the oil. Add salt and pepper. 2. Add ½ cup of water to the Ninja Foodi Smart XL Grill and select "Grill" mode. Regulate the settings at high. Place asparagus on the cook and crisp basket and cook for 2 minutes. 3. Select "air crisp" mode in the Ninja Foodi on 400°F/200°C and set the time for 4 minutes. Place asparagus in the Ninja Foodi once it shows "Add Food." 4. Air crisp for 4 minutes and dole out in a plate. Top with parmesan cheese.

Serving Suggestions: Serve with lemon wedges.

Variation Tip: You can use other varieties of vegetables too and serve topped with the sour cream.

Nutritional Information per Serving: Calories: 65 | Fat: 4.4g | Sat Fat: 1.1g | Carbohydrates: 4.6g | Fiber: 2.4g | Sugar: 2.2g | Protein: 3.7g

Sausage-Stuffed Zucchini

Prep Time: 35 minutes | Cook Time: 20 minutes | Servings: 6

Ingredients:

6 medium zucchinis	⅓ cup minced fresh parsley
1 pound sausage	2 tablespoons minced fresh oregano
2 medium tomatoes, seeded and chopped	2 tablespoons minced fresh basil
1 cup panko bread crumbs	¼ teaspoon pepper
⅓ cup grated Parmesan cheese	¾ cup shredded mozzarella cheese

Preparation:

1. Cut each zucchini lengthwise in half. Scoop out the pulp and slice it, leaving a ¼-inch shell. 2. In a large microwave-safe dish, place zucchini shells. Cover the microwave high for 2-3 minutes or until crisp-tender in batches. 3. Cook sausage and zucchini pulp in a large skillet over medium heat for 6-8 minutes, breaking sausage into crumbs. 4. Combine the tomatoes, bread crumbs, Parmesan cheese, herbs, and pepper in a mixing bowl. Fill zucchini shells with the mixture. 5. Select the "Bake" button on Ninja Foodi Smart XL Grill and regulate the settings at 325°F for 15 minutes. 6. Arrange them in the Ninja Foodi when it displays "Add Food." 7. Bake for about 15- 20 minutes. 8. Sprinkle with mozzarella cheese. Bake for another 5-8 minutes. 9. Serve and enjoy!

Serving Suggestions: Sprinkle with additional minced parsley.

Variation Tip: You can use dried oregano instead of minced oregano.

Nutritional Information per Serving: Calories: 206 | Fat: 9g | Sat Fat: 3g | Carbohydrates: 16g | Fiber: 3g | Sugar: 5g | Protein: 17g

Portobello Mushrooms Florentine

Prep Time: 5 minutes | Cook Time: 25 minutes | Servings: 2

Ingredients:

2 large portobello mushrooms
Cooking spray
⅛ teaspoon garlic salt
⅛ teaspoon pepper
½ teaspoon olive oil

1 small onion, chopped
1 cup fresh baby spinach
2 large eggs
⅛ teaspoon salt

Preparation:

1. Select the "Bake" button on Ninja Foodi Smart XL Grill and regulate the settings at 400°F for 15 minutes. 2. Spritz mushrooms with cooking spray. 3. Sprinkle garlic salt and pepper to taste. 4. Arrange them in the Ninja Foodi when it displays "Add Food." 5. Bake for about 10 minutes. 6. Meanwhile, heat oil in a nonstick skillet over medium-high heat and cook onion until tender. Stir in the spinach. 7. Whisk together the eggs and salt and pour into the skillet. Cook, constantly stirring, until no liquid egg is left, then spoon over mushrooms. 8. Serve and enjoy!

Serving Suggestions: Sprinkle with basil.
Variation Tip: You can also top it with feta cheese.
Nutritional Information per Serving: Calories: 126 | Fat: 5g | Sat Fat: 2g | Carbohydrates: 10g | Fiber: 3g | Sugar: 4g | Protein: 11g

Vegetable Skewers

Prep Time: 30 minutes | Cook Time: 10 minutes | Servings: 6

Ingredients:

¼ cup olive oil
2 tablespoons fresh lemon juice
2 tablespoons red wine vinegar
2 teaspoons freshly minced garlic
2 teaspoons dried oregano
1 teaspoon mint leaves, chopped

salt and black pepper, to taste
1 pound halloumi cheese, cut into ¾-inch cubes
2 medium zucchinis, cut into ½-inch rounds
1-pint grape tomatoes

Preparation:

1. In a bowl, add oil, lemon juice, vinegar, garlic, oregano, and mint. Season to taste with salt and pepper. 2. Toss in the cheese, zucchinis, and tomatoes to mix. 3. Thread cheese, zucchinis, and tomatoes onto pre-soaked skewers. 4. Select the "Bake" button on Ninja Foodi Smart XL Grill and regulate the settings at 325°F for 8 minutes. 5. Arrange the vegetables in the Ninja Foodi when it displays "Add Food." 6. Bake for about 8 minutes. 7. Dole out them when baked completely and serve warm.

Serving Suggestions: Serve with a warm pita.
Variation Tip: You can also add onions.
Nutritional Information per Serving: Calories: 220 | Fat: 16g | Sat Fat: 8g | Carbohydrates: 7g | Fiber: 1g | Sugar: 4g | Protein: 14g

Chicken Lettuce Wraps

Prep Time: 5 minutes | Cook Time: 25 minutes | Servings: 4

Ingredients:

¾ pound chicken breasts, cut into cubes
1 teaspoon ground ginger
¼ teaspoon salt
¼ teaspoon pepper
2 teaspoons olive oil
1½ cups shredded carrots

1¼ cups pitted fresh cherries, chopped
4 green onions, chopped
2 tablespoons rice vinegar
2 tablespoons teriyaki sauce
1 tablespoon honey
8 Bibb or Boston lettuce leaves

Preparation:

1. Sprinkle chicken with ginger, salt, and pepper, in a skillet and heat oil. 2. Cook for 3-5 minutes until the chicken is no longer pink. 3. Remove the pan from the heat. Stir in carrots, cherries, and green onions. Combine vinegar, teriyaki sauce, and honey in a small basin; stir into the chicken mixture. 4. Divide the filling among the lettuce leaves and fold the lettuce over the filling. 5. Choose the "Air Crisp" button on Ninja Foodi Smart XL Grill and regulate the settings at 325°F for 4 minutes. 6. Arrange them in the Ninja Foodi when it displays "Add Food." 7. Air crisp for about 4 minutes, tossing them in between. 8. Serve and enjoy!

Serving Suggestions: Sprinkle with cilantro.
Variation Tip: You can also add coarsely chopped almonds.
Nutritional Information per Serving: Calories: 257 | Fat: 10g | Sat Fat: 1g | Carbohydrates: 22g | Fiber: 4g | Sugar: 15g | Protein: 21g

Sesame Green Beans

Prep Time: 5 minutes | Cook Time: 10 minutes | Servings: 4

Ingredients:

2 cups green beans, fresh
3 tablespoons olive oil
4-6 fresh garlic cloves, minced or grated

2 tablespoons sesame oil
Sesame seeds to sprinkle
Salt and pepper

Preparation:

1. Lightly and evenly coat fresh green beans in oil. 2. Season to taste with salt and pepper. 3. Select the "Grill" button on Ninja Foodi Smart XL Grill and regulate the setting at MED for 6 minutes. 4. Arrange them in the Ninja Foodi when it displays "Add Food" and shower with olive oil. 5. Grill for about 6 minutes, turning them occasionally. 6. When the green beans are done, mix in the fresh garlic and cook until the green beans are tender. 7. Drizzle green beans with sesame oil and top with sesame seeds. 8. Serve and enjoy!

Serving Suggestions: Serve with steak.

Variation Tip: You can add red chili flakes.

Nutritional Information per Serving: Calories: 114 | Fat: 4g | Sat Fat: 0.8g | Carbohydrates: 17g | Fiber: 7g | Sugar: 3g | Protein: 4.4g

Sweet Potato & Chickpea Pitas

Prep Time: 10 minutes | Cook Time: 20 minutes | Servings: 6

Ingredients:

2 medium sweet potatoes, peeled and cubed
2 cans chickpeas, rinsed and drained
1 medium red onion, chopped
3 tablespoons canola oil, divided
½ teaspoon salt divided
2 garlic cloves, minced
1 cup plain Greek yogurt

1 tablespoon lemon juice
1 teaspoon ground cumin
2 cups baby spinach
12 whole-wheat pita pocket halves, warmed
¼ cup minced fresh cilantro

Preparation:

1. Microwave sweet potatoes for 5 minutes on high, covered, in a large microwave-safe bowl. 2. Toss with 2 tablespoons oil and ¼ teaspoon salt after adding chickpeas and onion. 3. Select the "Roast" button on Ninja Foodi Smart XL Grill and regulate the settings at MED for 10 minutes. 4. Arrange them in the Ninja Foodi when it displays "Add Food." 5. Roast for about 10 minutes, tossing once in between. 6. In a microwave-safe bowl, combine garlic and remaining oil; microwave on high for 1 to 1½ minutes. 7. Combine the yogurt, lemon juice, cumin, and the remaining salt in a mixing bowl. 8. Toss the spinach with the potato mixture. Fill pitas halfway with the filling, then top with the sauce. 9. Serve and enjoy!

Serving Suggestions: Sprinkle cilantro.

Variation Tip: You can sprinkle it with cheese.

Nutritional Information per Serving: Calories: 462 | Fat: 15g | Sat Fat: 3g | Carbohydrates: 72g | Fiber: 12g | Sugar: 13g | Protein: 14g

Coconut Sweet Potatoes

Prep Time: 10 minutes | Cook Time: 45 minutes | Servings: 4

Ingredients:

4 medium sweet potatoes
½ cup coconut Greek yogurt

1 medium apple, chopped
¼ cup toasted coconut flake

Preparation:

1. Select the "Bake" button on Ninja Foodi Smart XL Grill and regulate the settings at 400°F for 40 - 45 minutes. 2. Arrange sweet potatoes in the Ninja Foodi when it displays "Add Food." 3. Bake for about 40 - 45 minutes. 4. Cut an "X" in each sweet potato using a sharp knife. Then, using a fork, fluff the pulp. Add the remaining ingredients on top. 5. Serve and enjoy!

Serving Suggestions: Top with maple syrup.

Variation Tip: You can skip apples.

Nutritional Information per Serving: Calories: 321 | Fat: 3g | Sat Fat: 2g | Carbohydrates: 70g | Fiber: 8g | Sugar: 30g | Protein: 7g

Grilled Butternut Squash

Prep Time: 5 minutes | Cook Time: 10 minutes | Servings: 4

Ingredients:

4 cups butternut squash, peeled, and small diced

1 teaspoon olive oil
Salt and pepper to taste

Preparation:

1. Wash and carefully cut the butternut squash into workable pieces. 2. Cut the squash into small cubes. 3. Using a peeler or a knife, peel all of the squash. 4. Clean the seeds out of the bottom pieces using a big spoon. Remove the seed guts and throw them away. 5. Select the "Grill" button on Ninja Foodi Smart XL Grill and regulate the setting at MED for 8 minutes. 6. Arrange them in the Ninja Foodi when it displays "Add Food" and shower with olive oil. Sprinkle salt and pepper. 7. Grill for about 8 minutes, turning them occasionally. 8. Place on a serving plate. 9. Serve and enjoy!

Serving Suggestions: Serve with steaks.

Variation Tip: Add a tablespoon or two of brown sugar on top of the cooked squash.

Nutritional Information per Serving: Calories: 184 | Fat: 3g | Sat Fat: 0g | Carbohydrates: 43g | Fiber: 13g | Sugar: 8g | Protein: 4g

Spinach and Feta Pita

Prep Time: 10 minutes | Cook Time: 12 minutes | Servings: 6

Ingredients:

6 ounces sun-dried tomato pesto
6 whole wheat pita bread
2 plum tomatoes, chopped
1 bunch of spinach, rinsed and chopped
4 fresh mushrooms, sliced

½ cup crumbled feta cheese
2 tablespoons grated Parmesan cheese
3 tablespoons olive oil
ground black pepper, to taste

Preparation:

1. Spread tomato pesto on one side of each pita bread and set it on a baking sheet. 2. Toss tomatoes, spinach, mushrooms, feta cheese, and Parmesan cheese on top of the pitas. Drizzle with olive oil and season with pepper. 3. Select the "Bake" button on the Ninja Foodi Smart XL Grill and regulate the settings at 350°F for 15 minutes. 4. Arrange them in the Ninja Foodi when it displays "Add Food." 5. Bake for about 12 minutes. 6. Cut pitas into quarters. Serve and enjoy!

Serving Suggestions: Top with chopped cilantro.

Variation Tip: You can use any tomatoes.

Nutritional Information per Serving: Calories: 349 | Fat: 17g | Sat Fat: 3.9g | Carbohydrates: 41g | Fiber: 6.9g | Sugar: 2.8g | Protein: 11g

Tofu with Mushrooms

Prep Time: 15 minutes | Cook Time: 20 minutes | Servings: 8

Ingredients:

8 tablespoons Parmesan cheese, shredded
2 cups fresh mushrooms, finely chopped
2 blocks tofu, pressed and cubed into 1-inch

pieces
Salt and black pepper, to taste
8 tablespoons butter

Preparation:

1. Select the "Air Crisp" button on the Ninja Foodi Smart XL Grill and regulate the time for 2 minutes at 350°F. 2. Dust tofu with salt and black pepper in a bowl. 3. Put butter and tofu in a pot and sauté for 5 minutes. 4. Add mushrooms and Parmesan cheese and sauté for 3 minutes. 5. Place the tofu mixture in the Ninja Foodi when it displays "Add Food". 6. Air Crisp for 2 minutes and dole out in a platter to serve warm.

Serving Suggestions: Serve with tortillas.

Variation Tip: You can add any tasteful variety of mushrooms.

Nutritional Information per Serving: Calories: 142 | Fat: 13.9g | Sat Fat: 8.5g | Carbohydrates: 1.2g | Fiber: 0.4g | Sugar: 0.4g | Protein: 4.6g

Radicchio with Blue Cheese

Prep Time: 10 minutes | Cook Time: 15 minutes | Servings: 4

Ingredients:

3 tablespoons olive oil, divided	1 head radicchio
2 tablespoons white balsamic vinegar	2 tablespoons coarsely chopped pistachio
½ teaspoon Dijon mustard	nuts
salt and pepper to taste	2 tablespoons crumbled blue cheese

Preparation:

1. In a bowl, add olive oil, balsamic vinegar, Dijon mustard, salt, and pepper. Set aside the dressing. 2. Using a sharp knife, cut the radicchio head into four wedges. Brush the wedges with the 1 tablespoon of olive oil and sprinkle with a pinch of salt. 3. Select the "Grill" button on Ninja Foodi Smart XL Grill and regulate the setting at MED for 8 minutes. 4. Arrange them in the Ninja Foodi when it displays "Add Food" and shower with olive oil. 5. Grill for about 8 minutes, turning them occasionally. 6. Drizzle the dressing over the salad and sprinkle it with pistachios and blue cheese. 7. Serve and enjoy!

Serving Suggestions: Serve with fries.

Variation Tip: You can use white wine instead of vinegar.

Nutritional Information per Serving: Calories: 144 | Fat: 13g | Sat Fat: 2.4g | Carbohydrates: 4.7g | Fiber: 0.9g | Sugar: 1.7g | Protein: 2.5g

Zucchini and Yellow Squash

Prep Time: 5 minutes | Cook Time: 5 minutes | Servings: 8

Ingredients:

4 tablespoons avocado oil	1 tablespoon Sasquatch BBQ Moss
2 small zucchinis, sliced	1 teaspoon flaky salt
1 small yellow squash, sliced	¼ teaspoon freshly cracked pepper

Preparation:

1. Wash the vegetables and slice them into ¼-inch thick circles. 2. Choose the "Air Crisp" button on the Ninja Foodi Smart XL Grill and regulate the settings at 375°F for 4 minutes. 3. Arrange them in the Ninja Foodi when it displays "Add Food." 4. Sprinkle oil on top. 5. Air crisp for about 10 minutes, tossing them in between. 6. When done, sprinkle salt and pepper on top. Serve and enjoy!

Serving Suggestions: Sprinkle with a little additional Moss.

Variation Tip: You can use any oil.

Nutritional Information per Serving: Calories: 76 | Fat: 7g | Sat Fat: 1g | Carbohydrates: 3g | Fiber: 1g | Sugar: 2g | Protein: 1g

Stuffed Zucchini Rolls

Prep Time: 15 minutes | Cook Time: 8 minutes | Servings: 6

Ingredients:

3 medium zucchinis, cut into ¼-inch slices lengthwise	1 tablespoon fresh parsley, minced
	½ teaspoon fresh lemon juice
1 tablespoon olive oil	2 cups fresh baby spinach leaves,
Salt and ground black pepper, as required	trimmed
1½ ounces soft goat cheese	

Preparation:

1. Drizzle the zucchini slices with oil and sprinkle with salt and black pepper. 2. Arrange the lightly greased "Grill Grate" in the crisper basket in the cooking pot of Ninja Foodi Smart XL Grill. 3. Close the Grill with lid and press "Power" button. 4. Select "Grill" and then use the set of arrows to the left of the display to adjust the temperature to "MED". 5. Use the set of arrows to the right of the display to adjust the cook time to 8 minutes. 6. Press "Start/Stop" to begin preheating. When the display shows "Add Food", open the lid and place the zucchini slices onto the "Grill Grate". 7. With your hands, gently press down each zucchini slice. Close the Grill with lid. 8. After 4 minutes of cooking, flip the zucchini slices. 9. When the cooking time is completed, open the lid and place onto a platter. Set aside to cool completely. 10. In a clean bowl, blend together the goat cheese, parsley, and lemon juice and with a fork, mash them. 11. Place ½ teaspoon of cheese mixture over each zucchini slice about ½-inch from the end. 12. Top each slice with spinach and basil. 13. Roll the zucchini slices, starting from the filling side and serve.

Serving Suggestions: Serve alongside the yogurt sauce.

Variation Tip: You can use feta cheese instead of goat cheese.

Nutritional Information per Serving: Calories: 64 | Fat: 4.3g | Sat Fat: 1.4g | Carbohydrates: 4.5g | Fiber: 1.3g | Sugar: 1.8g | Protein: 3.1g

Jacket Potatoes

Prep Time: 10 minutes | Cook Time: 5 minutes | Servings: 2

Ingredients:

2 potatoes
1 tablespoon mozzarella cheese, shredded
1 tablespoon butter, softened
1 teaspoon chives, minced

1 tablespoon fresh parsley, chopped
3 tablespoons sour cream
Salt and black pepper, to taste

Preparation:

1. Select the "Grill" button on the Ninja Foodi Smart XL Grill and regulate the settings at Medium for 5 minutes. 2. Prick the potatoes with a fork and transfer the potatoes into the Ninja Foodi when it displays "Add Food". 3. Grill for 5 minutes, tossing once in between. 4. Dish out in a plate and let it cool slightly. 5. Merge together the remaining ingredients in a bowl until well combined. 6. Carve the potatoes from the center and stuff in the cheese mixture.

Serving Suggestions: You can serve it with tomato sauce.

Variation Tip: You can also add Monterey Jack cheese.

Nutritional Information per Serving: Calories: 277 | Fat: 12.3g | Sat Fat: 7.6g | Carbohydrates: 34.9g | Fiber: 5.2g | Sugar: 2.5g | Protein: 8.3g

Mini Pepper Nachos

Prep Time: 5 minutes | Servings: 4

Ingredients:

¼ cup jalapeno pepper, diced
Cooking spray
1 can chicken breast, drained
½ cup avocado, mashed
½ cup plain Greek yogurt

2 cups cheddar cheese, shredded, divided
1 teaspoon chili powder
24 mini bell peppers, halved with stem, seeds and membranes removed
¼ cup scallions, chopped

Preparation:

1. Heat greased pan and sauté jalapeno until tender. 2. Add chicken, jalapeno, avocado, yogurt, cheese, and chili powder in a bowl and mix well. 3. In a dish, place bell peppers, fill them with chicken mixture, and add some cheese. 4. Select the "Bake" button on the Ninja Foodi Smart XL Grill and regulate the settings at 350°F for 5 minutes. 5. Arrange them in the Ninja Foodi when it displays "Add Food." 6. Bake for about 5 minutes and sprinkle with chopped scallions.

Serving Suggestions: Serve with salsa.

Variation Tip: You can also use parmesan cheese instead of cheddar.

Nutritional Information per Serving: Calories: 330 | Fat:.13g | Sat Fat: 7.1g | Carbohydrates: 21g | Fiber: 3.4g | Sugar: 2.1g | Protein: 21g

Marinated Mushrooms

Prep Time: 5 minutes | Cook Time: 10 minutes | Servings: 4

Ingredients:

2 large portobello mushrooms
2 tablespoons olive oil
1 tablespoon red wine vinegar

¼ teaspoon salt
¼ teaspoon pepper

Preparation:

1. Drizzle olive oil over the mushroom cap, then season with salt, pepper, and vinegar. 2. Marinate for 30 minutes in the refrigerator. 3. Select the "Grill" button on Ninja Foodi Smart XL Grill and regulate the setting at MED for 8 minutes. 4. Arrange them in the Ninja Foodi when it displays "Add Food" and shower with olive oil. 5. Grill for about 8 minutes, turning them occasionally. 6. Serve and enjoy!

Serving Suggestions: Serve hot with some spicy sauce.

Variation Tip: You can use any oil.

Nutritional Information per Serving: Calories: 96 | Fat: 10g | Sat Fat: 3g | Carbohydrates: 1g | Fiber: 1g | Sugar: 1g | Protein: 1g

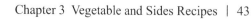

Baked Beet Chips

Prep Time: 15 minutes | Cook Time: 15 minutes | Servings: 4

Ingredients:

6-8 medium to large beets
Olive oil

1 tablespoon flaked sea salt
1 tablespoon dried chives

Preparation:

1. Remove the greens and roots from the beets. Under cold water, scrub the beets well. Cut into 1/16" thick slices of beets. 2. Select the "Bake" button on Ninja Foodi Smart XL Grill and regulate the settings at 400°F for 15 minutes. 3. Arrange them in the Ninja Foodi when it displays "Add Food." 4. Bake for about 15 minutes. 5. Crumble the dried chives into salt, while the beets are baking. 6. Let beets to cool. Then, transfer to a cooling rack to finish drying and crisping. 7. Serve and enjoy!

Serving Suggestions: Sprinkle pepper on top.

Variation Tip: You can also fry them instead of bake.

Nutritional Information per Serving: Calories: 71 | Fat: 0.3g | Sat Fat: 0g | Carbohydrates: 15g | Fiber: 4g | Sugar: 11g | Protein: 2g

Veggie Kabobs

Prep Time: 20 minutes | Cook Time: 10 minutes | Servings: 4

Ingredients:

For Marinade:
2 garlic cloves, chopped
2 tablespoons fresh ginger, chopped
1 teaspoon fresh oregano
1 teaspoon fresh basil

½ teaspoon cayenne powder
Salt and ground black pepper, as required
¼ cup olive oil

For Veggies:
2 large zucchinis, cut into thick slices
8 large button mushrooms, quartered
2 bell pepper, seeded and cubed

1 large onion, cubed
Olive oil cooking spray

Preparation:

1. In a food processor, add all marinade ingredients and pulse until well combined. 2. In a large-sized bowl, add all vegetables. 3. Pour marinade mixture over vegetables and toss to coat well. 4. Cover and refrigerate to marinate for at least 6-8 hours. 5. Remove the vegetables from marinade and thread onto pre-soaked wooden skewers. 6. Arrange the lightly greased "Grill Grate" in the crisper basket in the cooking pot of Ninja Foodi Smart XL Grill. 7. Close the Grill with lid and press "Power" button. 8. Select "Grill" and then use the set of arrows to the left of the display to adjust the temperature to "MED". 9. Use the set of arrows to the right of the display to adjust the cook time to 10 minutes. 10. Press "Start/Stop" to begin preheating. When the display shows "Add Food", open the lid and place the skewers onto the "Grill Grate". 11. With your hands, gently press down each skewer. Close the Grill with lid. 12. While cooking, flip the skewers ccasionally. 13. When the cooking time is completed, open the lid and serve hot.

Serving Suggestions: Serve alongside the ketchup.

Variation Tip: You can use multi-colored bell peppers.

Nutritional Information per Serving: Calories: 85 | Fat: 1.6g | Sat Fat: 0.3g | Carbohydrates: 16.4g | Fiber: 4.6g | Sugar: 8.3g | Protein: 4.7g

Rosemary Potatoes

Prep Time: 5 minutes | Cook Time: 10 minutes | Servings: 4

Ingredients:

1 pound red potatoes, quartered
8 large garlic cloves, smashed
3 large sprigs of rosemary

2 tablespoons unsalted butter
Salt & pepper, to taste
Olive oil

Preparation:

1. Add red potatoes, a pinch of salt and pepper, and 1-2 tablespoons of olive oil to a large mixing bowl. 2. Select the "Bake" button on the Ninja Foodi Smart XL Grill and regulate the settings at 350°F for 5 minutes. 3. Arrange them in the Ninja Foodi when it displays "Add Food." 4. Bake for about 5 minutes. 5. Toss all of the ingredients with the butter. Bake for another 4-5 minutes after covering with a dome. 6. Remove the potatoes when they are thoroughly cooked and serve them hot. 7. Serve and enjoy!

Serving Suggestions: Serve with steak.

Variation Tip: You can add red chili flakes.

Nutritional Information per Serving: Calories: 134 | Fat: 6.2g | Sat Fat: 3g | Carbohydrates: 18g | Fiber: 2g | Sugar: 1g | Protein: 2.2g

Lemony Portobello Mushrooms

Prep Time: 10 minutes | Cook Time: 14 minutes | Servings: 3

Ingredients:

12 ounces fresh portabella mushrooms, stalks removed
¼ cup olive oil

2 teaspoons fresh lemon juice
1 teaspoon garlic, finely minced
Salt, as required

Preparation:

1. In a bowl, add oil, lemon juice, garlic, and salt and beat until well combined. 2. Coat the mushrooms with oil mixture generously. 3. Arrange the lightly greased "Grill Grate" in the crisper basket in the cooking pot of Ninja Foodi Smart XL Grill. 4. Close the Grill with lid and press "Power" button. 5. Select "Grill" and then use the set of arrows to the left of the display to adjust the temperature to "HI". 6. Use the set of arrows to the right of the display to adjust the cook time to 14 minutes. 7. Press "Start/Stop" to begin preheating. When the display shows "Add Food", open the lid and place the mushrooms onto the "Grill Grate". 8. With your hands, gently press down each mushroom. Close the Grill with lid. 9. After 7 minutes of cooking, flip the mushrooms. 10. When the cooking time is completed, open the lid and serve hot.
Serving Suggestions: Serve with the garnishing of lemon zest.
Variation Tip: Make sure to clean the mushrooms properly.
Nutritional Information per Serving: Calories: 176 | Fat: 17.1g | Sat Fat: 2.5g | Carbohydrates: 6.1g | Fiber: 1.7g | Sugar: 2.1g | Protein: 2.9g

Seasoned Artichokes

Prep Time: 15 minutes | Cook Time: 13 minutes | Servings: 6

Ingredients:

4 large artichokes
1 lemon, quartered
2 garlic cloves, peeled
Salt, as required

3 tablespoons olive oil
1 tablespoon steak sauce
2 teaspoons balsamic vinegar
2 teaspoons Montreal Steak Seasoning

Preparation:

1. With a large chef knife, cut each artichoke into quarters. 2. Immediately rub the inside of each the artichoke with 1 lemon wedge. 3. In a large pan of the water, add remaining lemon wedges, garlic cloves, and salt. 4. Place the artichokes in the pot and bring to a boil. 5. Cook for about 8 minutes or until the artichoke heart is fork tender. 6. Remove from heat and place the artichokes in a colander to drain. 7. Meanwhile, in a small bowl, add the remaining ingredients and mix well. 8. Drizzle the marinade over the artichokes and gently toss to coat well. 9. Arrange the lightly greased "Grill Grate" in the crisper basket in the cooking pot of Ninja Foodi Smart XL Grill. 10. Close the Grill with lid and press "Power" button. 11. Select "Grill" and then use the set of arrows to the left of the display to adjust the temperature to "MED". 12. Use the set of arrows to the right of the display to adjust the cook time to 5 minutes. 13. Press "Start/Stop" to begin preheating. When the display shows "Add Food", open the lid and place the artichokes onto the "Grill Grate". 14. With your hands, gently press down each artichoke. Close the Grill with lid. 15. When the cooking time is completed, open the lid and serve hot.
Serving Suggestions: Serve alongside the dipping sauce of your choice.
Variation Tip: Choose plump artichokes.
Nutritional Information per Serving: Calories: 119 | Fat: 7.2g | Sat Fat: 1g | Carbohydrates: 12.7g | Fiber: 6g | Sugar: 1.6g | Protein: 3.7g

Red Chili Broccolini

Prep Time: 10 minutes | Cook Time: 4 minutes | Servings: 2

Ingredients:

8 ounces broccolini
2 tablespoons olive oil
2 tablespoons soy sauce
2 tablespoons balsamic vinegar

1 tablespoon sesame oil
1 medium red chili, thinly sliced
3 tablespoons fresh chervil, chopped

Preparation:

1. Brush the broccolini to with the olive oil lightly. 2. Arrange the lightly greased "Grill Grate" in the crisper basket in the cooking pot of Ninja Foodi Smart XL Grill. 3. Close the Grill with lid and press "Power" button. 4. Select "Grill" and then use the set of arrows to the left of the display to adjust the temperature to "MED". 5. Use the set of arrows to the right of the display to adjust the cook time to 4 minutes. 6. Press "Start/Stop" to begin preheating. When the display shows "Add Food", open the lid and place the broccolini onto the "Grill Grate". 7. With your hands, gently press down the broccolini. Close the Grill with lid. 8. After 2 minutes of cooking, flip the broccolini. 9. When the cooking time is completed, open the lid and place the broccolini onto a serving plate. 10. Meanwhile, mix together the remaining ingredients into a bowl. 11. Drizzle with chili mixture and serve.
Serving Suggestions: Serve with the topping of sesame seeds.
Variation Tip: Look for broccolini with bright-green crisp stalks.
Nutritional Information per Serving: Calories: 237 | Fat: 20.9g | Sat Fat: 3g | Carbohydrates: 10.3g | Fiber: 3.3g | Sugar: 2.3g | Protein: 4.9g

Herbed Eggplant

Prep Time: 15 minutes | Cook Time: 7 minutes | Servings: 4

Ingredients:

2 eggplants, cut into ¼-inch thick slices
Salt, as required
½ cup extra-virgin olive oil
2 tablespoons fresh oregano, chopped
2 tablespoons fresh parsley, chopped
3 garlic cloves, crushed
Ground black pepper, as required

Preparation:

1. In a strainer, place the eggplant slices and sprinkle with salt generously. Set aside for about 15 minutes. 2. With a paper towel, wipe each eggplant slice to remove the salt and moisture. 3. Whisk together olive oil, herbs, garlic, salt, and black pepper in a bowl. 4. In the bowl of oil mixture, add the eggplant slices and toss to coat. 5. Arrange the lightly greased "Grill Grate" in the crisper basket in the cooking pot of Ninja Foodi Smart XL Grill. 6. Close the Grill with lid and press "Power" button. 7. Select "Grill" and then use the set of arrows to the left of the display to adjust the temperature to "MED". 8. Use the set of arrows to the right of the display to adjust the cook time to 7 minutes. 9. Press "Start/Stop" to begin preheating. When the display shows "Add Food", open the lid and place the eggplant slices onto the "Grill Grate". 10. With your hands, gently press down the eggplant slices. Close the Grill with lid. 11. After 4 minutes of cooking, flip the eggplant slices. 12. When the cooking time is completed, open the lid and serve hot.
Serving Suggestions: Serve with the garnishing of extra fresh herbs.
Variation Tip: The skin of eggplants should be smooth and shiny.
Nutritional Information per Serving: Calories: 295 | Fat: 26g | Sat Fat: 3.7g | Carbohydrates: 18.4g | Fiber: 10.7g | Sugar: 8.4g | Protein: 3.1g

Smashed Potatoes

Prep Time: 15 minutes | Cook Time: 7 minutes | Servings: 6

Ingredients:

2 pounds Yukon gold potatoes
2 tablespoons vegetable oil
3 tablespoons butter, melted
¼ teaspoon granulated garlic
Salt and ground black pepper, as required
⅓ cup Parmesan cheese, shredded

Preparation:

1. Arrange the potatoes onto a metal sheet tray and drizzle with 2 tablespoons of oil. 2. With a potato masher, smash each potato lightly into ¼-½ inch thickness. 3. In a small clean bowl, stir together the butter and granulated garlic. 4. Brush each potato with butter mixture and then season with salt and black pepper. 5. Arrange the lightly greased "Grill Grate" in the crisper basket in the cooking pot of Ninja Foodi Smart XL Grill. 6. Close the Grill with lid and press "Power" button. 7. Select "Grill" and then use the set of arrows to the left of the display to adjust the temperature to "MED". 8. Use the set of arrows to the right of the display to adjust the cook time to 7 minutes. 9. Press "Start/Stop" to begin preheating. When the display shows "Add Food", open the lid and place the flattened potatoes onto the "Grill Grate". 10. Close the Grill with lid. 11. After 4 minutes of cooking, flip the potatoes and sprinkle with Parmesan cheese. 12. When the cooking time is completed, open the lid and serve hot.
Serving Suggestions: Serve with the garnishing of fresh herbs.
Variation Tip: Use unsalted butter.
Nutritional Information per Serving: Calories: 153 | Fat: 11.6g | Sat Fat: 5.3g | Carbohydrates: 10.4g | Fiber: 0.8g | Sugar: 0.4g | Protein: 2.9g

Sweet & Sour Carrots

Prep Time: 10 minutes | Cook Time: 12 minutes | Servings: 6

Ingredients:

3 tablespoons olive oil
3 teaspoons balsamic vinegar
2 tablespoons honey
1 teaspoon dried oregano, crushed
1 teaspoon ground cumin
½ teaspoon garlic powder
Salt and ground black pepper, as required
1½ pounds small carrots, peeled and halved lengthwise

Preparation:

1. In a bowl, blend together all ingredients except for carrots. 2. Add the carrots and toss to coat well. 3. Set aside, covered for about 1½ hours. 4. Arrange the lightly greased "Grill Grate" in the crisper basket in the cooking pot of Ninja Foodi Smart XL Grill. 5. Close the Grill with lid and press "Power" button. 6. Select "Grill" and then use the set of arrows to the left of the display to adjust the temperature to "MED". 7. Use the set of arrows to the right of the display to adjust the cook time to 12 minutes. 8. Press "Start/Stop" to begin preheating. When the display shows "Add Food", open the lid and place the carrot slices onto the "Grill Grate". 9. With your hands, gently press down the carrot slices. Close the Grill with lid. 10. While cooking, flip the carrot slices after every 3 minutes. 11. When the cooking time is completed, open the lid and serve hot.
Serving Suggestions: Serve with the garnishing of fresh parsley.
Variation Tip: Garlic powder can be replaced with fresh minced garlic.
Nutritional Information per Serving: Calories: 131 | Fat: 7.1g | Sat Fat: 1g | Carbohydrates: 17.4g | Fiber: 3g | Sugar: 11.4g | Protein: 1.1g

Lemony Yellow Squash

Prep Time: 15 minutes | Cook Time: 12 minutes | Servings: 4

Ingredients:

2 tablespoons canola oil
1 tablespoon fresh lemon juice
1 teaspoon dried rosemary, crushed
Salt and ground black pepper, as required

1 pound yellow squash, cut into ½-inch slices

Preparation:

1. In a bowl, blend together all ingredients except for squash slices. 2. Add the squash slices and toss to coat well. 3. Arrange the lightly greased "Grill Grate" in the crisper basket in the cooking pot of Ninja Foodi Smart XL Grill. 4. Close the Grill with lid and press "Power" button. 5. Select "Grill" and then use the set of arrows to the left of the display to adjust the temperature to "MED". 6. Use the set of arrows to the right of the display to adjust the cook time to 12 minutes. 7. Press "Start/Stop" to begin preheating. When the display shows "Add Food", open the lid and place the squash slices onto the "Grill Grate". 8. With your hands, gently press down the squash slices. Close the Grill with lid. 9. After 6 minutes of cooking, flip the squash slices. 10. When the cooking time is completed, open the lid and serve hot.
Serving Suggestions: Serve with the drizzling of melted butter.
Variation Tip: Feel free to use oil of your choice.
Nutritional Information per Serving: Calories: 82 | Fat: 7.3g | Sat Fat: 0.6g | Carbohydrates: 4.1g | Fiber: 1.4g | Sugar: 2g | Protein: 1.4g

Zucchini with Italian Dressing

Prep Time: 10 minutes | Cook Time: 8 minutes | Servings: 3

Ingredients:

1 large zucchini, cut into ¼-inch slices   ¼ cup Italian-style salad dressing

Preparation:

1. In a bowl, add zucchini and salad dressing and toss to coat. 2. Arrange the lightly greased "Grill Grate" in the crisper basket in the cooking pot of Ninja Foodi Smart XL Grill. 3. Close the Grill with lid and press "Power" button. 4. Select "Grill" and then use the set of arrows to the left of the display to adjust the temperature to "MED". 5. Use the set of arrows to the right of the display to adjust the cook time to 8 minutes. 6. Press "Start/Stop" to begin preheating. When the display shows "Add Food", open the lid and place the zucchini slices onto the "Grill Grate". 7. With your hands, gently press down each zucchini slice. Close the Grill with lid. 8. After 4 minutes of cooking, flip the zucchini slices. 9. When the cooking time is completed, open the lid and serve hot.
Serving Suggestions: Serve with a drizzling of lime juice.
Variation Tip: Make sure to cut zucchini into uniform-sized slices.
Nutritional Information per Serving: Calories: 111 | Fat: 8.6g | Sat Fat: 1.4g | Carbohydrates: 8.5g | Fiber: 1.8g | Sugar: 5.2g | Protein: 2.1g

Squash with Onion

Prep Time: 15 minutes | Cook Time: 15 minutes | Servings: 4

Ingredients:

½ cup plus 3 tablespoons vegetable oil, divided.
¼ cup white wine vinegar
1 garlic clove, grated
2 yellow squash, cut into ¼-inch thick slices lengthwise

1 red onion, cut into wedges
½ teaspoon salt
½ teaspoon ground black pepper
8 ounces feta cheese, crumbled
¼ teaspoon red pepper flakes

Preparation:

1. In a small-sized bowl, blend together ½ cup of oil, vinegar, and garlic. Set aside. 2. In a large-sized bowl, blend together the squash, onion, and remaining oil and toss to coat well. 3. Arrange the lightly greased "Grill Grate" in the crisper basket in the cooking pot of Ninja Foodi Smart XL Grill. 4. Close the Grill with lid and press "Power" button. 5. Select "Grill" and then use the set of arrows to adjust the temperature to "MAX". 6. Use the set of arrows to the right of the display to adjust the cook time to 15 minutes. 7. Press "Start/Stop" to begin preheating. When the display shows "Add Food", open the lid and place the yellow squash and onions onto the "Grill Grate". 8. With your hands, gently press down the vegetables. Close the Grill with lid. 9. After 6 minutes of cooking, flip the vegetables. 10. When the cooking time is completed, open the lid and transfer the vegetables onto a platter. 11. Top with feta cheese and then drizzle with vinegar mixture. 12. Sprinkle with red pepper flakes and serve.
Serving Suggestions: Serve with the garnishing of herbs.
Variation Tip: White wine vinegar can be replaced with fresh lime juice.
Nutritional Information per Serving: Calories: 522 | Fat: 50.8g | Sat Fat: 12.3g | Carbohydrates: 8.8g | Fiber: 1.8g | Sugar: 5.3g | Protein: 9.6g

Chapter 4 Fish and Seafood Recipes

Roasted Salmon

Prep Time: 10 minutes | Cook Time: 40 minutes | Servings: 4

Ingredients:

1 lb baby potatoes, halved and baked	2 teaspoons rosemary
Kosher salt to taste	5 garlic cloves, divided and minced
Pepper to taste	Extra virgin olive oil, as required
1 tablespoon + 1 teaspoon thyme, divided	1 lb salmon fillet

Preparation:

1. Season salmon with salt and pepper. Add in potatoes. 2. Drizzle 3 tablespoons oil on fillets and add garlic on top. 3. Select the "Roast" button on the Ninja Foodi Smart XL Grill and regulate the settings at MED for 18 minutes. 4. Arrange them in the Ninja Foodi when it displays "Add Food." 5. Roast for about 18 minutes, tossing once in between. 6. Dish out and drizzle lemon juice on them, serve and enjoy.

Serving Suggestions: Serve with fresh thyme and rosemary on top.

Variation Tip: You can add white pepper.

Nutritional Information per Serving: Calories: 253.9 | Fat: 1.1g | Sat Fat: 0.3g | Carbohydrates: 21g | Fiber: 2.6g | Sugar: 0g | Protein: 25g

Crispy Coconut Shrimp

Prep Time: 5 minutes | Cook Time: 35 minutes | Servings: 4

Ingredients:

1 pound shrimp	1 cup bread crumbs
½ teaspoon salt	½ cup shredded coconut
½ cup all-purpose flour	Olive oil
1 large egg, beaten	Cooking spray

Preparation:

1. Take three containers. Add flour and salt in one container, egg in the second container, and breadcrumbs and coconut in the third container. 2. First, dip the shrimp in the flour, dip into an egg. Then coat it with bread crumbs and coconut. 3. Choose the "Air Crisp" button on Ninja Foodi Smart XL Grill and regulate the settings at 375°F for 10 minutes. 4. Arrange them in the Ninja Foodi when it displays "Add Food." Spray oil on top. 5. Air crisp for about 10 minutes, tossing them in between. 6. When done, serve and enjoy!

Serving Suggestions: Serve with any sauce.

Variation Tip: You can also top it with fresh cilantro.

Nutritional Information per Serving: Calories: 294 | Fat: 19g | Sat Fat: 16g | Carbohydrates: 21g | Fiber: 5g | Sugar: 1.8g | Protein: 12g

Garlicky Shrimp

Prep Time: 8 minutes | Cook Time: 7 minutes | Servings: 1

Ingredients:

1 garlic clove, minced	½ teaspoon fresh lemon juice
½ tablespoon fresh cilantro, chopped	½ Serrano pepper, seeded and chopped
¼ pound shrimp, peeled and deveined	finely
½ tablespoon olive oil	

Preparation:

1. Marinate the shrimp with the ingredients except cilantro. 2. Select the "Grill" button on Ninja Foodi Smart XL Grill and regulate the setting at MED for 10 minutes. 3. Arrange them in the Ninja Foodi when it displays "Add Food" and shower with olive oil. 4. Grill for about 10 minutes, turning them occasionally. 5. Serve hot with the topping of cilantro.

Serving Suggestions: Serve it with mango salsa.

Variation Tip: You can add red pepper flakes to make spicy garlic shrimp.

Nutritional Information per Serving: Calories: 201 | Fat: 9g | Sat Fat: 1.6g | Carbohydrates: 3g | Fiber: 0.2g | Sugar: 0.2g | Protein: 26.1g

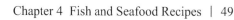

Honey Salmon

Prep Time: 10 minutes | Cook Time: 20 minutes | Servings: 6

Ingredients:

2 lb salmon fillet
Kosher salt to taste
2 tablespoons and ½ teaspoon olive oil
4 tablespoons mustard, whole grain

2 tablespoons honey
4 cloves garlic, minced
1 teaspoon paprika
½ teaspoon black pepper

Preparation:

1. Take a bowl and add salmon in it, season it and set aside. 2. Add honey, mustard, olive oil, garlic, and all peppers in a small bowl. Mix well. 3. Select the "Bake" button on the Ninja Foodi Smart XL Grill and regulate the settings at 375°F for 15 minutes. 4. Arrange them in the Ninja Foodi when it displays "Add Food." 5. Bake for 15-20 minutes. 6. Serve and enjoy.
Serving Suggestions: Serve with rice and enjoy.
Variation Tip: You can add cayenne pepper for taste.
Nutritional Information per Serving: Calories: 292 | Fat: 15.1g | Sat Fat: 2.2g | Carbohydrates: 7.3g | Fiber: 0.6g | Sugar: 2.1g | Protein: 30.7g

Salmon with Salsa

Prep Time: 10 minutes | Cook Time: 8 minutes | Servings: 1

Ingredients:

For Salsa:
¼ cup red bell pepper, seeded and chopped
1 tablespoon red onion, chopped
½ cup fresh pineapple chopped
½ tablespoon fresh lemon juice
Fresh ground black pepper to taste
For Salmon:
½ tablespoon extra-virgin olive oil
1 tablespoon fresh cilantro leaves, chopped
1 salmon fillets
Pinch of salt
Fresh ground black pepper to taste

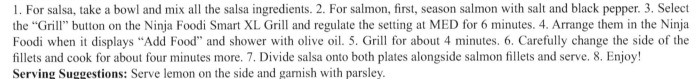

Preparation:

1. For salsa, take a bowl and mix all the salsa ingredients. 2. For salmon, first, season salmon with salt and black pepper. 3. Select the "Grill" button on the Ninja Foodi Smart XL Grill and regulate the setting at MED for 6 minutes. 4. Arrange them in the Ninja Foodi when it displays "Add Food" and shower with olive oil. 5. Grill for about 4 minutes. 6. Carefully change the side of the fillets and cook for about four minutes more. 7. Divide salsa onto both plates alongside salmon fillets and serve. 8. Enjoy!
Serving Suggestions: Serve lemon on the side and garnish with parsley.
Variation Tip: Cook the salmon until it is flaky and still pink on the inside.
Nutritional Information per Serving: Calories: 338 | Fat: 18.2g | Sat Fat: 2.6g | Carbohydrates: 10.4g | Fiber: 1.2g | Sugar: 7.1g | Protein: 35.5g

Baked Cod

Prep Time: 10 minutes | Cook Time: 20 minutes | Servings: 5

Ingredients:

4-6 cod fillet pieces
Sauce:
5 tablespoons lemon juice
5 tablespoons olive oil
Coating:
⅓ cup all-purpose flour
1 teaspoon ground coriander
¾ teaspoon sweet Spanish paprika
¼ cup parsley, chopped

2 tablespoons butter, melted
5 garlic cloves, minced

¾ teaspoon ground cumin
¾ teaspoon salt
½ teaspoon black pepper

Preparation:

1. Mix the ingredients of the sauce and set aside. 2. Take another bowl and add all the coating ingredients to it. Mix well and set it aside too. 3. Dip the fish in lemon syrup and then coat it with flour. 4. Select the "Bake" button on Ninja Foodi Smart XL Grill and regulate the settings at 400°F for 7 minutes. 5. Arrange them in the Ninja Foodi when it displays "Add Food." 6. Bake for about 7 minutes. 7. Drizzle the remaining syrup on top of it and bake for 10 minutes. 8. Serve and enjoy!
Serving Suggestions: Serve with boiled rice.
Variation Tip: Add in dried basil for more taste.
Nutritional Information per Serving: Calories: 319.3 | Fat: 19.8g | Sat Fat: 5g | Carbohydrates: 9.6g | Fiber: 1.2g | Sugar: 0.5g | Protein: 25.8g

Baked Fish with Chips

Prep Time: 10 minutes | Cook Time: 35 minutes | Servings: 4

Ingredients:

14 ounces fish fillet	2 tablespoon oil
1 cup breadcrumbs	1 teaspoon salt
1 large egg	2 russet potatoes
¼ cup flour	

Preparation:

1. Cut the potatoes into fresh fries. 2. Take a bowl, add potatoes, salt and oil and toss together. 3. Heat oil in a frying pan and fry the fries. 4. Meanwhile, add flour to a shallow bowl, beaten egg to a second bowl, and Panko to a third bowl. 5. First, coat the fish in the flour, dip it in egg, and last, cover it with breadcrumbs. 6. Remove the fries when done. 7. Select the "Bake" button on the Ninja Foodi Smart XL Grill and regulate the settings at 350°F for 15 minutes. 8. Arrange them in the Ninja Foodi when it displays "Add Food." 9. Bake for about 15 minutes. 10.Serve fish with fries.
Serving Suggestions: Serve with any sauce.
Variation Tip: You can use any fish (cod, tilapia, catfish).
Nutritional Information per Serving: Calories: 409 | Fat: 11g | Sat Fat: 1g | Carbohydrates: 44g | Fiber: 2g | Sugar: 2g | Protein: 30g

Mustard Baked Scampi

Prep Time: 10 minutes | Cook Time: 12 minutes | Servings: 4

Ingredients:

1 pound shrimps	1 teaspoon herbs
2 tablespoons unsalted butter, melted	½ teaspoon dry mustard
2 tablespoons extra virgin olive oil	¼ teaspoon salt
2 tablespoons finely minced shallot	¼ teaspoon freshly ground black pepper
2 garlic cloves, minced	2 tablespoons parsley, chopped

Preparation:

1. Take a bowl, add shrimp and remaining ingredients except the chopped parsley and mix. 2. Select the "Bake" button on Ninja Foodi Smart XL Grill and regulate the settings at 400°F for 9 minutes. 3. Arrange them in the Ninja Foodi when it displays "Add Food." 4. Bake for about 9 minutes. 5. When done, add parsley on top, bake for more than 2 minutes, and serve.
Serving Suggestions: Sprinkle lemon juice on top.
Variation Tip: You can also add breadcrumbs and bake for 2 minutes.
Nutritional Information per Serving: Calories: 366 | Fat: 19g | Sat Fat: 16g | Carbohydrates: 11g | Fiber: 1g | Sugar: 1.9g | Protein: 34g

Lobster Tails

Prep Time: 10 minutes | Cook Time: 10 minutes | Servings: 2

Ingredients:

2 lobster tails	1 clove garlic, grated
4 tablespoons butter	Salt and pepper, to taste
1 teaspoon lemon zest	2 lemon wedges

Preparation:

1. Butterfly lobster tails using kitchen shears to cut vertically through the centers of the hardtop. Next, cut to the bottoms of the shells. Separate the tail halves. 2. Take a saucepan and melt butter over medium heat. 3. Add lemon zest and garlic and cook until garlic is tender, for about 30 seconds. 4. Brush the butter mixture onto the lobster tails, then season it with salt and pepper. 5. Select the "Roast" button on the Ninja Foodi Smart XL Grill and regulate the settings at MED for 7 minutes. 6. Arrange them in the Ninja Foodi when it displays "Add Food." 7. Roast for about 7 minutes, turning once in between. 8. Serve with lemon wedges.
Serving Suggestions: Top with chopped parsley.
Variation Tip: You can also serve fresh cherry tomatoes with it.
Nutritional Information per Serving: Calories: 313 | Fat: 25.8g | Sat Fat: 16g | Carbohydrates: 3.3g | Fiber: 0.8g | Sugar: 0.1g | Protein: 18g

Air Fry Scallops

Prep Time: 5 minutes | Cook Time: 10 min | Servings: 2

Ingredients:

9 large fresh scallops
¼ teaspoon pepper
½ teaspoon Italian seasoning
½ teaspoon salt

2 garlic cloves, minced
3 tablespoons unsalted butter, melted
Fresh parsley, for garnish
Lemon wedges, for serving

Preparation:

1. Add salt and pepper to the scallops. 2. Set Ninja Foodi Smart XL Grill on Grill mode. Adjust the temperature to HI and set time to 10 minutes. 3. Once it displays "Add Food," place scallops on the Grill Grate, grill at LO for 10 minutes, and flip them halfway through the cooking time. 4. Meanwhile, mix garlic, spices, and herbs into the melted butter. 5. Transfer cooked scallops to a plate and drizzle with the garlic-herb butter. 6. Serve immediately.

Serving Suggestions: You can garnish it with parsley.

Variation Tip: Add some crushed chili to add heat to the dish.

Nutritional Information per Serving: Calories: 193 | Fat: 17g | Sat Fat: 11g | Carbohydrates: 3g | Fiber: 1g | Sugar: 1g | Protein: 7g

Grilled Tuna Burgers

Prep Time: 10 minutes | Cook Time: 20 minutes | Servings: 4

Ingredients:

1 large egg, beaten
½ cup dry bread crumbs
½ cup celery, finely chopped
⅓ cup mayonnaise

¼ cup finely chopped onion
2 tablespoons chili sauce
1 pouch of light tuna in water
4 hamburgers buns, split and toasted

Preparation:

1. Take a bowl, add the first 6 ingredients and fold in tuna. 2. Shape the tuna mixture into 4 patties. 3. Select the "Grill" button on Ninja Foodi Smart XL Grill and regulate the setting at MED for 12 minutes. 4. Arrange them in the Ninja Foodi when it displays "Add Food" and shower with olive oil. 5. Grill for about 12 minutes, turning them occasionally. 6. After 6 minutes, flip the sides and cook for another 6 minutes. 7. Set the patties on buns and serve.

Serving Suggestions: Serve with fries.

Variation Tip: You can also add tomatoes and lettuce to the buns.

Nutritional Information per Serving: Calories: 366 | Fat: 17g | Sat Fat: 3g | Carbohydrates: 35g | Fiber: 2g | Sugar: 3g | Protein: 17g

Basil Grilled Shrimp

Prep Time: 10 minutes | Cook Time: 15 minutes | Servings: 4

Ingredients:

⅓ cup lemon juice
¼ cup olive oil
2 tablespoons Dijon mustard
3 garlic cloves, minced
½ teaspoon salt

¼ teaspoon pepper
½ cup minced fresh basil, divided
2 pounds shrimp, peeled and deveined
2 teaspoons grated lemon zest

Preparation:

1. In a large mixing bowl, combine the lemon juice, oil, mustard, garlic, salt, and pepper; stir in ¼ cup of basil. Stir ¼ cup dressing into cooked couscous; set aside the rest. 2. Thread shrimp onto moistened wooden or metal skewers. 3. Select the "Grill" button on the Ninja Foodi Smart XL Grill and regulate the setting at MED for 15 minutes. 4. Arrange them in the Ninja Foodi when it displays "Add Food" and shower with olive oil. 5. Grill for about 15 minutes, turning them occasionally. 6. Remove the shrimp from the skewers and combine it with the leftover dressing. Serve alongside couscous. 7. Serve and enjoy!

Serving Suggestions: Sprinkle with the remaining basil and lemon zest.

Variation Tip: You can use any oil.

Nutritional Information per Serving: Calories: 363 | Fat: 12g | Sat Fat: 2g | Carbohydrates: 34g | Fiber: 0g | Sugar: 0g | Protein: 29g

Tuna Stuffed Avocados

Prep Time: 15 minutes | Servings: 1

Ingredients:

½ tablespoon red onion, chopped finely
4 tablespoons cooked tuna
½ tablespoon fresh cilantro, minced
½ large avocado halved and pitted

1 tablespoon fresh lime juice
Pinch of Cayenne pepper
Fresh ground black pepper to taste

Preparation:

1. Draw out the flesh from the center of the avocado and transfer it into a bowl. 2. Add chopped onion and lemon juice and mash until well combined. 3. Add tuna, cayenne, and black pepper and stir to combine everything well. 4. Divide the tuna mixture into both avocado halves evenly. 5. Select the "Bake" button on the Ninja Foodi Smart XL Grill and regulate the settings at 350°F for 5 minutes. 6. Arrange them in the Ninja Foodi when it displays "Add Food." 7. Bake for about 5 minutes. 8. Serve immediately and enjoy!

Serving Suggestions: Serve it with bread and savor the taste.

Variation Tip: Use fresh lime juice instead of bottled ones.

Nutritional Information per Serving: Calories: 1543 | Fat: 77.2g | Sat Fat: 15.9g | Carbohydrates: 13g | Fiber: 7.1g | Sugar: 1.5g | Protein: 191.1g

Lemon-Pepper Salmon

Prep Time: 15minutes Cook Time: 10 minutes| Servings: 4

Ingredients:

4 salmon fillets
2 lemons, sliced
½ teaspoon salt

1 tablespoon avocado oil
1 teaspoon fresh black pepper
1 teaspoon garlic powder

Preparation:

1. Season the salmon fillets with lemon, salt, garlic powder, black pepper, and avocado oil. 2. Select the "Grill" button on the Ninja Foodi Smart XL Grill and regulate the setting at MED for 10 minutes. 3. Arrange them in the Ninja Foodi when it displays "Add Food" and shower with olive oil. 4. Grill for about 10 minutes, turning them occasionally. 5. Remove the salmon fillets and put them on a serving platter. 6. Enjoy!

Serving Suggestions: Serve with chopped parsley on top.

Variation Tip: Use skin-on salmon fillets.

Nutritional Information per Serving: Calories: 167 | Fat: 7.6g | Sat Fat: 1.1g | Carbohydrates: 3.8g | Fiber: 1.2g | Sugar: 0.9g | Protein: 22.5g

Tuna Kabobs with Onion

Prep Time: 10 minutes | Cook Time: 15 minutes | Servings: 4

Ingredients:

1½ pounds tuna steaks, cut into chunks
2 medium red peppers, cut into small pieces

1 onion, cut into small pieces

Marinade:

¼ cup minced fresh cilantro
¼ cup sesame oil
3 tablespoons lime juice
2 tablespoons soy sauce

2 tablespoons extra virgin olive oil
1 tablespoon fresh ginger root, minced
2 garlic cloves, minced

Preparation:

1. Thread 4 metal or wooden skewers with tuna chunks. Thread 4 more skewers with tuna, pepper, and onion slices. 2. Mix up the marinade ingredients. Refrigerate for 30 minutes, and cover skewers with the marinade. 3. Select the "Grill" button on Ninja Foodi Smart XL Grill and regulate the setting at MED for 10 minutes. 4. Arrange them in the Ninja Foodi when it displays "Add Food" and shower with olive oil. 5. Grill for about 10 minutes, turning them occasionally. 6. Remove and put them on a serving platter. 7. Serve and enjoy!

Serving Suggestions: Served with salad.

Variation Tip: Top with lemon juice.

Nutritional Information per Serving: Calories: 389 | Fat: 16g | Sat Fat: 2g | Carbohydrates: 15g | Fiber: 4g | Sugar: 9g | Protein: 45g

Pretzel-Crushed Catfish

Prep Time: 15 minutes | Cook Time: 10 minutes | Servings: 4

Ingredients:

4 catfish fillets
½ teaspoon salt
2 large eggs
⅓ cup Dijon mustard
2 tablespoons milk

½ cup all-purpose flour
4 cups honey mustard miniature pretzels, coarsely crushed
Cooking spray

Preparation:

1. Take 3 bowls, add eggs, mustard, and milk in one bowl, and mix. Next, add flour in the second bowl and pretzels in the third bowl. 2. Season catfish with salt and pepper. First, coat in flour, dip in egg mixture, and coat in pretzels. 3. Choose the "Air Crisp" button on Ninja Foodi Smart XL Grill and regulate the settings at 325°F for 12 minutes. 4. Arrange them in the Ninja Foodi when it displays "Add Food." Spray oil on top. 5. Air crisp for about 12 minutes, tossing them in between. 6. When done, serve and enjoy.

Serving Suggestions: Serve with lemon slices.
Variation Tip: You can also serve it with macaronies.
Nutritional Information per Serving: Calories: 466 | Fat: 14g | Sat Fat: 3g | Carbohydrates: 45g | Fiber: 2g | Sugar: 2g | Protein: 33g

Herbed Sweet Salmon

Prep Time: 5minutes Cook Time: 10minutes Servings: 3

Ingredients:

1 pound salmon fillets
2 tablespoons butter
1½ tablespoons brown sugar
½ teaspoon parsley

½ teaspoon garlic powder
½ teaspoon salt
¼ teaspoon pepper

Preparation:

1. Add brown sugar, parsley, garlic, salt, and pepper in a bowl. Mix well. 2. Place salmon fillets in the mixture and rub them generously with it. 3. Select the "Grill" button on Ninja Foodi Smart XL Grill and regulate the setting at MED for 10 minutes. 4. Arrange them in the Ninja Foodi when it displays "Add Food" and shower with olive oil. 5. Grill for about 10 minutes, turning them occasionally. 6. Remove the salmon fillets and put them on a serving platter. 7. Enjoy!

Serving Suggestions: Serve with chopped mint leaves on the top.
Variation Tip: Use skinless salmon fillets.
Nutritional Information per Serving: Calories: 333 | Fat: 17g | Sat Fat: 6.2g | Carbohydrates: 16.7g | Fiber: 0.1g | Sugar: 16.1g | Protein: 29.5g

Salmon Cakes

Prep Time: 10 minutes | Cook Time: 30 minutes | Servings: 4

Ingredients:

3 teaspoons olive oil, divided
1 small onion, finely chopped
1 stalk celery, finely diced
2 tablespoons chopped fresh parsley
15 ounces canned salmon, drained

1 large egg, lightly beaten
1½ teaspoon Dijon mustard
1¾ cups fresh whole-wheat breadcrumbs
½ teaspoon freshly ground pepper

Preparation:

1. Heat 1½ teaspoons oil over medium-high heat in a large nonstick skillet. 2. Cook occasionally until the onion and celery are cooked for about 3 minutes. Remove from the fire and stir in the parsley. 3. In a medium mixing dish, place the salmon. Remove any bones and skin with a fork and flake them apart with a knife. Mix in the egg and mustard well. 4. Mix in the onion mixture, breadcrumbs, and pepper. Form the mixture into eight 2½-inch-wide patties. 5. Heat the remaining 1½ tablespoons oil in the same pan over medium heat. Cook for 2 to 3 minutes. 6. Turn them over onto the prepared baking sheet using a wide spatula. Carry on with the remaining patties in the same manner. 7. Select the "Bake" button on the Ninja Foodi Smart XL Grill and regulate the settings at 400°F for 15 to 20 minutes. 8. Arrange them in the Ninja Foodi when it displays "Add Food." 9. Bake for about 15 to 20 minutes. 10. Serve and enjoy!

Serving Suggestions: Serve with creamy dill sauce.
Variation Tip: You can also add cooked salmon.
Nutritional Information per Serving: Calories: 350 | Fat: 13g | Sat Fat: 1.4g | Carbohydrates: 23g | Fiber: 5g | Sugar: 5g | Protein: 34g

Tuna Kabobs

Prep Time: 15 minutes | Cook Time: 5 minutes | Servings: 2

Ingredients:

¾ ounce sesame oil
8 ounces fresh tuna steak, cut into 1-inch cubes

3-4 ounces teriyaki sauce
½ tablespoons ginger garlic paste
1 tablespoon fresh lemon juice

Preparation:

1. Mix together all the ingredients except for tuna steak in a bowl. 2. Add the tuna cubes and mix well. 3. Refrigerate to marinate for about 1 hour. 4. Thread the tuna cubes onto the skewers. 5. Arrange the lightly greased "Grill Grate" in the crisper basket in the cooking pot of Ninja Foodi Smart XL Grill. 6. Close the Grill with lid and press "Power" button. 7. Select "Grill" and then use the set of arrows to the left of the display to adjust the temperature to "HI". 8. Use the set of arrows to the right of the display to adjust the cook time to 5 minutes. 9. Press "Start/Stop" to begin preheating. When the display shows "Add Food", open the lid and place the skewers onto the "Grill Grate". 10. With your hands, gently press down each skewer. Close the Grill with lid. 11. While cooking, flip the skewers after every 2 minutes. 12. When the cooking time is completed, open the lid and serve hot.
Serving Suggestions: Serve with the dipping sauce of your choice.
Variation Tip: Use the best quality teriyaki sauce.
Nutritional Information per Serving: Calories: 363 | Fat: 20.1g | Sat Fat: 3.4g | Carbohydrates: 9.7g | Fiber: 0.6g | Sugar: 8.2g | Protein: 33.6g

Spicy Tilapia

Prep Time: 10 minutes | Cook Time: 15 minutes | Servings: 4

Ingredients:

4 tilapia fillets
1 teaspoon lemon pepper seasoning
1 teaspoon garlic powder

1 teaspoon onion powder
Salt and ground black pepper, as required
2 tablespoons olive oil

Preparation:

1. Mix the garlic powder, onion powder, lemon pepper seasoning, salt, and black pepper in a suitable mixing bowl. 2. Coat the tilapia fillets with oil and then rub them with a spice mixture. 3. Select the "Grill" button on the Ninja Foodi Smart XL Grill and regulate the setting at MED for 12 minutes. 4. Arrange them in the Ninja Foodi when it displays "Add Food" and shower with olive oil. 5. Grill for about 12 minutes, turning them occasionally. 6. Remove the tilapia fillets and put them on a serving platter. 7. Enjoy!
Serving Suggestions: Serve with your favorite salad.
Variation Tip: Use seasoning according to your choice.
Nutritional Information per Serving: Calories: 206 | Fat: 8.6g | Sat Fat: 1.7g | Carbohydrates: 0.2g | Fiber: 0.1g | Sugar: 0.4g | Protein: 31.9g

Cajun Cod Filets

Prep Time: 10 minutes | Cook Time: 15 minutes| Servings: 12

Ingredients:

3 pounds cod
6 tablespoons plantain flour
2 teaspoons smoked paprika
½ cup gluten-free flour

4 teaspoons Cajun seasoning
1 teaspoon garlic powder
Salt and pepper, to taste

Preparation:

1. Add plantain flour, smoked paprika, gluten-free flour, Cajun seasoning, garlic powder, salt, and pepper in a shallow dish. Whisk well. 2. Coat the fillets with flour mixture and refrigerate for about 2 hours. 3. Select the "Grill" button on Ninja Foodi Smart XL Grill and regulate the setting at MED for 6 minutes. 4. Arrange them in the Ninja Foodi when it displays "Add Food" and shower with olive oil. 5. Grill for about 16 minutes, turning them occasionally. 6. Remove the cod fillets and put them on a serving platter. 7. Enjoy!
Serving Suggestions: Serve with hot sauce.
Variation Tip: You can use regular flour instead.
Nutritional Information per Serving: Calories: 139 | Fat: 1.1g | Sat Fat: 0.2g | Carbohydrates: 4.4g | Fiber: 0.7g | Sugar: 0.2g | Protein: 26.3g

Salmon with Yogurt Sauce

Prep Time: 15 minutes | Cook Time: 12 minutes | Servings: 4

Ingredients:

½ cup plain Greek yogurt
3 garlic cloves, minced
2 tablespoons fresh dill, minced
2 tablespoons fresh lemon juice
1 tablespoon extra-virgin olive oil

1½ teaspoons ground coriander
1½ teaspoons ground cumin
Salt and ground black pepper, as required
4 (6-ounce) skinless salmon fillets

Preparation:

1. In a large bowl, add all the ingredients except the salmon and basil and mix well.
2. Transfer half of the yogurt mixture into another bowl and reserve for serving. 3. In the large bowl of the remaining yogurt mixture, add the salmon fillets and coat with the mixture well. 4. Refrigerate for about 25-30 minutes, flipping once half way through. 5. Remove the salmon fillets from the bowl and with the paper towels, discard the excess yogurt mixture. 6. Arrange the lightly greased "Grill Grate" in the crisper basket in the cooking pot of Ninja Foodi Smart XL Grill. 7. Close the Grill with lid and press "Power" button. Select "Grill" and then use the set of arrows to the left of the display to adjust the temperature to "MED". 8. Use the set of arrows to the right of the display to adjust the cook time to 12 minutes. 9. Press "Start/Stop" to begin preheating. When the display shows "Add Food", open the lid and place the salmon fillets onto the "Grill Grate". 10. With your hands, gently press down each salmon fillet. Close the Grill with lid. 11. After 6 minutes of cooking, flip the salmon fillets. 12. When the cooking time is completed, open the lid and serve hot with the topping of the reserved yogurt mixture and basil.

Serving Suggestions: Serve with a garnishing of fresh dill.

Variation Tip: Use plain yogurt.

Nutritional Information per Serving: Calories: 365 | Fat: 22.2g | Sat Fat: 4.6g | Carbohydrates: 4.3g | Fiber: 0.4g | Sugar: 2.4g | Protein: 35.6g

Sweet & Sour Salmon

Prep Time: 15 minutes | Cook Time: 23 minutes | Servings: 4

Ingredients:

4 teaspoons olive oil, divided
¼ cup dark brown sugar
¼ cup pineapple juice
2 tablespoons fresh lemon juice
2 tablespoons white distilled vinegar

½ teaspoon paprika
½ teaspoon cayenne powder
¼ teaspoon garlic powder
Salt and ground black pepper, as required
4 salmon fillets

Preparation:

1. In a saucepan, add 2 teaspoons of oil and remaining ingredients except for salmon fillets over medium-low heat and bring to a boil, stirring occasionally. 2. Reduce the heat to low and simmer, uncovered for about 15 minutes, stirring occasionally. 3. Preheat the barbecue grill to medium heat. 4. Grease the grill grate. 5. Rub the salmon fillets with remaining olive oil and then sprinkle with salt and black lightly. 6. Arrange the lightly greased "Grill Grate" in the crisper basket in the cooking pot of Ninja Foodi Smart XL Grill. 7. Close the Grill with lid and press "Power" button. 8. Select "Grill" and then use the set of arrows to the left of the display to adjust the temperature to "MED". 9. Use the set of arrows on the right of the display to adjust the cook time to 8 minutes. 10. Press "Start/Stop" to begin preheating. When the display shows "Add Food", open the lid and place the salmon fillets onto the "Grill Grate". 11. With your hands, gently press down each salmon fillet. Close the Grill with lid. 12. After 4 minutes of cooking, flip the salmon fillets. 13. When the cooking time is completed, open the lid and place the salmon fillets onto a plate. 14. Brush each fillet with the honey sauce and serve hot.

Serving Suggestions: Serve alongside the zucchini noodles.

Variation Tip: Use skinless salmon fillets.

Nutritional Information per Serving: Calories: 274 | Fat: 13.6g | Sat Fat: 2g | Carbohydrates: 11.5g | Fiber: 0.2g | Sugar: 10.6g | Protein: 27.7g

Salmon with Veggies

Prep Time: 10 minutes | Cook Time: 15 minutes | Servings: 4

Ingredients:

4 salmon fillets	4 tablespoons fresh parsley, roughly
3 tablespoons lemon juice	chopped
4 tablespoons fresh dill, roughly chopped	2 pounds asparagus
2 tablespoons olive oil	Salt and pepper, to taste

Preparation:

1. Mix lemon juice, olive oil, salt, pepper, dill, and parsley in a small dish. 2. Add salmon fillets to the mixture, coat well, and set aside. 3. Now, add asparagus to the dill mixture and mix well. 4. Select the "Grill" button on Ninja Foodi Smart XL Grill and regulate the setting at MED for 15 minutes. 5. Arrange them in the Ninja Foodi when it displays "Add Food" and shower with olive oil. 6. Grill for about 15 minutes, turning them occasionally. 7. Remove the salmon fillets and put them on a serving platter. 8. Enjoy!
Serving Suggestions: Serve with lemon wedges on the top.
Variation Tip: Don't use skinless salmon fillets.
Nutritional Information per Serving: Calories: 296 | Fat: 14.3g | Sat Fat: 2g | Carbohydrates: 6.1g | Fiber: 0.3g | Sugar: 5.7g | Protein: 37g

Tomato Grilled Tilapia

Prep Time: 10 minutes | Cook Time: 15 minutes | Servings: 4

Ingredients:

1 cup fresh cilantro leaves	ginger root
1 cup fresh parsley leaves	¾ teaspoon sea salt or kosher salt divided
2 tablespoons olive oil	2 cups grape tomatoes, halved lengthwise
2 teaspoons grated lemon zest	1½ cups fresh or frozen corn, thawed
2 tablespoons lemon juice	4 tilapia fillets
1 tablespoon coarsely chopped fresh	

Preparation:

1. In a food processor, combine the first 6 ingredients; add ½ teaspoon salt. Pulse the mixture until it is finely chopped. 2. Combine tomatoes and corn in a mixing bowl; whisk in 1 tablespoon of the herb mixture and the remaining salt. 3. Place each fillet on a heavy-duty foil sheet. Spoon tomato mixture alongside fish and top with herb mixture. Wrap the foil securely around the fish and vegetables. 4. Select the "Roast" button on Ninja Foodi Smart XL Grill and regulate the settings at MED for 10 minutes. 5. Arrange them in the Ninja Foodi when it displays "Add Food." 6. Roast for about 10 minutes, turning once in between. 7. Remove and put them on a serving platter. 8. Serve and enjoy!
Serving Suggestions: Served with salad.
Variation Tip: Top with lemon juice.
Nutritional Information per Serving: Calories: 270 | Fat: 9g | Sat Fat: 2g | Carbohydrates: 15g | Fiber: 4g | Sugar: 9g | Protein: 35g

Simple Salmon

Prep Time: 10 minutes | Cook Time: 12 minutes | Servings: 4

Ingredients:

4 (6-ounce) salmon fillets
Salt and ground black pepper, as required

Preparation:

1. Season the salmon fillets with salt and black pepper evenly. 2. Arrange the lightly greased "Grill Grate" in the crisper basket in the cooking pot of Ninja Foodi Smart XL Grill. 3. Close the Grill with lid and press "Power" button. 4. Select "Grill" and then use the set of arrows to the left of the display to adjust the temperature to "MED". 5. Use the set of arrows to the right of the display to adjust the cook time to 12 minutes. 6. Press "Start/Stop" to begin preheating. 7. When the display shows "Add Food", open the lid and place the salmon fillets onto the "Grill Grate". 8. With your hands, gently press down each salmon fillet. Close the Grill with lid. 9. After 4 minutes of cooking, flip the salmon fillets. 10. When the cooking time is completed, open the lid and serve hot.
Serving Suggestions: Serve alongside the asparagus.
Variation Tip: Salmon should look bright and shiny.
Nutritional Information per Serving: Calories: 225 | Fat: 10.5g | Sat Fat: 1.5g | Carbohydrates: 0g | Fiber: 0g | Sugar: 0g | Protein: 33g

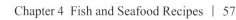

Lemony Salmon

Prep Time: 10 minutes | Cook Time: 14 minutes | Servings: 4

Ingredients:

2 garlic cloves, minced
1 tablespoon fresh lemon zest, grated
2 tablespoons extra-virgin olive oil
2 tablespoons fresh lemon juice

Salt and ground black pepper, as required
4 (6-ounce) boneless, skinless salmon fillets

Preparation:

1. In a bowl, place all ingredients except for salmon fillets and mix well. 2. Add the salmon fillets and coat with garlic mixture generously. 3. Set aside for about 20-30 minutes. 4. Arrange the lightly greased "Grill Grate" in the crisper basket in the cooking pot of Ninja Foodi Smart XL Grill. 5. Close the Grill with lid and press "Power" button. 6. Select "Grill" and then use the set of arrows to the left of the display to adjust the temperature to "MED". 7. Use the set of arrows to the right of the display to adjust the cook time to 14 minutes. 8. Press "Start/Stop" to begin preheating. When the display shows "Add Food", open the lid and place the salmon fillets onto the "Grill Grate". 9. With your hands, gently press down each salmon fillet. Close the Grill with lid. 10. After 7 minutes of cooking, flip the salmon fillets. 11. When the cooking time is completed, open the lid and serve hot.

Serving Suggestions: Serve with steamed veggies.
Variation Tip: You can use spices of your choice.
Nutritional Information per Serving: Calories: 281 | Fat: 16.3g | Sat Fat: 5.2g | Carbohydrates: 1g | Fiber: 0.2g | Sugar: 0.3g | Protein: 33.3g

Spiced Salmon

Prep Time: 10 minutes | Cook Time: 8 minutes | Servings: 6

Ingredients:

½ tablespoon ground ginger
½ tablespoon ground coriander
½ tablespoon ground cumin
½ teaspoon paprika
¼ teaspoon cayenne powder

Salt, as required
1 tablespoon fresh orange juice
1 tablespoon coconut oil, melted
2 pounds salmon fillets

Preparation:

1. In a bowl, add spices, salt, orange juice, and oil and mix until a paste forms. 2. Add salmon fillets and coat with mixture generously. 3. Refrigerate to marinate for about 30 minutes. 4. Arrange the lightly greased "Grill Grate" in the crisper basket in the cooking pot of Ninja Foodi Smart XL Grill. 5. Close the Grill with lid and press "Power" button. 6. Select "Grill" and then use the set of arrows to the left of the display to adjust the temperature to "HI". 7. Use the set of arrows to the right of the display to adjust the cook time to 8 minutes. 8. Press "Start/Stop" to begin preheating. When the display shows "Add Food", open the lid and place the salmon fillets onto the "Grill Grate". 9. With your hands, gently press down each salmon fillet. Close the Grill with lid. 10. After 4 minutes of cooking, flip the salmon fillets. 11. When the cooking time is completed, open the lid and serve hot.

Serving Suggestions: Serve alongside the lemon wedges.
Variation Tip: Adjust the ratio of spices according to your taste.
Nutritional Information per Serving: Calories: 225 | Fat: 11.8g | Sat Fat: 3.8g | Carbohydrates: 1g | Fiber: 0.2g | Sugar: 0.3g | Protein: 29.5g

Lobster Tail

Prep Time: 15 minutes | Cook Time: 5 minutes | Servings: 2

Ingredients:

2 lobster tails
2 tablespoons unsalted butter, melted
1 garlic clove, crushed

1 teaspoon dried parsley
Salt and ground black pepper, as required

Preparation:

1. With kitchen scissors, cut the lobster down the center of the tail. (Do not cut the fins). 2. Carefully pull apart the tail and with your fingers, bring the meat up to the top and close the shell. 3. In a small-sized bowl, blend together the butter, garlic, and parsley. 4. Brush each lobster with the butter mixture evenly. 5. Arrange the lightly greased "Grill Grate" in the crisper basket in the cooking pot of Ninja Foodi Smart XL Grill. 6. Close the Grill with lid and press "Power" button. 7. Select "Grill" and then use the set of arrows to the left of the display to adjust the temperature to "HI". 8. Use the set of arrows to the right of the display to adjust the cook time to 5 minutes. 9. Press "Start/Stop" to begin preheating. When the display shows "Add Food", open the lid and place the lobster tail onto the "Grill Grate". 10. With your hands, gently press down each lobster tail. Close the Grill with lid. 11. When the cooking time is completed, open the lid and serve hot.

Serving Suggestions: Serve with a drizzling of lemon juice.
Variation Tip: Don't overcook the lobster tails.
Nutritional Information per Serving: Calories: 282 | Fat: 13.2g | Sat Fat: 7.7g | Carbohydrates: 0.6g | Fiber: 0.1g | Sugar: 0g | Protein: 38g

Bacon-Wrapped Shrimp Kabobs

Prep Time: 20 minutes | Cook Time: 8 minutes | Servings: 3

Ingredients:

¼ cup olive oil
2 tablespoons fresh lime juice
½ chipotle pepper in adobo sauce, seeded and minced
1 garlic cloves, minced
1½ teaspoon powdered Erythritol
½ teaspoon red chili powder
½ teaspoon paprika

¼ teaspoon ground cumin
Salt and ground black pepper, as required
1 pound Medium raw shrimp, peeled and deveined
6 bacon slices, cut each into 3 equal pieces

Preparation:

1. In a bowl, add all the ingredients except the shrimp and bacon and mix well. 2. Add the shrimp and coat with the herb mixture generously. 3. Refrigerate to marinate for at least 30 minutes. 4. Wrap each shrimp in a piece of bacon and thread onto the presoaked wooden skewers. 5. Arrange the lightly greased "Grill Grate" in the crisper basket in the cooking pot of Ninja Foodi Smart XL Grill. 6. Close the Grill with lid and press "Power" button. 7. Select "Grill" and then use the set of arrows to the left of the display to adjust the temperature to "MED". 8. Use the set of arrows to the right of the display to adjust the cook time to 8 minutes. 9. Press "Start/Stop" to begin preheating. When the display shows "Add Food", open the lid and place the skewers onto the "Grill Grate". 10. With your hands, gently press down each skewer. Close the Grill with lid. 11. After 4 minutes of cooking, flip the skewers. 12. When the cooking time is completed, open the lid and serve hot.
Serving Suggestions: Serve with a drizzling of lemon juice.
Variation Tip: Use thick-cut bacon slices.
Nutritional Information per Serving: Calories: 641 | Fat: 43.7g | Sat Fat: 11.1g | Carbohydrates: 4.2g | Fiber: 0.7g | Sugar: 0.1g | Protein: 56g

Crusted Scallops

Prep Time: 15 minutes | Cook Time: 10 minutes | Servings: 4

Ingredients:

½ cup olive oil
¼ cup Parmesan cheese, shredded
½ cup fine Italian breadcrumbs
1 teaspoon dried parsley, crushed

½ teaspoon garlic salt
½ teaspoon ground black pepper
16 large sea scallops

Preparation:

1. In a shallow dish, place the oil. 2. In another shallow dish, mix together cheese, breadcrumbs, parsley, garlic salt, and black pepper. 3. Dip the scallops in oil and then roll in the cheese mixture evenly. 4. Arrange the scallops onto a large-sized plate in a single layer. 5. Refrigerate for at least 30 minutes. 6. Arrange the lightly greased "Grill Grate" in the crisper basket in the cooking pot of Ninja Foodi Smart XL Grill. 7. Close the Grill with lid and press "Power" button. 8. Select "Grill" and then use the set of arrows to the left of the display to adjust the temperature to "MED". 9. Use the set of arrows to the right of the display to adjust the cook time to 10 minutes. 10. Press "Start/Stop" to begin preheating. When the display shows "Add Food", open the lid and place the scallops onto the "Grill Grate". 11. With your hands, gently press down each scallop. Close the Grill with lid. 12. After 5 minutes of cooking, flip the scallops. 13. When the cooking time is completed, open the lid and serve hot.
Serving Suggestions: Serve with your favorite dipping sauce.
Variation Tip: Avoid shiny, wet or soft scallops.
Nutritional Information per Serving: Calories: 392 | Fat: 28.2g | Sat Fat: 4.7g | Carbohydrates: 12g | Fiber: 0.7g | Sugar: 0.9g | Protein: 22.8g

Garlicky Prawns

Prep Time: 15 minutes | Cook Time: 4 minutes | Servings: 5

Ingredients:

1½ pounds large prawns, peeled and deveined, with tails intact
3 large garlic cloves, minced
3 tablespoons extra-virgin olive oil

2 tablespoons fresh lemon juice
Salt and ground black pepper, as required

Preparation:

1. In a bowl, add all the ingredients and toss to coat well. 2. Arrange the lightly greased "Grill Grate" in the crisper basket in the cooking pot of Ninja Foodi Smart XL Grill. 3. Close the Grill with lid and press "Power" button. 4. Select "Grill" and then use the set of arrows to the left of the display to adjust the temperature to "HI". 5. Use the set of arrows to the right of the display to adjust the cook time to 4 minuutes. 6. Press "Start/Stop" to begin preheating. When the display shows "Add Food", open the lid and place the prawns onto the "Grill Grate". 7. With your hands, gently press down the prawns. Close the Grill with lid. 8. After 2 minutes of cooking, flip the prawns. 9. When the cooking time is completed, open the lid and serve hot.
Serving Suggestions: Serve with a drizzling of melted butter.
Variation Tip: Avoid the prawns that have cracked shells.
Nutritional Information per Serving: Calories: 238 | Fat: 10.8g | Sat Fat: 2g | Carbohydrates: 2.8g | Fiber: 0.1g | Sugar: 0.2g | Protein: 31.2g

Spicy Shrimp Kabobs

Prep Time: 15 minutes | Cook Time: 8 minutes | Servings: 4

Ingredients:

¼ cup olive oil
2 tablespoons fresh lime juice
1 teaspoon honey
½ teaspoon paprika

¼ teaspoon ground cumin
Salt and ground black pepper, as required
1¼ pounds medium raw shrimp, peeled and deveined

Preparation:

1. In a large bowl, add all the ingredients except for shrimp and mix well. 2. Add the shrimp and coat with the herb mixture generously. 3. Refrigerate to marinate for at least 30 minutes. 4. Arrange the lightly greased "Grill Grate" in the crisper basket in the cooking pot of Ninja Foodi Smart XL Grill. 5. Close the Grill with lid and press "Power" button. 6. Select "Grill" and then use the set of arrows to the left of the display to adjust the temperature to "MED". 7. Use the set of arrows to the right of the display to adjust the cook time to 8 minutes. 8. Press "Start/Stop" to begin preheating. When the display shows "Add Food", open the lid and place the skewers onto the "Grill Grate". 9. With your hands, gently press down each skewer. Close the Grill with lid. 10. After 4 minutes of cooking, flip the skewers. 11. When the cooking time is completed, open the lid and serve hot.
Serving Suggestions: Serve alongside the baby greens.
Variation Tip: Don't overcook te shrimp.
Nutritional Information per Serving: Calories: 284 | Fat: 15.1g | Sat Fat: 2.5g | Carbohydrates: 3.9g | Fiber: 0.1g | Sugar: 1.5g | Protein: 32.4g

Soy Orange Salmon

Prep Time: 15 minutes | Cook Time: 25 minutes | Servings: 4

Ingredients:

⅓ cup low-sodium soy sauce
⅓ cup fresh orange juice
¼ cup honey
1 scallion, chopped

1 teaspoon garlic powder
1 teaspoon ground ginger
1 (1½ pound) (¾-inch thick) salmon fillet

Preparation:

1. For marinade: in a bowl, add all ingredients except for salmon and mix well. 2. In a shallow bowl, add salmon and ⅔ cup of marinade and mix well. 3. Refrigerate to marinate for about 30 minutes, flipping occasionally. 4. Reserve the remaining marinade. 5. Arrange the lightly greased "Grill Grate" in the crisper basket in the cooking pot of Ninja Foodi Smart XL Grill. 6. Close the Grill with lid and press "Power" button. 7. Select "Grill" and then use the set of arrows to the left of the display to adjust the temperature to "MED". 8. Use the set of arrows to the right of the display to adjust the cook time to 25 minutes. 9. Press "Start/Stop" to begin preheating. When the display shows "Add Food", open the lid and place the salmon fillet onto the "Grill Grate". 10. With your hands, gently press down the salmon fillet. Close the Grill with lid. 11. After 13 minutes of cooking, flip the salmon fillets. 12. After 20 minutes of cooking, baste the salmon fillet with reserved marinade. 13. When the cooking time is completed, open the lid and place the salmon fillet onto a cutting board. 14. Cut the salmon into desired-sized fillets and serve.
Serving Suggestions: Serve with the garnishing of scallion greens.
Variation Tip: Adjust the ratio of honey according to to your taste.
Nutritional Information per Serving: Calories: 311 | Fat: 10.6g | Sat Fat: 1.5g | Carbohydrates: 22.1g | Fiber: 0.3g | Sugar: 20.7g | Protein: 34.8g

Simple Haddock

Prep Time: 10 minutes | Cook Time: 7 minutes | Servings: 4

Ingredients:

4 (4-ounce) haddock fillets

Salt and ground black pepper, as required

Preparation:

1. Sprinkle the haddock fillets with salt and black pepper generously. 2. Arrange the lightly greased "Grill Grate" in the crisper basket in the cooking pot of Ninja Foodi Smart XL Grill. 3. Close the Grill with lid and press "Power" button. Select "Grill" and then use the set of arrows to the left of the display to adjust the temperature to "MED". 4. Use the set of arrows to the right of the display to adjust the cook time to 7 minutes. Press "Start/Stop" to begin preheating. When the display shows "Add Food", open the lid and place the haddock fillets onto the "Grill Grate". 5. With your hands, gently press down each haddock fillet. Close the Grill with lid. 6. After 4 minutes of cooking, flip the haddock fillets. 7. When the cooking time is completed, open the lid and serve hot.
Serving Suggestions: Serve alongside the sauteed veggies.
Variation Tip: Fresh salmon should glisten, not look dull.
Nutritional Information per Serving: Calories: 127 | Fat: 24g | Sat Fat: 0.2g | Carbohydrates: 0g | Fiber: 0g | Sugar: 0g | Protein: 27.5g

Crab Cakes

Prep Time: 15 minutes | Cook Time: 10 minutes | Servings: 5

Ingredients:

12 ounces crabmeat	2 tablespoons fresh parsley, chopped
1 egg	3 scallions, chopped
2 teaspoons fresh lemon juice	½ cup Panko breadcrumbs
3 tablespoons mayonnaise	Salt and ground black pepper, as
1 teaspoon Sriracha sauce	required

Preparation:

1. Add crabmeat and remaining ingredients into a bowl and gently stir to combine. 2. Make 10 equal-sized patties from the mixture. 3. Arrange the lightly greased "Grill Grate" in the crisper basket in the cooking pot of Ninja Foodi Smart XL Grill. 4. Close the Grill with lid and press "Power" button. 5. Select "Grill" and then use the set of arrows to the left of the display to adjust the temperature to "MED". 6. Use the set of arrows to the right of the display to adjust the cook time to 10 minutes. 7. Press "Start/Stop" to begin preheating. When the display shows "Add Food", open the lid and place the patties onto the "Grill Grate". 8. With your hands, gently press down each patty. Close the Grill with lid. 9. After 5 minutes of cooking, flip the patties. 10. When the cooking time is completed, open the lid and serve hot.

Serving Suggestions: Serve with your favorite dipping sauce.

Variation Tip: Make sure to remove any cartilage from crabmeat.

Nutritional Information per Serving: Calories: 176 | Fat: 8.6g | Sat Fat: 1.4g | Carbohydrates: 6g | Fiber: 0.3g | Sugar: 0.9g | Protein: 10.2g

Glazed Halibut

Prep Time: 15 minutes | Cook Time: 12 minutes | Servings: 2

Ingredients:

1 orange, juiced	2 tablespoons extra-virgin olive oil
1 lime, juiced	2 tablespoons honey
1 tablespoon fresh parsley, minced	1 teaspoon salt
1 tablespoon garlic, minced	1 teaspoon ground black pepper
1 tablespoon fresh ginger, minced	2 frozen halibut fillets

Preparation:

1. For marinade: in a large-sized bowl, add all ingredients except for halibut fillets and mix well. 2. Add the halibut fillets and coat with mixture generously. 3. While unit is preheating, combine all ingredients except for halibut fillets, and mix well to incorporate. Then place fillets in the bowl and generously spoon marinade over them, coating evenly. 4. Arrange the lightly greased "Grill Grate" in the crisper basket in the cooking pot of Ninja Foodi Smart XL Grill. 5. Close the Grill with lid and press "Power" button. 6. Select "Grill" and then use the set of arrows to the left of the display to adjust the temperature to "MAX". 7. Use the set of arrows to the right of the display to adjust the cook time to 12 minutes. 8. Press "Start/Stop" to begin preheating. When the display shows "Add Food", open the lid and place the halibut fillets onto the "Grill Grate". 9. With your hands, gently press down each halibut fillet. 10. Place 1 spoon of marinade on the top of each fillet. Close the Grill with lid. 11. While cooking, flip the halibut fillets and coat with marinade after every 4 minutes. 12. When the cooking time is completed, open the lid and serve hot.

Serving Suggestions: Serve with a garnishing of sesame seeds.

Variation Tip: Fresh parsley can be replaced with dried parsley.

Nutritional Information per Serving: Calories: 404 | Fat: 18.3g | Sat Fat: 2.6g | Carbohydrates: 24g | Fiber: 0.9g | Sugar: 19.4g | Protein: 36.7g

Teriyaki Halibut

Prep Time: 10 minutes | Cook Time: 8 minutes | Servings: 4

Ingredients:

4 (6-ounce) skinless halibut fillets   1 cup teriyaki marinade

Preparation:

1. In a bowl, place all the halibut fillets and teriyaki marinade and mix well. 2. Refrigerate, covered to marinate for about 2-3 hours. 3. Arrange the lightly greased "Grill Grate" in the crisper basket in the cooking pot of Ninja Foodi Smart XL Grill. 4. Close the Grill with lid and press "Power" button. 5. Select "Grill" and then use the set of arrows to the left of the display to adjust the temperature to "MAX". 6. Use the set of arrows to the right of the display to adjust the cook time to 8 minutes. 7. Press "Start/Stop" to begin preheating. When the display shows "Add Food", open the lid and place the halibut fillets onto the "Grill Grate". 8. With your hands, gently press down each fillet. Close the Grill with lid. 9. After 6 minutes of cooking, flip the halibut fillets. 10. When the cooking time is completed, open the lid and serve hot.

Serving Suggestions: Serve with a garnishing of scallion greens.

Variation Tip: Rinse the halibut fillets thoroughly.

Nutritional Information per Serving: Calories: 269 | Fat: 4g | Sat Fat: 0.5g | Carbohydrates: 16g | Fiber: 0g | Sugar: 12g | Protein: 33g

Simple Cod

Prep Time: 10 minutes | Cook Time: 12 minutes | Servings: 2

Ingredients:

2 (6-ounce) cod fillets   Salt and ground black pepper, as required

Preparation:

1. Season the cod fillets with salt and black pepper. 2. Arrange the lightly greased "Grill Grate" in the crisper basket in the cooking pot of Ninja Foodi Smart XL Grill. 3. Close the Grill with lid and press "Power" button. 4. Select "Grill" and then use the set of arrows to the left of the displat to adjust the temperature to "MED". 5. Use the set of arrows to the right of the display to adjust the cook time to 12 minutes. 6. Press "Start/Stop" to begin preheating. When the display shows "Add Food", open the lid and place the cod fillets onto the "Grill Grate". 7. Place the cod fillets onto the "Grill Grate". 8. With your hands, gently press down each cod fillet. Close the Grill with lid. 9. When the cooking time is completed, open the lid and serve hot.

Serving Suggestions: Serve alongside the steamed green beans.

Variation Tip: Make sure you remove all the fish scales before cooking.

Nutritional Information per Serving: Calories: 137 | Fat: 1.5g | Sat Fat: 0g | Carbohydrates: 0g | Fiber: 0g | Sugar: 0g | Protein: 30.4g

Seasoned Tilapia

Prep Time: 5 minutes | Cook Time: 8 minutes | Servings: 4

Ingredients:

4 tilapia fillets   Salt and ground black pepper, as required
2 tablespoons BBQ seasoning

Preparation:

1. Season each tilapia fillet with BBQ seasoning, salt and black pepper. 2. Arrange the lightly greased "Grill Grate" in the crisper basket in the cooking pot of Ninja Foodi Smart XL Grill. 3. Close the Grill with lid and press "Power" button. 4. Select "Grill" and then use the set of arrows to the left of the display to adjust the temperature to "MED". 5. Use the set of arrows to the right of the display to adjust the cook time to 8 minutes. 6. Press "Start/Stop" to begin preheating. When the display shows "Add Food", open the lid and place the tilapia fillets onto the "Grill Grate". 7. With your hands, gently press down each tilapia fillet. Close the Grill with lid. 8. After 4 minutes of cooking, flip the tilapia fillets. 9. When the cooking time is completed, open the lid and serve hot.

Serving Suggestions: Serve with steamed green beans.

Variation Tip: Beware of strong fishy smells.

Nutritional Information per Serving: Calories: 122 | Fat: 1.3g | Sat Fat: 0.6g | Carbohydrates: 0.5g | Fiber: 0g | Sugar: 0g | Protein: 26.4g

Tilapia with Chimichurri Sauce

Prep Time: 20 minutes | Cook Time: 10 minutes | Servings: 4

Ingredients:

For Tilapia:
4 tilapia fillets
2 tablespoons BBQ seasoning
Salt and ground black pepper, as required
For Chimichurri Sauce
8 garlic cloves, minced
Salt, as required
1 teaspoon dried oregano
1 teaspoon ground black pepper
1 teaspoon red pepper flakes, crushed

2 teaspoons olive oil

4-5 teaspoons lemon zest, grated finely
4 ounces fresh lemon juice
1 bunch fresh flat leaf parsley
1 cup olive oil

Preparation:

1. For Chimichurri sauce: in a food processor, add all ingredients and pulse until well combined. 2. Transfer the sauce into a bowl and refrigerate to marinate for 30 minutes before serving. 3. Meanwhile, for tilapia: season each tilapia fillet with BBQ seasoning, salt, and black pepper. 4. Arrange the lightly greased "Grill Grate" in the crisper basket in the cooking pot of Ninja Foodi Smart XL Grill. 5. Close the Grill with lid and press "Power" button. 6. Select "Grill" and then use the set of arrows to the left of the display to adjust the temperature to "MED". 7. Use the set of arrows to the right of the display to adjust the cook time to 10 minutes. 8. Press "Start/Stop" to begin preheating. When the display shows "Add Food", open the lid and place the tilapia fillets onto the "Grill Grate". 9. With your hands, gently press down each tilapia fillet. Close the Grill with lid. 10. After 5 minutes of cooking, flip the tilapia fillets. 11. When the cooking time is completed, open the lid and divide tilapia fillets onto serving plates. 12. Top each fillet with Chimichurri sauce and serve.

Serving Suggestions: Serve with fresh salad.
Variation Tip: Feel free to use the seasoning of your choice.
Nutritional Information per Serving: Calories: 268 | Fat: 52.1g | Sat Fat: 5.5g | Carbohydrates: 3.9g | Fiber: 6.7g | Sugar: 0.9g | Protein: 27.2g

Garlicky Sword Fish

Prep Time: 10 minutes | Cook Time: 12 minutes | Servings: 4

Ingredients:

12 garlic cloves
⅓ cup olive oil
3 tablespoons fresh lemon juice
1½ teaspoons ground cumin

1 teaspoon ground coriander
1 teaspoon paprika
Salt and ground black pepper, as required
4 (7-ounce) swordfish steaks

Preparation:

1. In a food processor, add the garlic, lemon juice, oil, spices, salt, and black pepper and pulse until smooth. 2. Coat the swordfish steaks with the garlic mixture generously. 3. Arrange the swordfish steaks into a dish and refrigerate, covered for about 1 hour. 4. Arrange the lightly greased "Grill Grate" in the crisper basket in the cooking pot of Ninja Foodi Smart XL Grill. 5. Close the Grill with lid and press "Power" button. 6. Select "Grill" and then use the set of arrows to the left of the display to adjust the temperature to "HI". 7. Use the set of arrows to the right of the display to adjust the cook time to 10 minutes. 8. Press "Start/Stop" to begin preheating. 9. When the display shows "Add Food", open the lid and place the fish steaks onto the "Grill Grate". 10. With your hands, gently press down each fish steak. Close the Grill with lid. 11. After 5 minutes of cooking, flip the fish steaks. 12. When the cooking time is completed, open the lid and serve hot.

Serving Suggestions: Serve alongside the lemon slices.
Variation Tip: Use fresh garlic.
Nutritional Information per Serving: Calories: 473 | Fat: 27.4g | Sat Fat: 5.3g | Carbohydrates: 4g | Fiber: 0.6g | Sugar: 0.4g | Protein: 51.3g

Stuffed Swordfish

Prep Time: 15 minutes | Cook Time: 18 minutes | Servings: 2

Ingredients:

1 (8-ounce) (2-inch thick) swordfish steak
1½ tablespoons olive oil, divided
1 tablespoon fresh lemon juice
2 cups fresh spinach, torn

1 garlic clove, minced
¼ cup feta cheese, crumbled
Salt and black pepper, to taste

Preparation:

1. In a food processor, add the garlic, lemon juice, oil, salt, and black pepper and pulse until smooth. 2. Coat the swordfish steaks with the garlic mixture generously. 3. Arrange the swordfish steaks into a dish and refrigerate, covered for about 1 hour. 4. Carefully, cut a slit on one side of fish steak to create a pocket. 5. In a bowl, add 1 tablespoon of the oil and lemon juice and mix. 6. Coat both sides of fish with oil mixture evenly. 7. In a small skillet, add the remaining oil and garlic over medium heat and cook until heated. 8. Add the spinach and cook for about 2-3 minutes or until wilted. 9. Remove from the heat and set aside to cool slightly. 10. Stuff the fish pocket with spinach, followed by the feta cheese. 11. Arrange the lightly greased "Grill Grate" in the crisper basket in the cooking pot of Ninja Foodi Smart XL Grill. 12. Close the Grill with lid and press "Power" button. 13. Select "Grill" and then use the set of arrows to the left of the display to adjust the temperature to "MED". 14. Use the set of arrows to the right of the display to adjust the cook time to 14 minutes. 15. Press "Start/Stop" to begin preheating. When the display shows "Add Food", open the lid and place the fish pocket onto the "Grill Grate". 16. With your hands, gently press down the fish pocket. Close the Grill with lid. 17. After 8 minutes of cooking, flip the fish pocket. 18. When the cooking time is completed, open the lid and place the fish pocket onto a cutting board. 19. Cut the fish pocket into 2 equal-size pieces and serve.

Serving Suggestions: Serve with the garnishing of fresh herbs.

Variation Tip: Fresh spinach can be replaced with kale.

Nutritional Information per Serving: Calories: 326 | Fat: 20.5g | Sat Fat: 6g | Carbohydrates: 2.5g | Fiber: 0.7g | Sugar: 1.1g | Protein: 32.5g

Shrimp & Watermelon Kabobs

Prep Time: 15 minutes | Cook Time: 8 minutes | Servings: 6

Ingredients:

1 jalapeño pepper, chopped
1 large garlic clove, chopped
1 (1-inch) piece fresh ginger, mined
⅓ cup fresh mint leave

½ cup water
¼ cup fresh lime juice
24 Medium shrimp, peeled and deveined
4 cups seedless watermelon, cubed

Preparation:

1. In a food processor, add jalapeño, garlic, ginger, mint, water, and lime juice and pulse until smooth. 2. Transfer the mint mixture into a large-sized bowl. 3. Add the shrimp and coat with marinade generously. 4. Cover and refrigerate to marinate for at least 1-2 hours. 5. Remove shrimp from marinade and thread onto pre-soaked wooden skewers with watermelon. 6. Arrange the lightly greased "Grill Grate" in the crisper basket in the cooking pot of Ninja Foodi Smart XL Grill. 7. Close the Grill with lid and press "Power" button. 8. Select "Grill" and then use the set of arrows to the left of the display to adjust the temperature to "MED". 9. Use the set of arrows to the right of the the display to adjust the cook time to 8 minutes. 10. Press "Start/Stop" to begin preheating. When the display shows "Add Food", open the lid and place the skewers onto the "Grill Grate". 11. With your hands, gently press down each skewer. Close the Grill with lid. 12. After 4 minutes of cooking, flip the skewers. 13. When the cooking time is completed, open the lid and serve hot.

Serving Suggestions: Serve alongside fresh greens.

Variation Tip: Make sure to use seedless watermelon.

Nutritional Information per Serving: Calories: 190 | Fat: 1.8g | Sat Fat: 0.5g | Carbohydrates: 15.3g | Fiber: 0.9g | Sugar: 6.3g | Protein: 20.8g

Spiced Whole Trout

Prep Time: 10 minutes | Cook Time: 10 minutes | Servings: 2

Ingredients:

1 teaspoon vegetable oil
2 teaspoons fresh lemon juice
1 teaspoon ground cumin
1 teaspoon spicy Hungarian paprika

1 teaspoon red chili powder
Salt and ground black pepper, as required
1 whole trout, cleaned

Preparation:

1. In a bowl, blend together oil and remaining ingredients except for trout. 2. With a knife, make deep cuts in each side of trout. 3. Rub the trout with spice mixture generously. 4. Arrange the trout in a dish and refrigerate to marinate for at least 1 hour. 5. Arrange the lightly greased "Grill Grate" in the crisper basket in the cooking pot of Ninja Foodi Smart XL Grill. 6. Close the Grill with lid and press "Power" button. 7. Select "Grill" and then use the set of arrows to the left of the display to adjust the temperature to "MED". 8. Use the set of arrows to the right of the display to adjust the cook time to 10 minutes. 9. Press "Start/Stop" to begin preheating. When the display shows "Add Food", open the lid and place the trout onto the "Grill Grate". 10. With your hands, gently press down the trout. Close the Grill with lid. 11. After 5 minutes of cooking, flip the trout. 12. When the cooking time is completed, open the lid and serve hot.

Serving Suggestions: Serve with a drizzling of orange juice.

Variation Tip: The flesh of the fish should bounce back on touching it.

Nutritional Information per Serving: Calories: 565 | Fat: 29.6g | Sat Fat: 7.1g | Carbohydrates: 1.9g | Fiber: 1g | Sugar: 0.3g | Protein: 73.4g

Curried Shrimp Kabobs

Prep Time: 15 minutes | Cook Time: 6 minutes | Servings: 3

Ingredients:

2 garlic cloves, minced
3 tablespoons fresh lemon juice
1 tablespoon Dijon mustard
1 tablespoon maple syrup

1 tablespoon low-sodium soy sauce
2 teaspoons curry paste
1 pound medium shrimp, peeled and deveined

Preparation:

1. In a bowl, add garlic and remaining ingredients except for shrimp and mix until well combined. 2. Add shrimp and coat with marinade generously. 3. Cover the bowl of shrimp mixture and refrigerate to marinate for about 1 hour. 4. Thread the shrimp onto pre-soaked wooden skewers. 5. Arrange the lightly greased "Grill Grate" in the crisper basket in the cooking pot of Ninja Foodi Smart XL Grill. 6. Close the Grill with lid and press "Power" button. 7. Select "Grill" and then use the set of arrows to the left of the display to adjust the temperature to "HI". 8. Use the set of arrows to the right of the display to adjust the cook time to 6 minutes. 9. Press "Start/Stop" to begin preheating. When the display shows "Add Food", open the lid and place the skewers onto the "Grill Grate". 10. With your hands, gently press down each skewer. Close the Grill with lid. 11. After 3 minutes of cooking, flip the skewers. 12. When the cooking time is completed, open the lid and serve hot.

Serving Suggestions: Serve with the drizzling of lime juice.

Variation Tip: Use fresh shrimp.

Nutritional Information per Serving: Calories: 231 | Fat: 4.9g | Sat Fat: 0.9g | Carbohydrates: 9.3g | Fiber: 0.3g | Sugar: 4.7g | Protein: 35.4g

Simple Tuna

Prep Time: 10 minutes | Cook Time: 6 minutes | Servings: 4

Ingredients:

4 (6-ounce) (1-inch thick) tuna steaks   Salt and ground black pepper, as required
2 tablespoons extra-virgin olive oil, divided

Preparation:

1. Coat the tuna steaks with 1 tablespoon of the oil and sprinkle with salt and black pepper. 2. Set aside for about 5 minutes. 3. Arrange the lightly greased "Grill Grate" in the crisper basket in the cooking pot of Ninja Foodi Smart XL Grill. 4. Close the Grill with lid and press "Power" button. 5. Select "Grill" and then use the set of arrows to the left of the display to adjust the temperature to "HI". 6. Use the set of arrows to the right of the display to adjust the cook time to 6 minutes. 7. Press "Start/ Stop" to begin preheating. When the display shows "Add Food", open the lid and place the tuna steaks onto the "Grill Grate". 8. With your hands, gently press down each tuna steak. Close the Grill with lid. 9. After 3 minutes of cooking, flip the tuna steaks. 10. When the cooking time is completed, open the lid and serve hot.
Serving Suggestions: Serve alongside the salsa.
Variation Tip: Season the fish properly.
Nutritional Information per Serving: Calories: 239 | Fat: 8.5g | Sat Fat: 1g | Carbohydrates: 0g | Fiber: 0g | Sugar: 0g | Protein: 39.8g

Mustard Soy Salmon

Prep Time: 10 minutes | Cook Time: 10 minutes | Servings: 6

Ingredients:

⅓ cup olive oil   3 tablespoons low-   dried minced garlic
sodium soy sauce   6 (5-ounce) salmon fillets
2 tablespoons Dijon mustard   ½ teaspoon

Preparation:

1. In a small bowl, add the oil, soy sauce, mustard, and garlic and mix well. 2. In a large resealable plastic bag, place half of marinade and salmon fillets. 3. Seal the bag and shake to coat. 4. Refrigerate to marinate for about 30 minutes. 5. Reserve the remaining marinade. 6. Arrange the lightly greased "Grill Grate" in the crisper basket in the cooking pot of Ninja Foodi Smart XL Grill. 7. Close the Grill with lid and press "Power" button. 8. Select "Grill" and then use the set of arrows to the left of the display to adjust the temperature to "MED". 9. Use the set of arrows to the right of the display to adjust the cook time to 10 minutes. 10. Press "Start/Stop" to begin preheating. 11. When the display shows "Add Food", open the lid and place the salmon fillets onto the "Grill Grate". 12. With your hands, gently press down each fillet. Close the Grill with lid. 13. After 5 minutes of cooking, flip the salmon fillets. 14. When the cooking time is completed, open the lid and transfer the salmon fillets onto a platter. 15. Drizzle with reserved marinade and serve immediately.
Serving Suggestions: Serve with lemon wedges.
Variation Tip: Use low-sodium soy sauce.
Nutritional Information per Serving: Calories: 290 | Fat: 20.2g | Sat Fat: 2.9g | Carbohydrates: 0.9g | Fiber: 0.2g | Sugar: 0.5g | Protein: 28.2g

Roasted Spicy Catfish

Prep Time: 15 minutes | Cook Time: 14 minutes | Servings: 4

Ingredients:

4 catfish fillets   1 teaspoon garlic powder
4 tablespoons cornmeal polenta   Salt, as required
4 teaspoons Cajun seasoning   2 tablespoons olive oil
1 teaspoon paprika

Preparation:

1. Mix the cornmeal, Cajun seasoning, paprika, garlic powder, and salt in a bowl. 2. Add the catfish fillets and coat them evenly with the mixture. 3. Now, coat each fillet with oil. 4. Select the "Roast" button on Ninja Foodi Smart XL Grill and regulate the settings at MED for 15 minutes. 5. Arrange them in the Ninja Foodi when it displays "Add Food." 6. Roast for about 15 minutes, tossing once in between. 7. Remove the catfish fillets and put them on a serving platter. 8. Enjoy!
Serving Suggestions: Serve with your favorite salad.
Variation Tip: Use the seasoning according to your choice.
Nutritional Information per Serving: Calories: 321 | Fat: 20.3g | Sat Fat: 3.4g | Carbohydrates: 6.7g | Fiber: 0.3g | Sugar: 0.3g | Protein: 27.3g

Shrimp & Zucchini Kabobs

Prep Time: 15 minutes | Cook Time: 8 minutes | Servings: 4

Ingredients:

For Seasoning Mixture:

2 tablespoons paprika

½ tablespoon chili powder

½ tablespoon onion powder

½ tablespoon garlic powder

½ tablespoon dried thyme, crushed

½ tablespoon dried oregano, crushed

For Kabobs:

1 pound raw shrimp, peeled and deveined

2 zucchinis, cut in ½-inch cubes

2 tablespoons olive oil

Preparation:

1. For seasoning mixture: in a bowl, mix together all ingredients. 2. In a large bowl, add shrimp, zucchini, oil and seasoning and toss to coat well. 3. Thread shrimp and zucchini onto pre-soaked skewers. 4. Arrange the lightly greased "Grill Grate" in the crisper basket in the cooking pot of Ninja Foodi Smart XL Grill. 5. Close the Grill with lid and press "Power" button. 6. Select "Grill" and then use the set of arrows to the left of the display to adjust the temperature to "MED". 7. Use the set of arrows to the right of the display to adjust the cook time to 8 minutes. 8. Press "Start/Stop" to begin preheating. When the display shows "Add Food", open the lid and place the skewers onto the "Grill Grate". 9. With your hands, gently press down each skewer. Close the Grill with lid. 10. While cooking, flip the skewers after every 2 minutes. 11. When the cooking time is completed, open the lid and serve hot.

Serving Suggestions: Serve alongside the fresh salad.

Variation Tip: Adjust the ratio of seasoning according to your taste.

Nutritional Information per Serving: Calories: 232 | Fat: 9.8g | Sat Fat: 1.5g | Carbohydrates: 9.5g | Fiber: 3.2g | Sugar: 2.7g | Protein: 28g

Balsamic Baked Salmon

Prep Time: 10 minutes | Cook Time: 30 minutes | Servings: 8

Ingredients:

1 cup balsamic vinegar

¼ cup quality dark honey

4 garlic cloves, minced

½ teaspoon cayenne pepper

½ teaspoon Aleppo pepper

3 tablespoons Dijon mustard

2 tablespoons extra virgin olive oil

3 lb salmon fillet, no skin

Salt to taste

Pepper to taste

⅓ cup parsley leaves, chopped

⅓ cup fresh dill, chopped

Preparation:

1. Take a saucepan and put honey and balsamic vinegar into it. 2. Place saucepan over medium heat, and let it simmer. 3. Cook for 15 minutes. 4. In the saucepan, mixture adds garlic, spices, oil, and mustard. Mix well. 5. Season salmon with salt and pepper on both sides. 6. Brush the salmon with the saucepan mixture. 7. Select the "Bake" button on the Ninja Foodi Smart XL Grill and regulate the settings at 400°F for 15 minutes. 8. Arrange salmon in the Ninja Foodi when it displays "Add Food." 9. Bake for about 15 minutes. 10. Take out and serve.

Serving Suggestions: Serve with chopped parsley and dill on top.

Variation Tip: You can add crushed red chilies to add some spice.

Nutritional Information per Serving: Calories: 211 | Fat: 8.3g | Sat Fat: 1.6g | Carbohydrates: 8g | Fiber: 3.5g | Sugar: 4.9g | Protein: 25.6g

Salmon with Butter Sauce

Prep Time: 10 minutes | Cook Time: 10 minutes | Servings: 4

Ingredients:

For Salmon:

1 teaspoon garlic powder
1 teaspoon sea salt
½ teaspoon ground black pepper

2 pounds salmon fillets
1 tablespoon avocado oil
1-2 teaspoons fresh lemon juice

For Butter Sauce

4 tablespoons butter
2 garlic cloves, minced
2 tablespoons fresh lemon juice

1-2 teaspoons fresh parsley, chopped
Pinch of sea salt

Preparation:

1. In a small-sized bowl, blend together the garlic powder, salt, and back pepper. 2. Coat each salmon fillets with oil and then sprinkle with salt mixture. Then drizzle with lemon juice. 3. Set aside at room temperature for about 10 minutes. 4. Arrange the lightly greased "Grill Grate" in the crisper basket in the cooking pot of Ninja Foodi Smart XL Grill. 5. Close the Grill with lid and press "Power" button. 6. Select "Grill" and then use the set of arrows to the left of the display to adjust the temperature to "HI". 7. Use the set of arrows on the right of the display to adjust the cook time to 10 minutes. 8. Press "Start/Stop" to begin preheating. When the display shows "Add Food", open the lid and place the salmon fillets onto the "Grill Grate". 9. With your hands, gently press down each salmon fillet. Close the Grill with lid. 10. After 5 minutes of cooking, flip the salmon fillets. 11. Meanwhile, for butter sauce: in a non-stick frying pan, melt butter over low heat. 12. Stir in garlic and lemon juice and cook for about 1-2 minutes, stirring continuously. 13. Stir in parsley and salt and remove from the heat. 14. When the cooking time is completed, open the lid and transfer the salmon fillets onto a platter. 15. Top with butter sauce and serve.

Serving Suggestions: Serve with crusty bread.

Variation Tip: Olive oil can be used instead of vocado oil.

Nutritional Information per Serving: Calories: 649 | Fat: 41.2g | Sat Fat: 14.9g | Carbohydrates: 1.6g | Fiber: 0.4g | Sugar: 0.4g | Protein: 54g

Cheesy Lobster Sandwich

Prep Time: 15 minutes | Cook Time: 8 minutes | Servings: 4

Ingredients:

4 sourdough bread slices
4 tablespoons mayonnaise
8 Havarti cheese slices

4 ounces fresh lobster meat
Salt, as required

Preparation:

1. Arrange the bread slices onto a smooth surface. 2. Spread the mayonnaise on one side of each bread slice. 3. Place 2 cheese slices over each bread slice, followed by lobster meat and the remaining 2 cheese slices. 4. Sprinkle with salt evenly and cover with remaining slices. 5. Arrange the lightly greased "Grill Grate" in the crisper basket in the cooking pot of Ninja Foodi Smart XL Grill. 6. Close the Grill with lid and press "Power" button. 7. Select "Grill" and then use the set of arrows to the left of the display to adjust the temperature to "MED". 8. Use the set of arrows to the right of the display to adjust the cook time to 8 minutes. 9. Press "Start/Stop" to begin preheating. When the display shows "Add Food", open the lid and place the sandwiches onto the "Grill Grate". 10. With your hands, gently press down each sandwich. Close the Grill with lid. 11. After 4 minutes of cooking, flip the sandwiches. 12. When the cooking time is completed, open the lid and place the sandwiches onto a platter. 13. Cut 2 halves of each sandwich and serve warm.

Serving Suggestions: Serve alongside the mustard dip.

Variation Tip: You can use the bread of your choice.

Nutritional Information per Serving: Calories: 303 | Fat: 18.8g | Sat Fat: 9.9g | Carbohydrates: 16.3g | Fiber: 0.6g | Sugar: 3.1g | Protein: 18.5g

Zesty Salmon

Prep Time: 10 minutes | Cook Time: 10 minutes | Servings: 4

Ingredients:

2 tablespoons scallions, chopped
¾ teaspoon fresh ginger, minced
1 garlic clove, minced
½ teaspoon dried dill weed, crushed

¼ cup olive oil
2 tablespoons balsamic vinegar
2 tablespoons low-sodium soy sauce
4 (5-ounce) boneless salmon fillets

Preparation:

1. Add all ingredients except for salmon fillets in a large-sized bowl and mix well. 2. Add the salmon fillets and coat with marinade generously. 3. Cover and refrigerate to marinate for at least 4–5 hours. 4. Arrange the lightly greased "Grill Grate" in the crisper basket in the cooking pot of Ninja Foodi Smart XL Grill. 5. Close the Grill with lid and press "Power" button. 6. Select "Grill" and then use the set of arrows to the left of the display to adjust the temperature to "MED". 7. Use the set of arrows to the left of the display to adjust the cook time to 10 minutes. 8. Press "Start/Stop" to begin preheating. When the display shows "Add Food", open the lid and place the salmon fillets onto the "Grill Grate". 9. With your hands, gently press down each salmon fillet. Close the Grill with lid. 10. After 5 minutes of cooking, flip the salmon fillets. 11. When the cooking time is completed, open the lid and serve hot.

Serving Suggestions: Serve alongside the fresh salad.
Variation Tip: Dry the salmon fillets completely before applying marinade.
Nutritional Information per Serving: Calories: 303 | Fat: 21.4g | Sat Fat: 3.1g | Carbohydrates: 1.4g | Fiber: 0.2g | Sugar: 0.6g | Protein: 28.2g

Lemony Sardines

Prep Time: 15 minutes | Cook Time: 5 minutes | Servings: 4

Ingredients:

3 garlic cloves, minced
1 teaspoon dried rosemary, crushed
3 tablespoons fresh lemon juice
¼ cup olive oil

¼ teaspoon cayenne powder
Salt and ground black pepper, as required
1 pound fresh sardines, scaled and gutted

Preparation:

1. In a shallow baking dish, place all the ingredients except sardines and mix until well combined. 2. Place the sardines and coat with the mixture evenly. 3. Cover the baking dish and set aside to marinate for at least 1 hour. 4. Arrange the lightly greased "Grill Grate" in the crisper basket in the cooking pot of Ninja Foodi Smart XL Grill. 5. Close the Grill with lid and press "Power" button. 6. Select "Grill" and then use the set of arrows to the left of the display to adjust the temperature to "HI". 7. Use the set of arrows to the right of the display to adjust the cook time to 5 minutes. 8. Press "Start/Stop" to begin preheating. When the display shows "Add Food", open the lid and place the sardines onto the "Grill Grate". 9. With your hands, gently press down each sardine. Close the Grill with lid. 10. After 3 minutes of cooking, flip the sardines. 11. When the cooking time is completed, open the lid and serve hot.

Serving Suggestions: Serve with the drizzling of lime juice.
Variation Tip: Use freshly ground black pepper.
Nutritional Information per Serving: Calories: 351 | Fat: 25.8g | Sat Fat: 3.6g | Carbohydrates: 1.2g | Fiber: 0.3g | Sugar: 0.3g | Protein: 28.2g

Crispy Salmon

Prep Time: 10 minutes | Cook Time: 5 minutes | Servings: 4

Ingredients:

4 salmon fillets, skin on
Salt to taste
Pepper to taste
1½ tablespoons dry oregano

1 tablespoon garlic powder
¾ teaspoon paprika
Olive oil, as required
1½ lemon juice

Preparation:

1. Take a large bowl and add salmon to it. Season it with salt and pepper on both sides. 2. Add garlic, paprika, and oregano to a small bowl. Now again, season the fish with this mixture. 3. Choose the "Air Crisp" button on the Ninja Foodi Smart XL Grill and regulate the settings at 375°F for 5 minutes. 4. Arrange salmon in the Ninja Foodi when it displays "Add Food." 5. Air crisp for about 4 minutes, turning them in between. 6. Serve with lemon juice on top, and enjoy.

Serving Suggestions: Serve with lemon juice on top.
Variation Tip: You can use chili sauce for taste variation.
Nutritional Information per Serving: Calories: 92.3 | Fat: 1.5g | Sat Fat: 0.3g | Carbohydrates: 18.3g | Fiber: 6.9g | Sugar: 3.6g | Protein: 6.2g

Crab Cakes with Celery

Prep Time: 20 minutes | Cook Time: 10 minutes | Servings: 6

Ingredients:

1 medium sweet red pepper, finely chopped
1 celery rib, finely chopped
3 green onions, finely chopped
2 large egg whites
3 tablespoons reduced-fat mayonnaise
¼ teaspoon wasabi, prepared
¼ teaspoon salt
½ cup dry bread crumbs divided
½ cup lump crabmeat, drained
Cooking spray

Preparation:

1. Take a bowl to add sweet red pepper, celery rib, green onions, egg whites, mayonnaise, wasabi, salt, and ⅓ cup bread crumbs. Mix and gently fold the mixture into the crab. 2. Shape the crab mixture into ¾-inch thick patties. 3. Add the remaining crumbs to a bowl and gently coat the patties. 4. Select the "Bake" button on Ninja Foodi Smart XL Grill and regulate the settings at 375°F for 12 minutes. 5. Arrange them in the Ninja Foodi when it displays "Add Food." 6. Bake for about 12 minutes. 7. After 6 minutes, flip the sides, cook for more than 6 minutes, and serve.

Serving Suggestions: Serve with pickle sauce.

Variation Tip: You can use cream instead of mayonnaise.

Nutritional Information per Serving: Calories: 81 | Fat: 3.5g | Sat Fat: 0.6g | Carbohydrates: 8.4g | Fiber: 0.8g | Sugar: 1.9g | Protein: 5g

Herbed Salmon

Prep Time: 10 minutes | Cook Time: 8 minutes | Servings: 4

Ingredients:

2 garlic cloves, minced
1 teaspoon dried oregano, crushed
1 teaspoon dried basil, crushed
Salt and ground black pepper, as required
¼ cup olive oil
2 tablespoons fresh lemon juice
4 (4-ounce) salmon fillets

Preparation:

1. In a large-sized bowl, add all ingredients except salmon and mix well. 2. Add salmon fillets and coat with marinade generously. 3. Cover and refrigerate to marinate for at least 1 hour. 4. Arrange the lightly greased "Grill Grate" in the crisper basket in the cooking pot of Ninja Foodi Smart XL Grill. 5. Close the Grill with lid and press "Power" button. 6. Select "Grill" and then use the set of arrows to the left of the display to adjust the temperature to "MED". 7. Use the set of arrows to the right of the display to adjust the cook time to 8 minutes. 8. Press "Start/Stop" to begin preheating. When the display shows "Add Food", open the lid and place the salmon fillets onto the "Grill Grate". 9. With your hands, gently press down each salmon fillet. Close the Grill with lid. 10. After 4 minutes of cooking, flip the salmon fillets. 11. When the cooking time is completed, open the lid and serve hot.

Serving Suggestions: Serve alongside the grilled onions.

Variation Tip: Feel free to use fresh herbs.

Nutritional Information per Serving: Calories: 263 | Fat: 19.7g | Sat Fat: 2.9g | Carbohydrates: 0.9g | Fiber: 0.2g | Sugar: 0.2g | Protein: 22.2g

Chapter 5 Poultry Mains Recipes

Thyme Duck Breasts

Prep Time: 10 minutes | Cook Time: 16 minutes | Servings: 2

Ingredients:

2 shallots, sliced thinly
1 tablespoon fresh ginger, minced
2 tablespoons fresh thyme, chopped
Salt and ground black pepper, as required
2 duck breasts

Preparation:

1. In a large-sized bowl, place the shallots, ginger, thyme, salt, and black pepper, and mix well. 2. Add the duck breasts and coat with marinade evenly. 3. Refrigerate to marinate for about 2–12 hours. 4. Arrange the lightly greased "Grill Grate" in the crisper basket in the cooking pot of Ninja Foodi Smart XL Grill. 5. Close the Grill with lid and press "Power" button. 6. Select "Grill" and then use the set of arrows to the left of the display to adjust the temperature to "MED". 7. Use the set of arrows to the right of the display to adjust the cook time to 16 minutes. 8. Press "Start/Stop" to begin preheating. 9. When the display shows "Add Food", open the lid and place the duck breasts onto the "Grill Grate". 10. With your hands, gently press down each duck breast. Close the Grill with lid. 11. After 8 minutes of cooking, flip the duck breasts. 12. When the cooking time is completed, open the lid and serve hot.

Serving Suggestions: Serve alongside the steamed broccoli.
Variation Tip: Try to use Pekin duck breast.
Nutritional Information per Serving: Calories: 337 | Fat: 10.1g | Sat Fat: 0g | Carbohydrates: 3.4g | Fiber: 0g | Sugar: 0.8g | Protein: 55.5g

Sweet Chicken Skewers

Prep Time: 15 minutes | Cook Time: 13 minutes | Servings: 3

Ingredients:

4 scallions, chopped
1 tablespoon fresh ginger, finely grated
4 garlic cloves, minced
½ cup pineapple juice
½ cup soy sauce
¼ cup sesame oil
2 teaspoons sesame seeds
A pinch of black pepper
1 pound chicken tenders

Preparation:

1. Select the "Grill" button on Ninja Foodi Smart XL Grill and regulate the time for 10 minutes at HI. 2. Take a bowl and add all ingredients for chicken in it except for chicken. Mix well. 3. Add in chicken and marinade it, let sit for 10 minutes. 4. Place the chicken tenders in Ninja Foodi when it displays "Add Food". 5. Grill for 13 minutes, flipping after half time. 6. Meanwhile the chicken is being grilled, take another bowl and add all sauce ingredients in it. Mix well. 7. Once chicken is grilled, drizzle sauce over it and serve with rice.

Serving Suggestions: Serve with BBQ sauce.
Variation Tip: You can toast the sesame seeds too.
Nutritional Information per Serving: Calories: 523 | Fat: 30.6g | Sat Fat: 5.8g | Carbohydrates: 13.1g | Fiber: 1.5g | Sugar: 5.5g | Protein: 47.7g

Zesty Grilled Chicken

Prep Time: 35 minutes | Cook Time: 20 minutes | Servings: 2

Ingredients:

4 chicken breasts
⅓ cup olive oil
3 tablespoons soy sauce
2 tablespoons balsamic vinegar
¼ cup brown sugar
1 tablespoon worcestershire sauce
3 tablespoons minced garlic
Salt to taste
Pepper to taste

Preparation:

1. Select the "Grill" button on Ninja Foodi Smart XL Grill and regulate the time for 10 minutes at MED. 2. Take a bowl and add ingredients except for chicken in it. Mix well. 3. Add in chicken breasts in the sauce and let sit for 30 minutes. 4. Place the chicken breasts in Ninja Foodi when it displays "Add Food". 5. Grill for 20 minutes, flipping once after 10 minutes. 6. Once done, serve and enjoy!

Serving Suggestions: Serve with mash potatoes.
Variation Tip: You can add dried basil leaves for taste variation.
Nutritional Information per Serving: Calories: 419 | Fat: 22g | Sat Fat: 4g | Carbohydrates: 15g | Fiber: 0g | Sugar: 13g | Protein: 38g

Sweet & Sour Chicken Breasts

Prep Time: 15 minutes | Cook Time: 23 minutes | Servings: 4

Ingredients:

4 chicken breasts
⅓ cup olive oil
3 tablespoons soy sauce
1 tablespoon Worcestershire sauce
2 tablespoons balsamic vinegar
¼ cup brown sugar
3 teaspoons garlic, minced
Salt and ground black pepper, as required

Preparation:

1. With a fork, poke each chicken breast. 2. For marinade: in a large-sized bowl, blend together oil, soy sauce, Worcestershire sauce, vinegar, brown sugar, garlic, salt and black pepper. 3. In a small-sized bowl, place ¼ cup of the marinade and reserve in the refrigerator. 4. In the bowl of remaining marinade, add the chicken breasts and mix well. 5. Set aside for about 20 minutes. 6. Arrange the lightly greased "Grill Grate" in the crisper basket in the cooking pot of Ninja Foodi Smart XL Grill. 7. Close the Grill with lid and press "Power" button. 8. Select "Grill" and use the set of arrows to the left of the display to adjust the temperature to "MED." 9. Use the set of arrows to the right of the display to adjust the cook time to 23 minutes. 10. Press "Start/Stop" to begin preheating. 11. When the display shows "Add Food", open the lid and place the chicken breasts onto the "Grill Grate". 12. With your hands, gently press down each chicken breast. Close the Grill with lid. 13. After 10 minutes of cooking, flip the chicken breasts. 14. After 15 minutes of cooking, flip the chicken breasts and coat with half of the reserved marinade. 15. After 20 minutes of cooking, flip the chicken breasts and coat with the remaining reserved marinade. 16. When the cooking time is completed, press "Start/Stop" to stop cooking. 17. Open the lid and serve hot.

Serving Suggestions: Serve with garnishing of lemon slices.

Variation Tip: Try to use low-sodium soy sauce.

Nutritional Information per Serving: Calories: 345 | Fat: 18.7g | Sat Fat: 2.4g | Carbohydrates: 11.3g | Fiber: 0.1g | Sugar: 9.8g | Protein: 33.8g

Zesty Whole Chicken

Prep Time: 15 minutes | Cook Time: 45 minutes | Servings: 6

Ingredients:

1 (3½-pound) whole chicken, neck and giblets removed
3 tablespoons fresh lime juice
2 tablespoons extra-virgin olive oil
1 tablespoon garlic, minced
2 teaspoons lime zest, freshly grated
3 tablespoons Mexico Chile powder
1 teaspoon ground coriander
1 teaspoon ground cumin
Salt and ground black pepper, as required

Preparation:

1. Arrange the chicken onto a large cutting board, breast side down. 2. With a kitchen shear, start from thigh and cut along 1 side of the backbone and turn the chicken around. 3. Now, cut along the other side and discard the backbone. 4. Change the side and open it like a book and then flatten the backbone firmly. 5. In a clean glass bowl, blend together lime juice, oil, garlic, lime zest, chile powder, coriander, cumin, salt, and black pepper. 6. Rub the chicken with spice mixture evenly. 7. With plastic wrap, cover the chicken and refrigerator for about 24 hours. 8. Arrange the lightly greased "Grill Grate" in the crisper basket in the cooking pot of Ninja Foodi Smart XL Grill. 9. Close the Grill with lid and press "Power" button. 10. Select "Grill" and use the set of the arrows to the left of the display to adjust the temperature to "MED." 11. Use the set of arrows to the right of the display to adjust the cook time to 25 minutes. 12. Press "Start/Stop" to begin preheating. 13. When the display shows "Add Food", open the lid and place the chicken onto the "Grill Grate". 14. With your hands, gently press down the chicken. Close the Grill with lid. 15. After 25 minutes of cooking, flip the chicken. 16. Then grill the other side for 20 minutes. 17. When the cooking time is completed, open the lid and place the chicken onto a platter for about 10 minutes before carving. 18. Cut the chicken into desired-sized pieces and serve.

Serving Suggestions: Serve alongside the steamed green beans.

Variation Tip: Adjust the ratio of spices according to your taste.

Nutritional Information per Serving: Calories: 507 | Fat: 17.1g | Sat Fat: 4g | Carbohydrates: 0.8g | Fiber: 0.1g | Sugar: 0.1g | Protein: 82.2g

Chicken & Grapes Kabobs

Prep Time: 15 minutes | Cook Time: 10 minutes | Servings: 4

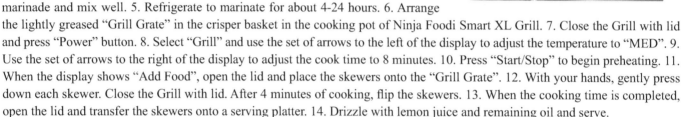

Ingredients:

⅓ cup extra-virgin olive oil, divided
2 garlic cloves, minced
1 tablespoon fresh rosemary, minced
1 tablespoon fresh oregano, minced
1 teaspoon fresh lemon zest, grated
½ teaspoon red chili flakes, crushed
1 pound boneless, skinless chicken breast, cut into ¾-inch cubes
1¾ cups green seedless grapes, rinsed
1 teaspoon salt
1 tablespoon fresh lemon juice

Preparation:

1. In a small-sized bowl, add ¼ cup of oil, garlic, fresh herbs, lemon zest, and chili flakes and beat until well combined. 2. Thread the chicken cubes and grapes onto 12 metal skewers. 3. In a large-sized baking dish, arrange the skewers. 4. Place the marinade and mix well. 5. Refrigerate to marinate for about 4-24 hours. 6. Arrange the lightly greased "Grill Grate" in the crisper basket in the cooking pot of Ninja Foodi Smart XL Grill. 7. Close the Grill with lid and press "Power" button. 8. Select "Grill" and use the set of arrows to the left of the display to adjust the temperature to "MED". 9. Use the set of arrows to the right of the display to adjust the cook time to 8 minutes. 10. Press "Start/Stop" to begin preheating. 11. When the display shows "Add Food", open the lid and place the skewers onto the "Grill Grate". 12. With your hands, gently press down each skewer. Close the Grill with lid. After 4 minutes of cooking, flip the skewers. 13. When the cooking time is completed, open the lid and transfer the skewers onto a serving platter. 14. Drizzle with lemon juice and remaining oil and serve.

Serving Suggestions: Serve with a green salad.

Variation Tip: Use seedless grapes.

Nutritional Information per Serving: Calories: 181 | Fat: 17.2g | Sat Fat: 2.6g | Carbohydrates: 8.8g | Fiber: 1.3g | Sugar: 6.7g | Protein: 0.6g

Herbed & Spiced Chicken Thighs

Prep Time: 10 minutes | Cook Time: 18 minutes | Servings: 6

Ingredients:

2 tablespoons fresh lime juice
½ tablespoon dried oregano, crushed
½ tablespoon dried thyme, crushed
1 tablespoon ground chipotle powder
1 tablespoon paprika
½ tablespoon garlic powder
Salt and ground black pepper, as required
6 (4-ounce) skinless, boneless chicken thighs

Preparation:

1. In a bowl, add lime juice and remaining ingredients except for chicken thighs and mix until well combined. 2. Coat the thighs with spice mixture generously. 3. Arrange the lightly greased "Grill Grate" in the crisper basket in the cooking pot of Ninja Foodi Smart XL Grill. 4. Close the Grill with lid and press "Power" button. 5. Select "Grill" and use the set of arrows to the left of the display to adjust the temperature to "MED". 6. Use the set of arrows to the right of the display to adjust the cook time to 18 minutes. 7. Press "Start/Stop" to begin preheating. 8. When the display shows "Add Food", open the lid and place the chicken thighs onto the "Grill Grate". 9. With your hands, gently press down each chicken thigh. Close the Grill with lid. 10. After 8 minutes of cooking, flip the chicken thighs. 11. When the cooking time is completed, open the lid and serve hot.

Serving Suggestions: Serve with a drizzling of fresh lemon juice.

Variation Tip: You can use spices of your choice.

Nutritional Information per Serving: Calories: 154 | Fat: 4.5g | Sat Fat: 1.6g | Carbohydrates: 2.4g | Fiber: 1.3g | Sugar: 0.4g | Protein: 25.8g

Chicken Fajitas

Prep Time: 15 minutes | Cook Time: 20 minutes | Servings: 6

Ingredients:

3 multi-colored bell peppers, seeded and sliced
½ cup sweet onion, chopped

6 boneless, skinless chicken breasts
2 tablespoons fajita seasoning
6 corn tortillas, warmed

Preparation:

1. Arrange the lightly greased "Grill Grate" in the crisper basket in the cooking pot of Ninja Foodi Smart XL Grill. 2. Close the Grill with lid and press "Power" button. 3. Select "Grill" and then use the set of arrows to the left of the display to adjust the temperature to "HI". 4. Use the set of arrows to the right of the display to adjust the cook time to 20 minutes. 5. Press "Start/Stop" to begin preheating. 6. When the display shows "Add Food", open the lid and place the bell pepper and onion slices onto the "Grill Grate". 7. Arrange the chicken breasts on top of veggies and sprinkle with seasoning. 8. With your hands, gently press down each chicken breast. Close the Grill with lid. 9. After 10 minutes of cooking, flip the chicken breasts. 10. When the cooking time is completed, open the lid and transfer the chicken breasts and vegetables onto a platter. 11. Cut each chicken breast into desired-sized pieces and mix with vegetables. 12. Place the chicken mixture onto reach tortilla and serve.
Serving Suggestions: Serve the fajitas with the topping of sour cream.
Variation Tip: Adjust the ratio of seasoning according to your taste.
Nutritional Information per Serving: Calories: 301 | Fat: 9.2g | Sat Fat: 2.4g | Carbohydrates: 18.2g | Fiber: 2.5g | Sugar: 3.6g | Protein: 34.9g

Greek Chicken

Prep Time: 20 minutes | Cook Time: 15 minutes | Servings: 4

Ingredients:

For chicken:
4 chicken breasts
¼ cup extra-virgin olive oil
2 teaspoons dried oregano
For sauce:
½ cup finely grated cucumber
1 cup of greek yogurt

1 teaspoon garlic powder
1 tablespoon lemon juice

2 teaspoons apple cider vinegar
1 tablespoon of garlic powder

Preparation:

1. Select the "Grill" button on the Ninja Foodi Smart XL Grill and regulate the time for 10 minutes at HI. 2. Take a bowl and add all ingredients for chicken in it except for chicken in it. Mix well. 3. Add in chicken and marinade it, let sit for 10 minutes. 4. Place the chicken tenders in Ninja Foodi when it displays "Add Food". 5. Grill for 15 minutes, flipping after half time. 6. Meanwhile the chicken is being grilled, take another bowl and add all sauce ingredients in it. Mix well. 7. Once chicken is grilled, drizzle sauce over it and serve with rice.
Serving Suggestions: Serve with green onions on top.
Variation Tip: You can use any yogurt instead of Greek yogurt.
Nutritional Information per Serving: Calories: 521 | Fat: 20g | Sat Fat: 4g | Carbohydrates: 26g | Fiber: 2g | Sugar: 18g | Protein: 59g

Simple Chicken Breasts

Prep Time: 5 minutes | Cook Time: 8 minutes | Servings: 4

Ingredients:

4 (6-ounce) chicken breasts
Salt and ground black pepper, as required

2 tablespoons olive oil

Preparation:

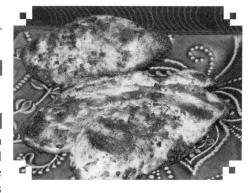

1. With a meat mallet, pound the chicken breasts thinly. 2. Season each chicken with salt and black pepper and then brush with oil. 3. Arrange the lightly greased "Grill Grate" in the crisper basket in the cooking pot of Ninja Foodi Smart XL Grill. 4. Close the Grill with lid and press "Power" button. 5. Select "Grill" and use the set of arrows to the left side of the display to adjust temperature to "MED." 6. Use the set of arrows to the right side of the display to adjust the cook time to 8 minutes. 7. Press "Start/Stop" to begin preheating. 8. When the display shows "Add Food", open the lid and place the chicken breasts onto the "Grill Grate". 9. With your hands, gently press down each chicken breast. Close the Grill with lid. 10. After 4 minutes of cooking, flip the chicken breasts. 11. When the cooking time is completed, open the lid and serve hot.
Serving Suggestions: Serve with your favorite fresh salad.
Variation Tip: Select chicken breasts with a pinkish hue.
Nutritional Information per Serving: Calories: 307 | Fat: 15.7g | Sat Fat: 3.6g | Carbohydrates: 0g | Fiber: 0g | Sugar: 0g | Protein: 39.4g

Lemony Chicken Tenders

Prep Time: 10 minutes | Cook Time: 9 minutes | Servings: 4

Ingredients:

2 tablespoons fresh lemon juice	1 teaspoon lemon zest, grated
3 teaspoons olive oil	Salt and ground black pepper, as required
1½ teaspoons garlic, minced	1 pound chicken tenders

Preparation:

1. For marinade: in a large ceramic bowl, add all ingredients except for chicken and mix well. 2. Add chicken tenders and toss to coat. 3. Cover the bowl and refrigerate to marinate for about 2 hours. 4. Remove the chicken tenders from the bowl and shake off excess marinade. 5. Arrange the lightly greased "Grill Grate" in the crisper basket in the cooking pot of Ninja Foodi Smart XL Grill. 6. Close the Grill with lid and press "Power" button. 7. Select "Grill" and use the set of the arrows to the left side of the display to adjust temperature to "MED." 8. Use the set of the arrows to the right side of the display to adjust the cook time to 8 minutes. 9. Press "Start/Stop" to begin preheating. 10. When the display shows "Add Food", open the lid and place the chicken tenders onto the "Grill Grate". 11. With your hands, gently press down each chicken tender. Close the Grill with lid. 12. After 4 minutes of cooking, flip the chicken tenders. 13. When the cooking time is completed, open the lid an serve hot.

Serving Suggestions: Serve alongside ketchup.

Variation Tip: For the best result, use freshly squeezed lemon juice.

Nutritional Information per Serving: Calories: 249 | Fat: 12g | Sat Fat: 2.9g | Carbohydrates: 0.6g | Fiber: 0.1g | Sugar: 0.2g | Protein: 33g

Sweet & Spicy Chicken Thighs

Prep Time: 10 minutes | Cook Time: 17 minutes | Servings: 4

Ingredients:

2 tablespoons dark brown sugar	⅛ teaspoons cayenne powder
2 teaspoons ground allspice	Salt and ground black pepper, as required
½ teaspoon ground cinnamon	2 pounds bone-in, skin on chicken thighs
½ teaspoon ground cumin	

Preparation:

1. In a bowl, mix together the brown sugar, spices, salt and black pepper. 2. Rub the chicken thighs with spice mixture generously. 3. Arrange the lightly greased "Grill Grate" in the crisper basket in the cooking pot of Ninja Foodi Smart XL Grill. 4. Close the Grill with lid and press "Power" button. 5. Select "Grill" and use the set of arrows to the left of the display to adjust the temperature to "MED". 6. Use the set of arrows to the right of the display to adjust the cook time to 17 minutes. 7. Press "Start/Stop" to begin preheating. 8. When the display shows "Add Food", open the lid and place the chicken thighs onto the "Grill Grate". 9. With your hands, gently press down each chicken thigh. Close the Grill with lid. 10. After 9 minutes of cooking, flip the chicken thighs. 11. When the cooking time is completed, open the lid and serve hot.

Serving Suggestions: Serve with fresh spinach.

Variation Tip: Brown sugar can be replaced with white sugar too.

Nutritional Information per Serving: Calories: 244 | Fat: 8.3g | Sat Fat: 2g | Carbohydrates: 5.5g | Fiber: 0.4g | Sugar: 4.4g | Protein: 40.7g

Chicken Liver Kabobs

Prep Time: 15 minutes | Cook Time: 8 minutes | Servings: 3

Ingredients:

1 pound chicken livers, trimmed and cubed
1 small garlic clove, minced
2 tablespoons low-sodium soy sauce
1 tablespoon red boat fish sauce
2 teaspoons sugar

Preparation:

1. In a medium-sized bowl, combine the garlic, soy sauce, fish sauce, and sugar. 2. Add in the chicken livers coat well. 3. Place in the refrigerator to marinate for at least 30 minutes. 4. Thread the liver cubes onto pre-soaked wooden skewer. 5. Arrange the lightly greased "Grill Grate" in the crisper basket in the cooking pot of Ninja Foodi Smart XL Grill. 6. Close the Grill with lid and press "Power" button. 7. Select "Grill" and then use the set of arrows to the left of the display to adjust the temperature to "MED". 8. Use the set of arrows to the right of the display to adjust the cook time to 8 minutes. 9. Press "Start/Stop" to begin preheating. 10. When the display shows "Add Food", open the lid and place the skewers onto the "Grill Grate". 11. With your hands, gently press down each skewer. Close the Grill with lid. 12. After 4 minutes of cooking, flip the skewers. 13. When the cooking time is completed, open the lid and serve hot.

Serving Suggestions: Serve alongside the spicy sauce.

Variation Tip: Make sure to trim chicken liver properly.

Nutritional Information per Serving: Calories: 263 | Fat: 9.9g | Sat Fat: 3.1g | Carbohydrates: 3.3g | Fiber: 1g | Sugar: 2.7g | Protein: 39g

Tandoori Chicken Legs

Prep Time: 15 minutes | Cook Time: 20 minutes | Servings: 4

Ingredients:

4 chicken legs
3 tablespoons lemon juice
3 teaspoons ginger paste
3 teaspoons garlic paste
Salt to taste
4 tablespoons yogurt
2 tablespoons tandoori masala powder
2 teaspoons red chili powder
1 teaspoon garam masala powder
1 teaspoon ground cumin
1 teaspoon ground coriander
1 teaspoon ground turmeric
Pepper to taste
Pinch of orange food color

Preparation:

1. Select the "Grill" button on the Ninja Foodi Smart XL Grill and regulate the time for 10 minutes at HI. 2. Take a large bowl and add all ingredients in it except for chicken legs. 3. Mix well and marinade chicken legs with this mixture. Set aside for 5 hours. 4. Place the chicken in Ninja Foodi when it displays "Add Food". 5. Grill for 20 minutes, flipping each side after half time. 6. Serve and enjoy!

Serving Suggestions: Can be served with rice.

Variation Tip: You can skip the food color if you want.

Nutritional Information per Serving: Calories: 32 | Fat: 0.9g | Sat Fat: 0.3g | Carbohydrates: 4.3g | Fiber: 0.9g | Sugar: 1.5g | Protein: 1.7g

BBQ Chicken Breasts

Prep Time: 10 minutes | Cook Time: 22 minutes | Servings: 4

Ingredients:

4 (8-ounce) frozen boneless, skinless chicken breasts
2 tablespoons olive oil, divided

Salt and ground black pepper, as required
1 cup BBQ sauce

Preparation:

1. Brush the chicken breasts with ½ tablespoon of oil evenly and season with salt and black pepper. 2. Arrange the lightly greased "Grill Grate" in the crisper basket in the cooking pot of Ninja Foodi Smart XL Grill. 3. Close the Grill with lid and press "Power" button. 4. Select "Grill" and use the set of arrows to the left of the display to adjust the temperature to "MED". 5. Use the set of arrows to the right of the display to adjust the cook time to 22 minutes. 6. Press "Start/Stop" to begin preheating. 7. When the display shows "Add Food", open the lid and place the chicken breasts onto the "Grill Grate". 8. With your hands, gently press down the chicken breasts. Close the Grill with lid. 9. After 10 minutes of cooking, flip the chicken breasts. 10. After 15 minutes of cooking, flip the chicken breasts and coat the upper side with BBQ sauce generously. 11. After 20 minutes of cooking, flip the chicken breasts and coat the upper side with BBQ sauce generously. 12. When the cooking time is completed, open the lid and serve hot. 13. Place the chicken breasts onto a platter for about 5 minutes before serving.
Serving Suggestions: Serve with the drizzling of extra sauce.
Variation Tip: Feel free to use BBQ sauce of your choice.
Nutritional Information per Serving: Calories: 585 | Fat: 24g | Sat Fat: 5.6g | Carbohydrates: 22.7g | Fiber: 6.7g | Sugar: 16.3g | Protein: 65.6g

Honey Garlic Chicken

Prep Time: 10 minutes | Cook Time: 18 minutes | Servings: 6

Ingredients:

1 tablespoon adobe seasoning
1½ teaspoons sazon seasoning
½ teaspoon ground black pepper

1½ pounds boneless, skinless chicken breasts, cut into tenders
6 ounces honey garlic sauce

Preparation:

1. In a large-sized bowl, blend together the adobo seasoning, sazon seasoning and black pepper. 2. Add the chicken tenders and coat with the seasoning mixture generously. 3. Add the honey garlic sauce and mix well. 4. Cover the bowl and refrigerate to marinate for 30-60 minutes. 5. Arrange the lightly greased "Grill Grate" in the crisper basket in the cooking pot of Ninja Foodi Smart XL Grill. 6. Close the Grill with lid and press "Power" button. 7. Select "Grill" and then use the set of arroes to the left of the display to adjust the temperature to "HI." 8. Use the set of arrows to the right of the display to adjust the cook time to 18 minutes. 9. Press "Start/Stop" to begin preheating. 10. When the display shows "Add Food", open the lid and place the chicken tenders onto the "Grill Grate". 11. With your hands, gently press down each chicken tender. Close the Grill with lid. 12. After 9 minutes of cooking, flip the chicken tenders. 13. When the cooking time is completed, open the lid and serve hot.
Serving Suggestions: Serve alongside baby greens.
Variation Tip: You can adjust the seasoning ratio according to your choice.
Nutritional Information per Serving: Calories: 348 | Fat: 8.4g | Sat Fat: 2.3g | Carbohydrates: 33.2g | Fiber: 0.1g | Sugar: 13.2g | Protein: 33.1g

Simple Chicken Thighs

Prep Time: 5 minutes | Cook Time: 12 minutes | Servings: 6

Ingredients:

3 pounds boneless, skinless chicken thighs   Salt, as required

Preparation:

1. Season the chicken thighs with salt evenly. 2. Arrange the lightly greased "Grill Grate" in the crisper basket in the cooking pot of Ninja Foodi Smart XL Grill. 3. Close the Grill with lid and press "Power" button. 4. Select "Grill" and use the set of arrows to the left of the display to adjust the temperature to "MED". 5. Use the set of arrows to the right of the display to adjust the cook time to 14 minutes. 6. Press "Start/Stop" to begin preheating. 7. When the display shows "Add Food", open the lid and place the chicken thighs onto the "Grill Grate". 8. With your hands, gently press down each chicken thigh. Close the Grill with lid. 9. After 7 minutes of cooking, flip the chicken thighs. 10. When the cooking time is completed, open the lid and serve hot.

Serving Suggestions: Serve with the garnishing of scallion greens.
Variation Tip: Don't use chicken thighs with faded color.
Nutritional Information per Serving: Calories: 243 | Fat: 12.2g | Sat Fat: 3g | Carbohydrates: 0g | Fiber: 0g | Sugar: 0g | Protein: 38.5g

Peach Glazed Chicken Breasts

Prep Time: 15 minutes | Cook Time: 18 minutes | Servings: 4

Ingredients:

4 (6-ounce) skinless, boneless chicken breast halves
Salt and ground black pepper, as required
¾ cup peach preserves

1 tablespoon extra-virgin olive oil
1 tablespoon soy sauce
½ tablespoon Dijon mustard
½ tablespoon garlic, finely chopped

Preparation:

1. Season the chicken breast halves with salt and black pepper evenly. 2. In a bowl, add the peach preserves, olive oil, soy sauce, mustard, garlic, salt, and black pepper and mix well. 3. Arrange the lightly greased "Grill Grate" in the crisper basket in the cooking pot of Ninja Foodi Smart XL Grill. 4. Close the Grill with lid and press "Power" button. 5. Select "Grill" and use the set of arrows to the left of the display to adjust the temperature to "MED". 6. Use the set of arrows to the right of the display to adjust the cook time to 18 minuets. 7. Press "Start/Stop" to begin preheating. 8. When the display shows "Add Food", open the lid and place the chicken breast halves onto the "Grill Grate". 9. With your hands, gently press down each chicken breast. Close the Grill with lid. 10. After 7 minutes of cooking, flip the chicken breasts. 11. After 13 minutes of cooking, flip the chicken breasts and coat with the peach sauce evenly. 12. When the cooking time is completed, open the lid and serve hot.
Serving Suggestions: Enjoy alongside the grilled peaches.
Variation Tip: Use high-quality peach preserves.
Nutritional Information per Serving: Calories: 414 | Fat: 9.7g | Sat Fat: 2.8g | Carbohydrates: 42.1g | Fiber: 0.8g | Sugar: 29.2g | Protein: 38.6g

Marinated Chicken Breasts

Prep Time: 10 minutes | Cook Time: 14 minutes | Servings: 4

Ingredients:

4 (4-ounce) boneless, skinless chicken breasts
2 tablespoons olive oil
2 tablespoons fresh lemon juice

1 garlic clove, minced
1 teaspoon red pepper flakes
Salt and ground black pepper, as required

Preparation:

1. For marinade: in a large-sized bowl, add oil, lemon juice, garlic, red pepper flakes, salt, and black pepper and beat until well combined. 2. In a large-sized resealable plastic bag, place chicken and ¾ cup marinade. 3. Seal bag and shake to coat well. 4. Refrigerate overnight. 5. Cover the bowl of remaining marinade and refrigerate before serving. 6. Arrange the lightly greased "Grill Grate" in the crisper basket in the cooking pot of Ninja Foodi Smart XL Grill. 7. Close the Grill with lid and press "Power" button. 8. Select "Grill" and then use the arrow on the left side of display to adjust to "MED". 9. Then press the arrow on the right side to adjust the cook time to 14 minutes. 10. Press "Start/Stop" to begin preheating. 11. When the display shows "Add Food", open the lid and place the chicken breasts onto the "Grill Grate". 12. With your hands, gently press down each chicken breast. Close the Grill with lid. 13. After 7 minutes of cooking, flip the chicken breasts. 14. When the cooking time is completed, open the lid and serve hot.
Serving Suggestions: Serve with the topping of lemon wedges.
Variation Tip: Check the meat "best by" date.
Nutritional Information per Serving: Calories: 280 | Fat: 15.5g | Sat Fat: 3.4g | Carbohydrates: 0.7g | Fiber: 0.2g | Sugar: 0.2g | Protein: 33g

Roasted Herb Chicken

Prep Time: 10 minutes | Cook Time: 30 minutes | Servings: 7

Ingredients:

2 tablespoons butter
3 cups cornbread and sausage stuffing
3 garlic cloves, minced
1 teaspoon lemon zest, grated
1 teaspoon dried thyme, crushed
1 teaspoon dried oregano, crushed
1 teaspoon dried rosemary, crushed

1 teaspoon smoked paprika
Salt to taste
Pepper to taste
2 tablespoons lemon juice
2 tablespoons sesame oil
1 whole chicken

Preparation:

1. Select the "Roast" button on Ninja Foodi Smart XL Grill and regulate the time for 20 minutes at HI. 2. Take a bowl and add garlic, lemon zest, herbs and spices. 3. Rub the chicken evenly with herb mixture. 4. Drizzle some oil and lemon juice on the chicken. Set aside overnight. 5. Place the chicken wings in Ninja Foodi when it displays "Add Food". 6. Roast for 30 minutes, flipping the side after 15 minutes. 7. Serve and enjoy.
Serving Suggestions: Serve with mayo dip.
Variation Tip: You can skip cayenne pepper
Nutritional Information per Serving: Calories: 860 | Fat: 50g | Sat Fat: 24g | Carbohydrates: 1.3g | Fiber: 2g | Sugar: 0.2g | Protein: 71.1g

Lemony Chicken Breast

Prep Time: 15 minutes | Cook Time: 14 minutes | Servings: 4

Ingredients:

For Chicken Breasts:
¼ cup extra-virgin olive oil
1½-2 tablespoons fresh lemon juice
2 teaspoons dried oregano
1 teaspoon garlic powder

Salt and ground black pepper, as required
4 chicken breasts

For Tzatziki Sauce:
½ cup cucumber, finely grated
1 cup plain Greek yogurt
1½-2 tablespoons fresh lemon juice

2 teaspoons apple cider vinegar
1 tablespoon garlic powder

Preparation:

1. For chicken marinade, in a bowl, whisk together the oil, lemon juice, oregano, garlic powder, salt, and black pepper. 2. In a Ziploc bag, place the chicken breasts and marinade. 3. Seal the bag tightly and shake to coat. 4. Refrigerate to marinate for at least 2 hours. 5. Meanwhile, for tzatziki sauce: in a bowl, add all ingredients and stir to combine. 6. Refrigerate to chill before serving. 7. Arrange the lightly greased "Grill Grate" in the crisper basket in the cooking pot of Ninja Foodi Smart XL Grill. 8. Close the Grill with lid and press "Power" button. 9. Select "Grill" and use the set of arrows to the left of the display to adjust the temperature to "MED". 10. Use the set of arrows to the right of the display to adjust the cook time to 14 minutes. 11. Press "Start/Stop" to begin preheating. 12. When the display shows "Add Food", open the lid and place the chicken breasts onto the "Grill Grate". 13. With your hands, gently press down each chicken breast. Close the Grill with lid. 14. After 7 minutes of cooking, flip the chicken breasts. 15. When the cooking time is completed, open the lid and then serve hot alongside the tzatziki sauce.

Serving Suggestions: Serve with the drizzling of some lemon juice.
Variation Tip: For a thick tzatziki sauce, squeeze the excess liquid out of the grated cucumber.
Nutritional Information per Serving: Calories: 318 | Fat: 15.5g | Sat Fat: 2.5g | Carbohydrates:7.1 | Fiber: 0.7g | Sugar: 5.3g | Protein: 37g

Sweet Gingered Chicken Breasts

Prep Time: 10 minutes | Cook Time: 20 minutes | Servings: 4

Ingredients:

4 skinless, boneless chicken breasts
1 (1-inch) piece fresh ginger, minced
2 garlic cloves, minced
1 cup fresh pineapple juice
¼ cup low-sodium soy sauce

¼ cup extra-virgin olive oil
1 teaspoon ground cinnamon
1 teaspoon ground cumin
Salt, as required

Preparation:

1. In a Ziploc bag, add chicken breasts and remaining ingredients. 2. Seal the bag of chicken mixture tightly and shake to coat well. 3. Refrigerate to marinade for about 1 hour. 4. Arrange the lightly greased "Grill Grate" in the crisper basket in the cooking pot of Ninja Foodi Smart XL Grill. 5. Close the Grill with lid and press "Power" button. 6. Select "Grill" and use the set of arrows to the left of the display to adjust the temperature to "MED". 7. Use the set of arrows to the right of the display to adjust the cook time to 20 minutes. 8. Press "Start/Stop" to begin preheating. 9. When the display shows "Add Food", open the lid and place the chicken breasts onto the "Grill Grate". 10. With your hands, gently press down each chicken breast. Close the Grill with lid. 11. After 10 minutes of cooking, flip the chicken breasts. 12. When the cooking time is completed, open the lid and serve hot.

Serving Suggestions: Serve alongside the fresh greens.
Variation Tip: Use fresh chicken breasts.
Nutritional Information per Serving: Calories: 268 | Fat: 17.9g | Sat Fat: 3.7g | Carbohydrates: 10.2g | Fiber: 0.5g | Sugar: 7.3g | Protein: 33.1g

Paprika Chicken Thighs

Prep Time: 5 minutes | Cook Time: 15 minutes | Servings: 4

Ingredients:

4 (6-ounce) skinless chicken thighs
2 tablespoons smoked paprika

Salt and ground black pepper, as required

Preparation:

1. Season the chicken thighs with smoked paprika, salt, and black pepper. 2. Arrange the lightly greased "Grill Grate" in the crisper basket in the cooking pot of Ninja Foodi Smart XL Grill. 3. Close the Grill with lid and press "Power" button. 4. Select "Grill" and use the set of arrows to the left of the display to adjust the temperature to "MED". 5. Use the set of arrows to the right of the display to adjust the cook time to 15 minutes. 6. Press "Start/Stop" to begin preheating. 7. When the display shows "Add Food", open the lid and place the chicken thighs onto the "Grill Grate". 8. With your hands, gently press down each chicken thigh. Close the Grill with lid. 9. After 8 minutes of cooking, flip the chicken thighs. 10. When the cooking time is completed, open the lid and serve hot.

Serving Suggestions: Serve with a drizzling of melted butter.
Variation Tip: You can adjust the quantity of paprika according to your taste.
Nutritional Information per Serving: Calories: 206 | Fat: 7.2g | Sat Fat: 1.6g | Carbohydrates: 1.9g | Fiber: 1.3g | Sugar: 0.4g | Protein: 33.6g

Parsley Chicken Breasts

Prep Time: 15 minutes | Cook Time: 16 minutes | Servings: 6

Ingredients:

½ cup avocado oil
½ cup fresh parsley leaves
1 lemon, juiced and zested
1¼ teaspoons salt

½ teaspoon ground black pepper
24 ounces boneless, skinless chicken
breasts

Preparation:

1. For marinade: in a high-power blender, add the avocado oil, parsley, lemon juice, zest, salt, and black pepper and pulse for about 1 minute. 2. In a small-sized bowl, place ¼ cup of the marinade and reserve in the refrigerator. 3. In a large-sized or zip-top bag, place the chicken breasts and remaining marinade. 4. Seal the bag tightly and shake to coat. 5. Refrigerate to marinate for at least 30 minutes or up to 4 hours. 6. Remove the chicken breasts from the bag and discard the marinade. 7. Arrange the lightly greased "Grill Grate" in the crisper basket in the cooking pot of Ninja Foodi Smart XL Grill. 8. Close the Grill with lid and press "Power" button. 9. Select "Grill" and use the set of arrows to the left side of the display to adjust temperature to "MED". 10. Use the set of arrows to the right side of the display to adjust the cook time to 16 minutes. 11. Press "Start/Stop" to begin preheating. When the display shows "Add Food", open the lid and place the chicken breasts onto the "Grill Grate". 12. With your hands, gently press down each chicken breast. Close the Grill with lid. 13. After 8 minutes of cooking, flip the chicken breasts and brush each with reserved marinade. 14. When the cooking time is completed, open the lid and serve hot.

Serving Suggestions: Serve with your favorite salad.
Variation Tip: Select chicken with a pinkish hue.
Nutritional Information per Serving: Calories: 379 | Fat: 27.1g | Sat Fat: 5g | Carbohydrates: 0.8g | Fiber: 0.3g | Sugar: 0.1g | Protein: 33g

Vinegar Chicken Breasts

Prep Time: 10 minutes | Cook Time: 14 minutes | Servings: 4

Ingredients:

¼ cup balsamic vinegar
2 tablespoons olive oil
1½ teaspoons fresh lemon juice

½ teaspoon lemon-pepper seasoning
4 (6-ounce) boneless, skinless chicken
breast halves, pounded slightly

Preparation:

1. In a glass baking dish, place the vinegar, oil, and lemon-pepper seasoning and mix well. 2. Add the chicken breasts and coat with the mixture generously. 3. Refrigerate to marinate for about 25-30 minutes. 4. Arrange the lightly greased "Grill Grate" in the crisper basket in the cooking pot of Ninja Foodi Smart XL Grill. 5. Close the Grill with lid and press "Power" button. 6. Select "Grill" and use the set of arrows to the left of the display to adjust the temperature to "MED". 7. Use the set of arrows to the right of the display to adjust the cook time to 14 minutes. 8. Press "Start/Stop" to begin preheating. 9. When the display shows "Add Food", open the lid and place the skewers onto the "Grill Grate". 10. With your hands, gently press down each skewer. Close the Grill with lid. 11. After 7 minutes of cooking, flip the skewers.
12. When the cooking time is completed, open the lid and serve hot.

Serving Suggestions: Serve with the garnishing of fresh herbs.
Variation Tip: Feel free to use the seasoning of your choice.
Nutritional Information per Serving: Calories: 258 | Fat: 11.3g | Sat Fat: 1g | Carbohydrates: 0.4g | Fiber: 0.1g | Sugar: 0.1g | Protein: 36.1g

Zesty Chicken Breasts

Prep Time: 10 minutes | Cook Time: 20 minutes | Servings: 4

Ingredients:

2 scallions, chopped
1 (1-inch) piece fresh ginger, minced
2 garlic cloves, minced
¼ cup olive oil
2 tablespoons fresh lime juice
2 tablespoons low-sodium soy sauce

1 teaspoon ground cinnamon
1 teaspoon ground cumin
1 teaspoon ground turmeric
Ground black pepper, as required
4 (5-ounce) boneless, skinless chicken
breasts

Preparation:

1. In a large-sized Ziploc bag, add all the ingredients and seal it. 2. Shake the bag to coat the chicken with marinade well. 3. Refrigerate to marinate for about 20 minutes to 1 hour. 4. Arrange the lightly greased "Grill Grate" in the crisper basket in the cooking pot of Ninja Foodi Smart XL Grill. 5. Close the Grill with lid and press "Power" button. 6. Select "Grill" and use the set of arrows to the left of the display to adjust the temperature to "MED". 7. Use the set of arrows to the right of the display to adjust the cook time to 20 minutes. 8. Press "Start/Stop" to begin preheating. 9. When the display shows "Add Food", open the lid and place the chicken breasts onto the "Grill Grate". 10. With your hands, gently press down each chicken breast. Close the Grill with lid. 11. After 10 minutes of cooking, flip the chicken breasts. 12. When the cooking time is completed, open the lid and serve hot.

Serving Suggestions: Serve with the topping of pesto.
Variation Tip: For best result, use freshly squeezed lime juice.
Nutritional Information per Serving: Calories: 273 | Fat: 14.7g | Sat Fat: 1.8g | Carbohydrates: 2.7g | Fiber: 0.7g | Sugar: 0.7g | Protein: 33.8g

Spiced Whole Chicken

Prep Time: 15 minutes | Cook Time: 50 minutes | Servings: 8

Ingredients:

1 tablespoon brown sugar	Salt and ground black pepper, as required
1 tablespoon paprika	1 (4-pound) whole chicken, neck and
1 tablespoon garlic powder	giblets removed

Preparation:

1. Arrange the chicken onto a large cutting board, breast side down. 2. With a kitchen shear, start from thigh and cut along 1 side of the backbone and turn the chicken around. 3. Now, cut along the other side and discard the backbone. 4. Change the side and open it like a book and then flatten the backbone firmly. 5. In a small bowl, blend together the brown sugar, paprika, garlic powder, salt, and black pepper. 6. Rub the chicken with spice mixture generously. 7. Arrange the lightly greased "Grill Grate" in the crisper basket in the cooking pot of Ninja Foodi Smart XL Grill. 8. Close the Grill with lid and press "Power" button. 9. Select "Grill" and use the set of the display to adjust the temperature to "MED." 10. Use the arrow on the right side to adjust the cook time to 25 minutes. 11. Press "Start/Stop" to begin preheating. 12. When the display shows "Add Food", open the lid and place the chicken onto the "Grill Grate". 13. With your hands, gently press down the chicken. 14. Close the Grill with lid and the cook time begins counting down. 15. After 25 minutes of cooking, flip the chicken. 16. Grill the other side again for 25 minutes. 17. When the cooking time is completed, open the lid and place the chicken onto a platter for about 10 minutes before carving. 18. Cut the chicken into desired-sized pieces and serve.

Serving Suggestions: Serve alongside the grilled veggies.

Variation Tip: Fresh chicken should have a pinkish color.

Nutritional Information per Serving: Calories: 441 | Fat: 16.9g | Sat Fat: 4.7g | Carbohydrates:2.4 | Fiber: 0.4g | Sugar: 1.5g | Protein: 65.9g

Chicken & Pineapple Kabobs

Prep Time: 15 minutes | Cook Time: 12 minutes | Servings: 6

Ingredients:

2 tablespoons unsweetened applesauce	1 teaspoon red pepper flakes, crushed
3 tablespoons balsamic vinegar	3 cups skinless, boneless chicken, cubed
2 tablespoons olive oil	2½ cups fresh pineapple cubes
3 tablespoons fresh ginger, chopped	2 bell peppers, seeded and cubed
3 tablespoons fresh garlic, chopped	

Preparation:

1. In a large-sized bowl, mix together the applesauce, vinegar, oil, ginger, garlic, and red pepper flakes. 2. Add the chicken cubes and coat with marinade generously. 3. Refrigerate, covered for about 2-3 hours. 4. Thread chicken, pineapple, and bell pepper onto pre-soaked wooden skewers. 5. Arrange the lightly greased "Grill Grate" in the crisper basket in the cooking pot of Ninja Foodi Smart XL Grill. 6. Close the Grill with lid and press "Power" button. 7. Select "Grill" and use the set of arrows to the left of the display to adjust the temperature to "MED". 8. Use the set of arrows to the right of the display to adjust the cook time to 12 minutes. 9. Press "Start/Stop" to begin preheating. 10. When the display shows "Add Food", open the lid and place the skewers onto the "Grill Grate". 11. With your hands, gently press down each skewer. Close the Grill with lid. 12. While cooking, flip the skewers occasionally. 13. When the cooking time is completed, open the lid and serve hot.

Serving Suggestions: Serve with your favorite salad.

Variation Tip: Soak the bamboo skewers in water for at least 30 minutes before using.

Nutritional Information per Serving: Calories: 240 | Fat: 10.3g | Sat Fat: 2.2g | Carbohydrates: 16.1g | Fiber: 2.1g | Sugar: 9.5g | Protein: 21.6g

Garlicky Chicken Breasts

Prep Time: 10 minutes | Cook Time: 12 minutes | Servings: 4

Ingredients:

4 (4-ounce) boneless, skinless chicken breast halves
3 garlic cloves, finely chopped
3 tablespoons fresh parsley, chopped
3 tablespoons olive oil

3 tablespoons lemon juice
1 teaspoon paprika
½ teaspoon dried oregano
Salt and ground black pepper, as required

Preparation:

1. With a fork, pierce chicken breasts several times. 2. In a large bowl, add all the ingredients except the chicken breasts and mix until well combined. 3. Add the chicken breasts and coat with the marinade generously. 4. Refrigerate to marinate for about 2-3 hours. 5. Arrange the lightly greased "Grill Grate" in the crisper basket in the cooking pot of Ninja Foodi Smart XL Grill. 6. Close the Grill with lid and press "Power" button. 7. Select "Grill" and use the set of arrows to the left of display to adjust the temperature to "MED". Use the set of arrows to the right side of display to adjust the cook time to 12 minutes. 8. Press "Start/Stop" to begin preheating. 9. When the display shows "Add Food", open the lid and place the chicken breasts onto the "Grill Grate". 10. With your hands, gently press down each chicken breast. Close the Grill. 11. After 6 minutes of cooking, flip the chicken breasts. 12. When the cooking time is completed, open the lid and serve hot.

Serving Suggestions: Serve with the garnishing of lemon zest.

Variation Tip: Fresh parsley can be replaced with the fresh herb of your choice.

Nutritional Information per Serving: Calories: 216 | Fat: 11.3g | Sat Fat: 2.1g | Carbohydrates: 1.3g | Fiber: 0.4g | Sugar: 0.3g | Protein: 26.6g

Chicken & Veggie Kabobs

Prep Time: 15 minutes | Cook Time: 8 minutes | Servings: 6

Ingredients:

¼ cup Parmigiano Reggiano cheese, grated
3 tablespoons butter
2 garlic cloves, minced
1 cup fresh basil leaves, chopped

Salt and ground black pepper, as required
1¼ pounds boneless, skinless chicken breast, cut into 1-inch cubes
1 large green bell pepper, seeded and cubed
24 cherry tomatoes

Preparation:

1. Add cheese, butter, garlic, basil, salt and black pepper in a food processor and pulse until smooth. 2. Transfer the basil mixture into a large-sized bowl. 3. Add the chicken cubes and mix well. 4. Cover the bowl and refrigerate to marinate for at least 4-5 hours. 5. Thread the chicken, bell pepper cubes and tomatoes onto presoaked wooden skewers. 6. Arrange the lightly greased "Grill Grate" in the crisper basket in the cooking pot of Ninja Foodi Smart XL Grill. 7. Close the Grill with lid and press "Power" button. 8. Select "Grill" and then use the set of arrows to the left of the display to adjust the temperature to "HI". 9. Use the set of arrows to the right of the display to adjust the cook time to 8 minutes. 10. Press "Start/Stop" to begin preheating. 11. When the display shows "Add Food", open the lid and place the skewers onto the "Grill Grate". 12. With your hands, gently press down each skewer. Close the Grill with lid. 13. While cooking, flip the skewers occasionally. 14. When the cooking time is completed, open the lid and serve hot.

Serving Suggestions: Serve with a drizzling of lemon juice.

Variation Tip: Cherry tomatoes can be replaced with grape tomatoes.

Nutritional Information per Serving: Calories: 201 | Fat: 10.6g | Sat Fat: 1.7g | Carbohydrates: 4.3g | Fiber: 1.1g | Sugar: 2.6g | Protein: 22.3g

Marinated Spicy Chicken Thighs

Prep Time: 15 minutes | Cook Time: 12 minutes | Servings: 4

Ingredients:

½ ounce dried chipotle chile pepper
½ ounce dried ancho chile pepper
¼ cup water
¼ of red onion, cut into small chunks
2 garlic cloves, peeled
½ teaspoon dried oregano

1 teaspoon sea salt
½ teaspoon ground cumin
½ teaspoon ground black pepper
1 tablespoon olive oil
4 (4-ounce) skinless, boneless chicken thighs, pounded slightly

Preparation:

1. In a bowl, place chipotle chile pepper and ancho chile pepper and top with water. 2. Cover the bowl and set aside for at least 10-12 hours. 3. Drain the water and remove seeds from peppers. 4. In a blender, add the chile peppers, onion, garlic, oregano, sea salt, cumin and black pepper and pulse until coarse paste forms. 5. Add olive oil and pulse until smooth. 6. In a resealable plastic bag, place chicken and then seal the bag. Shake to coat well. 7. Refrigerate to marinate for at least 8 hours. 8. Arrange the lightly greased "Grill Grate" in the crisper basket in the cooking pot of Ninja Foodi Smart XL Grill. 9. Close the Grill with lid and press "Power" button. 10. Select "Grill" and use the set of arrows to the left of the display to adjust the temperature to "MED". 11. Use the set of arrows to the right of the display to adjust the cook time to 12 minutes. 12. Press "Start/Stop" to begin preheating. 13. When the display shows "Add Food", open the lid and place the chicken thighs onto the "Grill Grate". 14. With your hands, gently press down each chicken thigh. Close the Grill with lid. 15. After 6 minutes of cooking, flip the chicken thighs. 16. When the cooking time is completed, open the lid and serve hot.

Serving Suggestions: Serve alongside the yogurt sauce.
Variation Tip: Coat the chicken thighs with spice mixture evenly.
Nutritional Information per Serving: Calories: 309 | Fat: 14.2g | Sat Fat: 3.4g | Carbohydrates: 1.9g | Fiber: 0.6g | Sugar: 0.6g | Protein: 41.4g

Lime Maple Chicken Breasts

Prep Time: 10 minutes | Cook Time: 16 minutes | Servings: 5

Ingredients:

¼ cup extra-virgin olive oil
¼ cup fresh lime juice
2 tablespoons maple syrup
1 garlic clove, minced

Salt and ground black pepper, as required
5 (6-ounce) boneless, skinless chicken breasts

Preparation:

1. In a large-sized bowl, add oil, lemon juice, maple syrup, garlic, salt, and black pepper and beat until well combined. 2. In a large-sized resealable plastic bag, place the chicken and ¾ cup of marinade. 3. Seal the bag and shake to coat well. 4. Refrigerate for about 6-8 hours. 5. Cover the bowl of remaining marinade and refrigerate before serving. 6. Arrange the lightly greased "Grill Grate" in the crisper basket in the cooking pot of Ninja Foodi Smart XL Grill. 7. Close the Grill with lid and press "Power" button. 8. Select "Grill" and then use the set of arrows to the left of the display to adjust the temperature to "MED". 9. Use the set of arrows to the right of the display to adjust the cook time to 16 minutes. 10. Press "Start/Stop" to begin preheating. 11. When the display shows "Add Food", open the lid and place the chicken breasts onto the "Grill Grate". 12. With your hands, gently press down each chicken breast. Close the Grill with lid. 13. After 8 minutes of cooking, flip the chicken breasts. 14. When the cooking time is completed, open the lid and serve hot.

Serving Suggestions: Serve with the garnishing of scallions.
Variation Tip: Maple syrup can be replaced with honey.
Nutritional Information per Serving: Calories: 292 | Fat: 12.4g | Sat Fat: 1.4g | Carbohydrates: 5.7g | Fiber: 0g | Sugar: 4.8g | Protein: 39.5g

Chicken & Avocado Burgers

Prep Time: 15 minutes | Cook Time: 10 minutes | Servings: 4

Ingredients:

½ of avocado, peeled, pitted and cut into chunks
½ cup Parmesan cheese, grated
1 garlic clove, minced
Salt and ground black pepper, as required
1 pound ground chicken

Preparation:

1. In a clean bowl, add avocado chunks, Parmesan cheese, garlic, salt, and black pepper and toss to combine. 2. In the bowl of avocado mixture, add the ground chicken and gently stir to combine. 3. Divide the chicken mixture into 4 equal-sized portions and shape each in a patty. 4. Arrange the lightly greased "Grill Grate" in the crisper basket in the cooking pot of Ninja Foodi Smart XL Grill. 5. Close the Grill with lid and press "Power" button. 6. Select "Grill" and then use the set of arrows to the left of the display to adjust the temperature to "MED". 7. Use the set of arrows to the right of the display to adjust the cook time to 10 minutes. 8. Press "Start/Stop" to begin preheating. 9. When the display shows "Add Food", open the lid and place the patties onto the "Grill Grate". 10. With your hands, gently press down each patty. Close the Grill with lid. 11. After 5 minutes of cooking, flip the patties. 12. When the cooking time is completed, open the lid and serve hot.

Serving Suggestions: Serve with your favorite salad.

Variation Tip: Use ripe avocado.

Nutritional Information per Serving: Calories: 238 | Fat: 13.3g | Sat Fat: 4.2g | Carbohydrates: 2.4g | Fiber: 1.7g | Sugar: 0.1g | Protein: 27.5g

Soy Sauce Turkey Breast

Prep Time: 10 minutes | Cook Time: 30 minutes | Servings: 14

Ingredients:

2 garlic cloves, minced
1 tablespoon fresh basil, finely chopped
½ teaspoon ground black pepper
2 (3-pound) boneless turkey breast halves
6 whole cloves
¼ cup soy sauce
¼ cup vegetable oil
2 tablespoons fresh lemon juice
1 tablespoon brown sugar

Preparation:

1. In a small-sized, clean bowl, blend together the garlic, basil, and black pepper. 2. Rub each turkey breast with garlic mixture evenly. 3. Insert 1 whole clove into each end of all turkey breasts and one in the center. 4. In a glass baking dish, add soy sauce, oil, lemon juice, and brown sugar and whisk until well blended. 5. Add the turkey breasts and coat with mixture generously. 6. Cover the baking dish and refrigerate to marinate for at least 4 hours. 7. Remove the turkey breasts from the baking dish and discard the excess marinade. 8. Arrange the lightly greased "Grill Grate" in the crisper basket in the cooking pot of Ninja Foodi Smart XL Grill. 9. Close the Grill with lid and press "Power" button. 10. Select "Grill" and then use the set of arrows to the left of the display to adjust the temperature to "MED". 11. Use the set of arrows to the right of the display to adjust the cook time to 30 minutes. 12. Press "Start/Stop" to begin preheating. 13. When the display shows "Add Food", open the lid and place the turkey breasts onto the "Grill Grate". 14. With your hands, gently press down each turkey breast. Close the Grill with lid. 15. After 15 minutes of cooking, flip the turkey breasts. 16. When the cooking time is completed, open the lid and place the turkey breasts onto a platter for about 10 to 15 minutes before slicing. 17. Cut each turkey breast into desired-sized slices and serve.

Serving Suggestions: Serve with fresh greens.

Variation Tip: Beware of flat spots on meat, which can indicate thawing and refreezing.

Nutritional Information per Serving: Calories: 230 | Fat: 4.8g | Sat Fat: 0.8g | Carbohydrates: 1.2g | Fiber: 0.1g | Sugar: 0.8g | Protein: 48.5g

BBQ Chicken Thighs

Prep Time: 10 minutes | Cook Time: 10 minutes | Servings: 6

Ingredients:

¾ cup BBQ sauce
4 tablespoons peach preserve
1½ tablespoons fresh lemon juice

Salt and ground black pepper, as required
4 bone-in chicken thighs

Preparation:

1. In a bowl, add the barbecue sauce, peach preserves, lemon juice, salt, and black pepper in a bowl and with a whisk, mix until well combined. 2. Add the chicken thighs and coat with mixture generously. 3. Refrigerate to marinate for 4 hours. 4. Arrange the lightly greased "Grill Grate" in the crisper basket in the cooking pot of Ninja Foodi Smart XL Grill. 5. Close the Grill with lid and press "Power" button. 6. Select "Grill" and use the set of arrows to the left of the display to adjust the temperature to "HI". 7. Use the set of arrows to the right of the display to adjust the cook time to 10 minutes. 8. Press "Start/Stop" to begin preheating. 9. When the display shows "Add Food", open the lid and place the chicken thighs onto the "Grill Grate". 10. With your hands, gently press down each chicken thigh. Close the Grill with lid. 11. After 5 minutes of cooking, flip the chicken thighs. 12. When the cooking time is completed, open the lid and serve hot.

Serving Suggestions: Serve with the garnishing of fresh parsley.

Variation Tip: Use high-quality BBQ sauce.

Nutritional Information per Serving: Calories: 450 | Fat: 12.8g | Sat Fat: 3.5g | Carbohydrates: 30.9g | Fiber: 0.5g | Sugar: 22g | Protein: 49.3g

Sweet & Sour Turkey Wings

Prep Time: 15 minutes | Cook Time: 49 minutes | Servings: 6

Ingredients:

6 turkey wings
8 cups water
¼ cup red wine vinegar
2 tablespoons dark soy sauce
1½ tablespoons light brown sugar

¾ teaspoon dried thyme
1 teaspoon Tabasco sauce
3 garlic cloves, finely chopped
2 scallions, finely chopped

Preparation:

1. In a pan of water, add the turkey wings and bring to a boil. 2. Cover the pan with a lid and boil for about 15 minutes. 3. Remove the pan of turkey from heat and set aside. 4. Arrange the lightly greased "Grill Grate" in the crisper basket in the cooking pot of Ninja Foodi Smart XL Grill. 5. Close the Grill with lid and press "Power" button. 6. Select "Grill" and then use the set of arrows to the left of the display to adjust temperature to "MED". 7. Use the set of arrows to the right of the display to adjust the cook time 29 minutes. 8. Press "Start/Stop" to begin preheating. 9. When the display shows "Add Food", open the lid. 10. Remove the wings from pan of water and place onto the "Grill Grate". 11. With your hands, gently press down each wing. Close the Grill with lid. 12. Meanwhile, for sauce: in a bowl, mix together all the remaining ingredients. 13. After 12 minutes of cooking, flip the wings and coat with the sauce evenly. 14. After 24 minutes of cooking, flip the wings and coat with the sauce evenly. 15. When the cooking time is completed, open the lid and transfer the wings onto a platter. 16. Coat the wings with any remaining sauce and serve immediately.

Serving Suggestions: Serve with a garnishing of scallion greens.

Variation Tip: Red wine vinegar can be replaced with balsamic vinegar too.

Nutritional Information per Serving: Calories: 6118 | Fat: 37.8g | Sat Fat: 0g | Carbohydrates: 3.3g | Fiber: 0.2g | Sugar: 2.4g | Protein: 62.7g

Glazed Chicken Thighs

Prep Time: 15 minutes | Cook Time: 12 minutes | Servings: 4

Ingredients:

1 cup low-sodium soy sauce
3 tablespoons rice vinegar
2 tablespoons mirin
2 tablespoons brown sugar, packed

2 teaspoons powdered ginger
1½ pounds boneless, skinless chicken thighs

Preparation:

1. In a bowl, place all ingredients except for chicken thighs and mix until well combined. 2. Add the chicken thighs and refrigerate to marinate for about 20-30 minutes. 3. Remove the chicken thighs from the bowl, reserving the marinade. 4. Arrange the lightly greased "Grill Grate" in the crisper basket in the cooking pot of Ninja Foodi Smart XL Grill. 5. Close the Grill with lid and press "Power" button. 6. Select "Grill" and use the set of arrows to the left of the display to adjust the temperature to "HI". 7. Use the set of arrows to the right of the display to adjust the cook time to 12 minutes. 8. Press "Start/Stop" to begin preheating. 9. When the display shows "Add Food", open the lid and place the chicken thighs onto the "Grill Grate". 10. With your hands, gently press down each chicken thigh. Close the Grill with lid. 11. After 6 minutes of cooking, flip the chicken thighs. 12. Meanwhile, place the marinade into a small saucepan over medium heat and bring to a boil. 13. Reduce the heat to low and simmer until desired thickness of marinade. 14. When the cooking time is completed, open the lid and transfer the chicken thighs onto a platter. 15. Top with the thickened marinade and serve immediately.

Serving Suggestions: Serve with the garnishing of sesame seeds.

Variation Tip: Sweet marsala wine can be used instead of mirin.

Nutritional Information per Serving: Calories: 383 | Fat: 12.7g | Sat Fat: 3.5g | Carbohydrates: 12.6g | Fiber: 0.1g | Sugar: 10.4g | Protein: 53.3g

Chicken & Broccoli Kabobs

Prep Time: 15 minutes | Cook Time: 16 minutes | Servings: 6

Ingredients:

1½ pounds skinless, boneless chicken breasts, cubed
2 tablespoons olive oil
2 tablespoons dried marjoram, crushed

2 garlic cloves, minced
2 tablespoons tomato paste
4 cups broccoli florets
Ground black pepper, as required

Preparation:

1. In a bowl, add the chicken, oil, marjoram, garlic, tomato paste, broccoli, and black pepper and mix well. 2. Cover the bowl of chicken mixture and set aside at room temperature for about 10-15 minutes. 3. Thread the chicken and broccoli onto pre-soaked wooden skewers. 4. Arrange the lightly greased "Grill Grate" in the crisper basket in the cooking pot of Ninja Foodi Smart XL Grill. 5. Close the Grill with lid and press "Power" button. 6. Select "Grill" and then use the set of arrows to the left of the display to adjust the temperature to "MED". 7. Press "Start/Stop" to begin preheating. 8. When the display shows "Add Food", open the lid and place the skewers onto the "Grill Grate". 9. With your hands, gently press down each skewer. Close the Grill with lid. 10. After 8 minutes of cooking, flip the skewers. 11. When the cooking time is completed, open the lid and serve hot.

Serving Suggestions: Serve with the garnishing of parsley.

Variation Tip: You can also use metal skewers instead of wooden skewers.

Nutritional Information per Serving: Calories: 210 | Fat: 9g | Sat Fat: 2.2g | Carbohydrates: 5.7g | Fiber: 2.1g | Sugar: 1.7g | Protein: 27.4g

Honey Mustard Chicken Drumsticks

Prep Time: 10 minutes | Cook Time: 25 minutes | Servings: 8

Ingredients:

3 garlic cloves, minced
⅓ cup honey
¼ cup Dijon mustard
2 tablespoons low-sodium soy sauce

2 tablespoons mustard powder
Ground black pepper, as required
4 pounds chicken drumsticks

Preparation:

1. In a bowl, add garlic and remaining ingredients except for chicken drumsticks and mix until well combined. 2. Coat the chicken drumsticks with spice mixture generously. 3. Cover the bowl of chicken drumsticks and refrigerate to marinate for at least 2 hours. 4. Remove the chicken drumsticks from the bowl, reserving the marinade. 5. Arrange the lightly greased "Grill Grate" in the crisper basket in the cooking pot of Ninja Foodi Smart XL Grill. 6. Close the Grill with lid and press "Power" button. 7. Select "Grill" and use the set of arrows to the left of the display to adjust the temperature to "MED". 8. Use the set of arrows to the right of the display to adjust the cook time to 25 minutes. 9. Press "Start/Stop" to begin preheating. 10. When the display shows "Add Food", open the lid and place the chicken drumsticks onto the "Grill Grate". 11. With your hands, gently press down each chicken drumstick. Close the Grill with lid. 12. While cooking, flip and coat the drumsticks with reserved marinade after every 10 minutes. 13. When the cooking time is completed, open the lid and serve hot.

Serving Suggestions: Serve with the dipping sauce of your choice.

Variation Tip: Use skinless chicken Drumsticks.

Nutritional Information per Serving: Calories: 448 | Fat: 14.1g | Sat Fat: 3.5g | Carbohydrates: 13.7g | Fiber: 0.7g | Sugar: 12.1g | Protein: 63.8g

Teriyaki Chicken Kabobs

Prep Time: 15 minutes | Cook Time: 8 minutes | Servings: 6

Ingredients:

1 tablespoon honey
3 tablespoons teriyaki sauce
2 tablespoons low-sodium soy sauce
1 tablespoon garlic, crushed
2 tablespoons fresh lemon juice

2 tablespoons olive oil
Ground black pepper, as required
2 pounds boneless, skinless chicken breast, cut into 1-inch pieces

Preparation:

1. In a bowl, place all ingredients except for chicken pieces and vegetables and mix well. 2. Add the chicken pieces and coat with the mixture generously. 3. Cover the bowl and refrigerate to marinate for about 1 hour. 4. Remove the chicken pieces and vegetables from the bowl and thread onto skewers. 5. Arrange the lightly greased "Grill Grate" in the crisper basket in the cooking pot of Ninja Foodi Smart XL Grill. 6. Close the Grill with lid and press "Power" button. 7. Select "Grill" and use the set of arrows to the left of the display to adjust the temperature to "HI". 8. Use the set of arrows to the right of the display to adjust the cook time to 8 minutes. 9. Press "Start/Stop" to begin preheating. 10. When the display shows "Add Food", open the lid and place the skewers onto the "Grill Grate". 11. With your hands, gently press down each skewer. Close the Grill with lid. 12. After 4 minutes of cooking, flip the skewers. 13. When the cooking time is completed, open the lid and serve hot.

Serving Suggestions: Serve alongside the steamed rice.

Variation Tip: Honey can be replaced with maple syrup.

Nutritional Information per Serving: Calories: 226 | Fat: 8.6g | Sat Fat: 0.7g | Carbohydrates: 5.2g | Fiber: 0.1g | Sugar: 4.6g | Protein: 36.1g

Glazed Turkey Cutlets

Prep Time: 10 minutes | Cook Time: 10 minutes | Servings: 4

Ingredients:

2 tablespoons Dijon mustard
tablespoons honey
2 tablespoons dry sherry
½ tablespoons light soy sauce

¼ teaspoon ginger powder
4 (6-ounce) (½-inch thick) turkey breast cutlets

Preparation:

1. In a bowl, place all the ingredients except for turkey cutlets and mix until well combined. 2. Place the turkey cutlets and coat with marinade generously. 3. Refrigerate to marinate for at least 30 minutes. 4. Arrange the lightly greased "Grill Grate" in the crisper basket in the cooking pot of Ninja Foodi Smart XL Grill. 5. Close the Grill with lid and press "Power" button. 6. Select "Grill" and then use the set of arrows to the left of the display to adjust the temperature to "MED". 7. Use the set of arrows to the right of the display to adjust the cook time to 10 minutes. 8. Press "Start/Stop" to begin preheating. 9. When the display shows "Add Food", open the lid and place the turkey cutlets onto the "Grill Grate". 10. With your hands, gently press down each turkey cutlet. Close the Grill with lid. 11. After 5 minutes of cooking, flip the turkey cutlets. 12. When the cooking time is completed, open the lid and serve hot.

Serving Suggestions: Serve with cranberry sauce.

Variation Tip: Avoid using turkey breast cutlets with flat spots.

Nutritional Information per Serving: Calories: 222 | Fat: 3.1g | Sat Fat: 0.6g | Carbohydrates: 16.7g | Fiber: 1.1g | Sugar: 14.7g | Protein: 29.5g

Glazed Turkey Tenderloins

Prep Time: 10 minutes | Cook Time: 20 minutes | Servings: 8

Ingredients:

1 large shallot, quartered
1 (¾-inch) piece fresh ginger, chopped
2 small garlic cloves, chopped
1 tablespoon honey
¼ cup olive oil

¼ cup soy sauce
2 tablespoons fresh lime juice
Ground black pepper, as required
4 (½-pound) turkey breast tenderloins

Preparation:

1. In a food processor, add shallot, ginger, and garlic and pulse until minced. 2. Add the remaining ingredients except for turkey tenderloins and pulse until well combined. 3. Transfer the mixture into a large bowl. 4. Add the turkey tenderloins and coat with mixture generously. 5. Arrange the lightly greased "Grill Grate" in the crisper basket in the cooking pot of Ninja Foodi Smart XL Grill. 6. Close the Grill with lid and press "Power" button. 7. Select "Grill" and then use the set of arrows to the left of the display to adjust the temperature to "MED". 8. Use the set of arrows to the right to adjust the cook time to 20 minutes. 9. Press "Start/Stop" to begin preheating. 10. When the display shows "Add Food", open the lid and place the turkey tenderloins onto the "Grill Grate". 11. With your hands, gently press down each turkey tenderloin. Close the Grill with lid. 12. After 10 minutes of cooking, flip the turkey tenderloins. 13. When the cooking time is completed, open the lid and place the turkey tenderloins onto a cutting board. 14. Cut each tenderloin into desired-sized slices and serve.

Serving Suggestions: Serve alongside the roasted Brussels sprout.

Variation Tip: You can use tamari instead of soy sauce.

Nutritional Information per Serving: Calories: 188 | Fat: 8.2g | Sat Fat: 1.3g | Carbohydrates: 8.5g | Fiber: 0.7g | Sugar: 6.3g | Protein: 20g

Simple Turkey Burgers

Prep Time: 15 minutes | Cook Time: 10 minutes | Servings: 4

Ingredients:

1 pound ground turkey
1 large egg, lightly beaten
½ cup seasoned breadcrumbs

Salt and ground black pepper, as required
1 tablespoon olive oil

Preparation:

1. In a large bowl, add the ground turkey, egg, breadcrumbs, salt, and black pepper and mix until well combined. 2. Make 4 (½-inch-thick) patties from the mixture. 3. With your thumb, press a shallow indentation in the center of each patty. 4. Brush both sides of each patty with oil. 5. Arrange the lightly greased "Grill Grate" in the crisper basket in the cooking pot of Ninja Foodi Smart XL Grill. 6. Close the Grill with lid and press "Power" button. 7. Select "Grill" and then use the set of arrows to the left of the display to adjust the temperature to "MED". 8. Use the set of arrows to the right of the display to adjust the cook time to 10 minutes. 9. Press "Start/Stop" to begin preheating. 10. When the display shows "Add Food", open the lid and place the patties onto the "Grill Grate". 11. With your hands, gently press down each patty. Close the Grill with lid. 12. After 5 minutes of cooking, flip the patties. 13. When the cooking time is completed, open the lid and serve hot.

Serving Suggestions: Serve alongside the buttered potatoes.

Variation Tip: You can use breadcrumbs of your choice.

Nutritional Information per Serving: Calories: 265 | Fat: 14.6g | Sat Fat: 2.9g | Carbohydrates: 8.6g | Fiber: 0.5g | Sugar: 0.1g | Protein: 27.4g

Chipotle Turkey Burger

Prep Time: 15 minutes | Cook Time: 10 minutes | Servings: 4

Ingredients:

1 pound extra lean ground turkey
2-2¼ tablespoons chipotle chile in adobo sauce, pureed

1 garlic clove, minced
1 tablespoon red chili powder
Salt and ground black pepper, as required

Preparation:

1. In a bowl, add ground turkey and remaining ingredients and mix until well combined. 2. Refrigerate for about 6-8 hours. 3. Make 4 equal-sized patties from the mixture. 4. With your thumb, make a slight dent in the center of each patty. 5. Arrange the lightly greased "Grill Grate" in the crisper basket in the cooking pot of Ninja Foodi Smart XL Grill. 6. Close the Grill with lid and press "Power" button. 7. Select "Grill" and then use the set of arrows to the left of the display to adjust the temperature to "MED". 8. Use the set of arrows to the right of the display to adjust the cook time to 10 minutes. 9. Press "Start/Stop" to begin preheating. 10. When the display shows "Add Food", open the lid and place the patties onto the "Grill Grate". 11. With your hands, gently press down each patty. Close the Grill with lid. 12. After 5 minutes of cooking, flip the patties. 13. When the cooking time is completed, open the lid and serve hot.

Serving Suggestions: Serve these patties in your favorite burger.

Variation Tip: You can skip the red chili powder.

Nutritional Information per Serving: Calories: 180 | Fat: 8.4g | Sat Fat: 2.6g | Carbohydrates: 1.5g | Fiber: 0.7g | Sugar: 0.3g | Protein: 21.6g

Turkey & Apple Burgers

Prep Time: 15 minutes | Cook Time: 12 minutes | Servings: 2

Ingredients:

6 ounces lean ground turkey
½ of small apple, peeled, cored and grated
2 tablespoons red onion, minced
1 small garlic clove, minced
½ tablespoon fresh ginger, minced
1 tablespoon fresh cilantro, chopped
¼ teaspoon ground cumin
Salt and ground black pepper, as required
Non-stick cooking spray

Preparation:

1. In a bowl, add all the ingredients except and mix until well combined. 2. Shape the mixture into 2 patties. 3. Spray each patty with cooking spray. 4. Arrange the lightly greased "Grill Grate" in the crisper basket in the cooking pot of Ninja Foodi Smart XL Grill. 5. Close the Grill with lid and press "Power" button. 6. Select "Grill" and then use the set of arrows to the left of the display to adjust the temperature to "MED". 7. Use the set of arrows to the right of the display to adjust the cook time to 12 minutes. 8. Press "Start/Stop" to begin preheating. 9. When the display shows "Add Food", open the lid and place the patties onto the "Grill Grate". 10. With your hands, gently press down each patty. Close the Grill with lid. 11. After 6 minutes of cooking, flip the patties. 12. When the cooking time is completed, open the lid and serve hot.

Serving Suggestions: Serve alongside the spinach and tomato salad.

Variation Tip: Don't use tart apple.

Nutritional Information per Serving: Calories: 167 | Fat: 6.5g | Sat Fat: 1.5g | Carbohydrates: 10.6g | Fiber: 2.4g | Sugar: 6.4g | Protein: 18g

Turkey Meatballs Kabobs

Prep Time: 15 minutes | Cook Time: 14 minutes | Servings: 4

Ingredients:

1 yellow onion, chopped roughly
½ cup lemongrass, chopped roughly
2 garlic cloves, chopped roughly
1½ pounds lean ground turkey
1 teaspoon sesame oil
½ tablespoons low-sodium soy sauce
1 tablespoon arrowroot starch
⅛ teaspoon powdered stevia
Salt and ground black pepper, as required

Preparation:

1. In a food processor, add the onion, lemongrass, and garlic and pulse until finely chopped. 2. Transfer the onion mixture into a large-sized bowl. 3. Add the remaining ingredients and mix until well combined. 4. Make 12 equal-sized balls from meat mixture. 5. Thread the balls onto the presoaked wooden skewers. 6. Arrange the lightly greased "Grill Grate" in the crisper basket in the cooking pot of Ninja Foodi Smart XL Grill. 7. Close the Grill with lid and press "Power" button. 8. Select "Grill" and then use the set of arrows to the left of the display to adjust the temperature to "MED". 9. Use the set of arrows to the right of the display to adjust the cook time to 14 minutes. 10. Press "Start/Stop" to begin preheating. 11. When the display shows "Add Food", open the lid and place the skewers onto the "Grill Grate". 12. With your hands, gently press down each skewer. Close the Grill with lid. 13. After 7 minutes of cooking, flip the skewers. 14. When the cooking time is completed, open the lid and serve hot.

Serving Suggestions: Serve alongside the tzatziki sauce.

Variation Tip: Make sure to use lean ground turkey.

Nutritional Information per Serving: Calories: 276 | Fat: 13.4g | Sat Fat: 4g | Carbohydrates: 5.6g | Fiber: 0.6g | Sugar: 1.3g | Protein: 34.2g

Chapter 6 Beef, Pork, and Lamb Recipes

Creamy Saucy Beef

Prep Time: 20 minutes | Cook Time: 60 minutes | Servings: 4

Ingredients:

2 beef tenderloin center-cut filet trimmed
Kosher salt to taste

1 package crescent roll sheet, cooked
Mushroom sauce

Preparation:

1. Season the beef tenderloin with salt and set aside for 3 hours. 2. Select the "Grill" button on Ninja Foodi Smart XL Grill and regulate the time for 15 minutes at LO. 3. Place the beef in Ninja Foodi when it displays "Add Food". 4. Grill for 60 minutes, flipping the sides after 30 minutes. 5. Once done serve with crescent rolls with mushroom sauce on top.

Serving Suggestions: Serve with a bread loaf.
Variation Tip: You can some red chili flakes.
Nutritional Information per Serving: Calories: 265 | Fat: 13g | Sat Fat: 4.9g | Carbohydrates: 0g | Fiber: 0g | Sugar: 0g | Protein: 34.8g

Beef Kebabs Skewers

Prep Time: 15minutes | Cook Time: 8 minutes | Servings: 10

Ingredients:

1-2 steaks, cubed
1 onion, cut in squares
1 bundle mushrooms
10 cherry tomatoes

1 bell pepper, cubed
2 cups Italian dressing
Wooden skewers

Preparation:

1. Select the "Grill" button on the Ninja Foodi Smart XL Grill and regulate the time for 10 minutes at HI. 2. Season the steak with dressing. 3. Set steaks, onion, cherry tomatoes, mushrooms in skewers. 4. Place the chicken tenders in Ninja Foodi when it displays "Add Food". 5. Grill for 8 minutes, flipping after half time. 6. Serve warm and enjoy.

Serving Suggestions: Serve with garlic mayo sauce.
Variation Tip: You can also add tofu in skewers.
Nutritional Information per Serving: Calories: 416 | Fat: 33g | Sat Fat: 7g | Carbohydrates: 17g | Fiber: 1g | Sugar: 14g | Protein: 12g

Honey Roasted Pork Ribs

Prep Time: 10 minutes | Cook Time: 20 minutes | Servings: 4

Ingredients:

¼ cup honey, divided
¾ cup BBQ sauce
2 tablespoons tomato ketchup
1 tablespoon Worcestershire sauce

1 tablespoon soy sauce
½ teaspoon garlic powder
White pepper, to taste
1¾ pounds pork ribs

Preparation:

1. Select the "Roast" button on the Ninja Foodi Smart XL Grill and regulate the settings at MED for 20 minutes. 2. In a bowl, mingle 3 tablespoons of honey and the remaining ingredients except pork ribs. 3. Add the pork ribs and generously coat with the honey mixture. 4. Refrigerate to marinate for about 30 minutes. 5. Arrange the pork ribs in the Ninja Foodi when it displays "Add Food". 6. Roast for 20 minutes, flipping once in the middle way. 7. Remove from Ninja Foodi Smart XL Grill and dish out the ribs. 8. Trickle with the remaining honey and immediately serve.

Serving Suggestions: You can serve them with fresh baby greens.
Variation Tip: You can use fresh garlic too instead of garlic powder.
Nutritional Information per Serving: Calories: 691 | Fat: 35.3g | Sat Fat: 12.5g | Carbohydrates: 37.7g | Fiber: 0.4g | Sugar: 32.2g | Protein: 53.1g

Mignon Steak

Prep Time: 10 minutes | Cook Time: 10 minutes | Servings: 2

Ingredients:

2-4 filet mignon

½ tablespoons steak seasoning

cooking spray

Preparation:

1. Season the filet mignon with seasoning and spray some cooking spray on it. 2. Select the "Grill" button on the Ninja Foodi Smart XL Grill and regulate the time for 10 minutes at HI. 3. Place the steak in Ninja Foodi when it displays "Add Food". 4. Grill for 10 minutes, flipping sides after 5 minutes. 5. Serve warm and enjoy!

Serving Suggestions: Serve with chopped cilantro on top.

Variation Tip: Add some black pepper.

Nutritional Information per Serving: Calories: 460 | Fat: 29g | Sat Fat: 11g | Carbohydrates: 1g | Fiber: 12g | Sugar: 8 | Protein: 45g

Breaded Pork Chops

Prep Time: 15 minutes | Cook Time: 15 minutes | Servings: 3

Ingredients:

2 (6-ounces) pork chops

Salt and black pepper, to taste

¼ cup plain flour

1 egg

4 ounces breadcrumbs

1 tablespoon vegetable oil

Preparation:

1. Select the "Air Crisp" button on Ninja Foodi Smart XL Grill and regulate the settings at 365°F for 15 minutes. 2. Dust each pork chop evenly with salt and black pepper. 3. In a shallow bowl, place the flour. 4. In a second bowl, crack the egg and beat well. 5. Mingle breadcrumbs and oil in a third bowl and combine well until crumbled. 6. Coat flour on the pork chop, then fold into the egg and finally, coat breadcrumbs mixture on the pork chops. 7. Arrange the pork chops in the Ninja Foodi when it displays "Add Food". 8. Air crisp for about 15 minutes, flipping once in between. 9. Dole out in a platter and serve warm.

Serving Suggestions: Serve these breaded pork chops with creamed spinach.

Variation Tip: You can also use butter or olive oil.

Nutritional Information per Serving: Calories: 611 | Fat: 36.3g | Sat Fat: 12.4g | Carbohydrates: 35.3g | Fiber: 2g | Sugar: 2.5g | Protein: 33.5g

Short Beef Ribs

Prep Time: 20 minutes | Cook Time: 16 minutes | Servings: 8

Ingredients:

4 pounds bone-in beef short ribs

⅓ cup scallions, chopped

1 tablespoon fresh ginger, finely grated

1 cup low-sodium soy sauce

½ cup rice vinegar

1 tablespoon sriracha

2 tablespoons brown sugar

1 teaspoon ground black pepper

Preparation:

1. Take a bowl and add all ingredients in it except for beef ribs. 2. Marinade beef ribs with it and leave overnight. 3. Select the "Roast" button on the Ninja Foodi Smart XL Grill and regulate the time for 10 minutes at HI. 4. Place the beef ribs in Ninja Foodi when it displays "Add Food". 5. Roast for 16 minutes, flipping the sides after 4 minutes. 6. Take out from Ninja Foodi and serve.

Serving Suggestions: Serve with ranch sauce.

Variation Tip: You can add some hot sauce too.

Nutritional Information per Serving: Calories: 475 | Fat: 41.1g | Sat Fat: 18g | Carbohydrates: 5.6g | Fiber: 0.3g | Sugar: 4.3g | Protein: 18.2g

Beef with Onion

Prep Time: 30 minutes | Cook Time: 10 minutes | Servings: 2

Ingredients:

1 pound top round beef, cut into cubes
½ onion, chopped
2 tablespoons Worcestershire sauce
1 tablespoon avocado oil
1 teaspoon onion powder
1 teaspoon garlic powder
Salt to taste
Pepper to taste

Preparation:

1. Select the "Grill" button on the Ninja Foodi Smart XL Grill and regulate the time for 10 minutes at MED. 2. Take a bowl and add in all ingredients in it. Mix well and set aside for 30 hours. 3. Place the beef in Ninja Foodi when it displays "Add Food". 4. Grill for 10 minutes and serve.

Serving Suggestions: Serve with garlic rice.

Variation Tip: You can use variety of onions like yellow onion, red onion.

Nutritional Information per Serving: Calories: 532 | Fat: 21.1g | Sat Fat: 7.2g | Carbohydrates: 8g | Fiber: 1.1g | Sugar: 5g | Protein: 72.6g

Beef Tacos

Prep Time: 10 minutes | Cook Time: 10 minutes | Servings: 6

Ingredients:

6 (12-inch) flour tortillas
2 pounds ground beef
12 ounces nacho cheese
2 cups sour cream
2 cups lettuce, shredded
3 tomatoes, sliced
2 cups Mexican blend cheese, shredded
Olive oil cooking spray

Preparation:

1. Select the "Grill" button on Ninja Foodi Smart XL Grill and regulate the time for 10 minutes at HI. 2. Place the ground beef in Ninja Foodi when it displays "Add Food". 3. Grill for 10 minutes. 4. Once done, take out from Ninja Foodi and set aside. 5. In a large skillet, put oil and add all other ingredients over medium heat except tortillas. 6. Cook for 6 minutes and take the mixture out. 7. Now fill the mixture in half of tortilla and fold it, repeat until all tortillas are filled with mixture. 8. Enjoy yummy tacos.

Serving Suggestions: Serve with lemons and green chili sauce.

Variation Tip: Add some basil leaves in it.

Nutritional Information per Serving: Calories: 1026 | Fat: 59.5g | Sat Fat: 33.2g | Carbohydrates: 49.5g | Fiber: 2.8g | Sugar: 4.6g | Protein: 74.6

Pork Tenderloin with Bell Peppers

Prep Time: 15 minutes | Cook Time: 20 minutes | Servings: 3

Ingredients:

1 large red bell pepper, chopped
1 red onion, thinly sliced
2 teaspoons Herbs de Provence
Salt and ground black pepper, as required
1 tablespoon olive oil
10½-ounces pork tenderloin, cut into 4 pieces
½ tablespoon Dijon mustard

Preparation:

1. Select the "Bake" button on Ninja Foodi Smart XL Grill and regulate the settings at 390°F for 20 minutes. 2. In a bowl, merge the bell pepper, onion, Herbs de Provence, salt, black pepper, and ½ tablespoon of oil and toss to coat well. 3. Scrub the pork pieces with Dijon mustard, salt, and black pepper. 4. Trickle with the remaining oil. 5. Place bell pepper mixture in the Ninja Foodi when it displays "Add Food" and top with pork pieces. 6. Bake for about 20 minutes, flipping once in between. 7. Dole out in a platter and serve warm.

Serving Suggestions: Serve with fried rice.

Variation Tip: Add in some paprika powder for taste variation.

Nutritional Information per Serving: Calories: 211 | Fat: 8.4g | Sat Fat: 1.9g | Carbohydrates: 6.6g | Fiber: 1.4g | Sugar: 3.6g | Protein: 26.9g

Sweet and Sour Pork Chops

Prep Time: 15 minutes | Cook Time: 25 minutes | Servings: 6

Ingredients:

6 pork loin chops
1 tablespoon meat tenderizer
Salt and black pepper, to taste
2 garlic cloves, minced

2 tablespoons honey
2 tablespoons soy sauce
1 tablespoon balsamic vinegar
¼ teaspoon ground ginger

Preparation:

1. Select the "Roast" button on Ninja Foodi Smart XL Grill and regulate the settings at MED for 15 minutes. 2. Dust the pork chops with meat tenderizer, salt, and black pepper. 3. Mingle the remaining ingredients in a large bowl and coat pork chops with this marinade. 4. Cover and refrigerate for about 8 hours. 5. Arrange the pork chops in the Ninja Foodi when it displays "Add Food". 6. Roast for 15 minutes, flipping once in the middle way. 7. Dish out and serve warm.

Serving Suggestions: Serve these pork chops with rice.

Variation Tip: Bring the pork ribs to room temperature before cooking.

Nutritional Information per Serving: Calories: 282 | Fat: 19.9g | Sat Fat: 7.5g | Carbohydrates: 6.6g | Fiber: 0.1g | Sugar: 5.9g | Protein: 18.4g

Herbed Pork Chops

Prep Time: 15 minutes | Cook Time: 15 minutes | Servings: 4

Ingredients:

½ tablespoon fresh cilantro, chopped
½ tablespoon fresh parsley, chopped
2 tablespoons olive oil
1 tablespoon ground coriander
Salt, to taste

2 (6-ounces) (1-inch thick) pork chops
2 garlic cloves, minced
½ tablespoon fresh rosemary, chopped
¾ tablespoon Dijon mustard
1 teaspoon sugar

Preparation:

1. Select the "Grill" button on the Ninja Foodi Smart XL Grill and regulate the settings at MED for 15 minutes. 2. Mingle garlic, herbs, oil, mustard, coriander, sugar, and salt in a bowl. 3. Add the pork chops and generously coat with marinade. 4. Cover and refrigerate for about 3 hours. 5. Arrange the pork ribs in the Ninja Foodi when it displays "Add Food". 6. Grill for about 20 minutes, tossing once in the middle way. 7. Dole out in a platter and serve warm.

Serving Suggestions: Serve these pork chops with curried potato salad.

Variation Tip: You can add basil instead of rosemary.

Nutritional Information per Serving: Calories: 342 | Fat: 28.3g | Sat Fat: 9g | Carbohydrates: 2g | Fiber: 0.3g | Sugar: 1.1g | Protein: 19.4g

Bacon Wrapped Pork Tenderloin

Prep Time: 15 minutes | Cook Time: 20 minutes | Servings: 4

Ingredients:

1 (1½ pound) pork tenderloins
4 bacon strips

2 tablespoons Dijon mustard

Preparation:

1. Select the "Air Crisp" button on Ninja Foodi Smart XL Grill and regulate the settings at 400°F for 20 minutes. 2. Coat the pork tenderloin evenly with Dijon mustard. 3. Wrap the tenderloin with the bacon strips. 4. Arrange the pork tenderloin in the Ninja Foodi when it displays "Add Food". 5. Air crisp for about 20 minutes, flipping once in between. 6. Dole out in a platter and serve warm.

Serving Suggestions: Serve with mashed potatoes.

Variation Tip: You can omit Dijon mustard from this recipe.

Nutritional Information per Serving: Calories: 447 | Fat: 23.1g | Sat Fat: 8g | Carbohydrates: 0.4g | Fiber: 0.3g | Sugar: 0.1g | Protein: 55.1g

Glazed Pork Shoulder

Prep Time: 15 minutes | Cook Time: 20 minutes | Servings: 6

Ingredients:

⅓ cup soy sauce
2 tablespoons sugar
1 tablespoon honey

2 pounds pork shoulder, cut into 1½-inch thick slices

Preparation:

1. Select the "Roast" button on the Ninja Foodi Smart XL Grill and regulate the settings at MED for 20 minutes. 2. In a bowl, mingle all the soy sauce, sugar, and honey. 3. Add the pork and generously coat with the marinade. 4. Cover and refrigerate to marinate for about 6 hours. 5. Arrange the pork shoulder in the Ninja Foodi when it displays "Add Food". 6. Roast for 20 minutes, flipping once in the middle way. 7. Dish out in a platter and carve into desired-sized slices to serve.

Serving Suggestions: Enjoy this glazed pork shoulder with grilled potatoes.
Variation Tip: Coconut aminos can replace soy sauce in this recipe for low carb diet.
Nutritional Information per Serving: Calories: 475 | Fat: 32.4g | Sat Fat: 11.9g | Carbohydrates: 8g | Fiber: 0.1g | Sugar: 7.1g | Protein: 36.1g

Pork Loin with Potatoes

Prep Time: 15 minutes | Cook Time: 25 minutes | Servings: 6

Ingredients:

3 tablespoons olive oil, divided
2 pounds pork loin
1 teaspoon fresh parsley, chopped
3 large red potatoes, chopped

½ teaspoon red pepper flakes, crushed
Salt and black pepper, to taste
½ teaspoon garlic powder

Preparation:

1. Select the "Bake" button on Ninja Foodi Smart XL Grill and regulate the settings at 325°F for 25 minutes. 2. Scrub the pork loin with oil and then, dust evenly with parsley, salt, and black pepper. 3. In a large bowl, merge the potatoes, remaining oil, garlic powder, red pepper flakes, salt, and black pepper and toss to coat well. 4. Place loin in the Ninja Foodi when it displays "Add Food" and arrange potato slices around it. 5. Bake for about 25 minutes, flipping once in between. 6. Dish out in a platter and serve warm.

Serving Suggestions: Serve with other stir-fried vegetables in addition to potatoes.
Variation Tip: You can add white pepper for taste variation.
Nutritional Information per Serving: Calories: 556 | Fat: 28.3g | Sat Fat: 9g | Carbohydrates: 29.6g | Fiber: 3.2g | Sugar: 1.9g | Protein: 44.9g

Glazed Ham

Prep Time: 15 minutes | Cook Time: 35 minutes | Servings: 4

Ingredients:

1 cup whiskey
1 pound ham

2 tablespoons French mustard
2 tablespoons honey

Preparation:

1. Select the "Roast" button on Ninja Foodi Smart XL Grill and regulate the settings at MED for 30 minutes. 2. In a bowl, merge the whiskey, mustard, and honey. 3. Place the ham in the Ninja Foodi cooking pot. 4. Trickle with half of the honey mixture and coat well. 5. Arrange the ham in the Ninja Foodi when it displays "Add Food". 6. Roast for 15 minutes and flip the side of the ham. 7. Trickle with the remaining honey mixture and roast for another 20 minutes. 8. Dish out and serve hot.

Serving Suggestions: Serve with fries or rice.
Variation Tip: You can add maple syrup instead of honey for a different deliciousness.
Nutritional Information per Serving: Calories: 356 | Fat: 9.8g | Sat Fat: 3.3g | Carbohydrates: 13.1g | Fiber: 1.5g | Sugar: 8.7g | Protein: 18.9g

Simple Lamb Chops

Prep Time: 10 minutes | Cook Time: 20 minutes | Servings: 4

Ingredients:

1 tablespoon olive oil
Salt and black pepper, to taste

4 (4-ounces) lamb chops

Preparation:

1. Select the "Air Crisp" button on Ninja Foodi Smart XL Grill and regulate the settings at 390°F for 20 minutes. 2. In a large bowl, merge together the oil, salt, and black pepper. 3. Add the chops and evenly coat with the mixture. 4. Arrange chops in the Ninja Foodi when it displays "Add Food" and top with pork pieces. 5. Air crisp for about 20 minutes, flipping once in between. 6. Dole out in a platter and serve warm.

Serving Suggestions: You can serve it with fig and arugula salad.

Variation Tip: The addition of dried herbs will add a delish touch in lamb chops.

Nutritional Information per Serving: Calories: 241 | Fat: 11.8g | Sat Fat: 3.5g | Carbohydrates: 0g | Fiber: 0g | Sugar: 0g | Protein: 31.8g

Nut Crusted Rack of Lamb

Prep Time: 15 minutes | Cook Time: 25 minutes | Servings: 5

Ingredients:

1 tablespoon olive oil
1 garlic clove, minced
Salt and black pepper, as required
1¾ pounds rack of lamb

1 egg, beaten
1 tablespoon breadcrumbs
3 ounces pistachios, finely chopped

Preparation:

1. Select the "Grill" button on Ninja Foodi Smart XL Grill and regulate the settings at MED for 25 minutes. 2. In a bowl, mingle together the oil, garlic, salt, and black pepper. 3. Coat the rack of lamb evenly with oil mixture. 4. In another bowl, merge together the breadcrumbs and pistachios. 5. Coat the rack of lamb in egg and coat with pistachio mixture. 6. Arrange the rack of lamb in the Ninja Foodi when it displays "Add Food". 7. Grill for about 25 minutes, flipping once in between. 8. Dole out in a platter and serve warm after cutting into desired-sized slices.

Serving Suggestions: Serve with stir-fried vegetables.

Variation Tip: You can also use almonds in this recipe.

Nutritional Information per Serving: Calories: 362 | Fat: 23.7g | Sat Fat: 5.7g | Carbohydrates: 5.8g | Fiber: 1.8g | Sugar: 1.3g | Protein: 32.3g

Herbed Lamb Chops

Prep Time: 10 minutes | Cook Time: 12 minutes | Servings: 4

Ingredients:

1 tablespoon fresh lemon juice
1 tablespoon olive oil
1 teaspoon dried rosemary
1 teaspoon dried thyme
1 teaspoon dried oregano

½ teaspoon ground cumin
½ teaspoon ground coriander
Salt and black pepper, to taste
4 (4-ounces) lamb chops

Preparation:

1. Select the "Grill" button on Ninja Foodi Smart XL Grill and regulate the settings at MED for 12 minutes. 2. In a large bowl, merge the lemon juice, oil, herbs, and spices. 3. Add the chops and coat evenly with the herb mixture. 4. Refrigerate to marinate for about 1 hour. 5. Arrange the lamb chops in the Ninja Foodi when it displays "Add Food". 6. Grill for about 12 minutes, flipping once in between. 7. Dole out in a platter and serve warm.

Serving Suggestions: Serve it with hummus.

Variation Tip: You can also add some red chili flakes.

Nutritional Information per Serving: Calories: 246 | Fat: 12g | Sat Fat: 3.5g | Carbohydrates: 0.8g | Fiber: 0.4g | Sugar: 0.1g | Protein: 32g

Spiced Lamb Steaks

Prep Time: 15 minutes | Cook Time: 20 minutes | Servings: 3

Ingredients:

5 garlic cloves, peeled
1 teaspoon garam masala
½ teaspoon ground cumin
½ teaspoon cayenne pepper
1½ pounds boneless lamb sirloin steaks

½ onion, roughly chopped
1 tablespoon fresh ginger, peeled
1 teaspoon ground fennel
½ teaspoon ground cinnamon
Salt and black pepper, to taste

Preparation:

1. Select the "Grill" button on Ninja Foodi Smart XL Grill and regulate the settings at MED for 20 minutes. 2. In a blender, merge the onion, garlic, ginger, and spices and pulse until smooth. 3. Shift the mixture into a large bowl and add the lamb steaks. 4. Coat generously with the mixture and refrigerate for 12-24 hours. 5. Arrange the lamb steaks in the Ninja Foodi when it displays "Add Food". 6. Grill for about 20 minutes, flipping once in between. 7. Dole out in a platter and serve warm after cutting into desired-sized slices.

Serving Suggestions: Serve with roasted vegetables.
Variation Tip: You can also add white pepper to taste.
Nutritional Information per Serving: Calories: 222 | Fat: 9.8g | Sat Fat: 3.6g | Carbohydrates: 5.6g | Fiber: 1.3g | Sugar: 0.9g | Protein: 26.6g

Garlic Lamb Loin Chops

Prep Time: 10 minutes | Cook Time: 20 minutes | Servings: 8

Ingredients:

3 garlic cloves, crushed
1 tablespoon fresh lemon juice
1 teaspoon olive oil
1 tablespoon Za'atar

Salt and black pepper, to taste
8 (3½-ounces) lamb loin chops, bone-in and trimmed

Preparation:

1. Select the "Roast" button on the Ninja Foodi Smart XL Grill and regulate the settings at MED for 20 minutes. 2. In a large bowl, merge together the garlic, lemon juice, oil, Za'atar, salt, and black pepper. 3. Add chops and generously coat with the mixture. 4. Arrange chops into the Ninja Foodi when it displays "Add Food". 5. Roast for 20 minutes, flipping once in the middle way. 6. Dish out in a platter and serve warm.

Serving Suggestions: Serve with some lemon juice on top.
Variation Tip: You can also use pork chops in this recipe.
Nutritional Information per Serving: Calories: 192 | Fat: 7.9g | Sat Fat: 2.7g | Carbohydrates: 0.4g | Fiber: 0g | Sugar: 0.1g | Protein: 28g

Pesto Coated Rack of Lamb

Prep Time: 15 minutes | Cook Time: 25 minutes | Servings: 4

Ingredients:

½ bunch fresh mint
1 garlic clove
¼ cup extra-virgin olive oil

½ tablespoon honey
Salt and black pepper, as required
1 (1½-pounds) rack of lamb

Preparation:

1. Select the "Grill" button on Ninja Foodi Smart XL Grill and regulate the settings at MED for 25 minutes. 2. For Pesto: In a blender, merge the mint, garlic, oil, honey, salt, and black pepper and pulse until smooth. 3. Coat the pesto on the rack of lamb evenly. 4. Arrange the rack of lamb in the Ninja Foodi when it displays "Add Food". 5. Grill for about 25 minutes, flipping once in between. 6. Dole out in a platter and serve warm after cutting into desired-sized slices.

Serving Suggestions: Serve with boiled potatoes.
Variation Tip: You can also add some fresh parsley.
Nutritional Information per Serving: Calories: 410 | Fat: 27.7g | Sat Fat: 7.1g | Carbohydrates: 3.9g | Fiber: 1.2g | Sugar: 2.2g | Protein: 35.1g

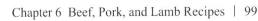

Herbed Leg of Lamb

Prep Time: 15 minutes | Cook Time: 1 hour 15 minutes | Servings: 5

Ingredients:

2 pounds bone-in leg of lamb
2 tablespoons olive oil
Salt and black pepper, to taste

2 fresh rosemary sprigs
2 fresh thyme sprigs

Preparation:

1. Select the "Bake" button on Ninja Foodi Smart XL Grill and regulate the settings at 325°F for 75 minutes. 2. Coat the leg of lamb with oil and dust with salt and black pepper. 3. Wrap herb sprigs around the leg of lamb. 4. Arrange the leg of lamb in the Ninja Foodi when it displays "Add Food". 5. Bake for about 1 hour 15 minutes, flipping once in between. 6. Dish out the leg of lamb in a platter and wrap with foil. 7. Cut the leg of lamb into desired size pieces and serve.

Serving Suggestions: Serve with cilantro leaves on top.

Variation Tip: You can also drizzle the leg of lamb with BBQ sauce.

Nutritional Information per Serving: Calories: 292 | Fat: 13.7g | Sat Fat: 4.1g | Carbohydrates: 0.6g | Fiber: 0.4g | Sugar: 0g | Protein: 37g

Garlic Lamb Roast

Prep Time: 20 minutes | Cook Time: 1 hour 20 minutes | Servings: 8

Ingredients:

2¾ pounds lamb leg roast
3 garlic cloves, cut into thin slices
2 tablespoons extra-virgin olive oil

1 tablespoon dried rosemary, crushed
Salt and black pepper, to taste

Preparation:

1. Select the "Roast" button on Ninja Foodi Smart XL Grill and regulate the settings at MED for 1 hour 20 minutes. 2. In a small bowl, merge the oil, rosemary, salt, and black pepper. 3. With the tip of a sharp knife, carve deep slits on the top of lamb roast and insert the garlic slices in it. 4. Rub the lamb roast evenly with the oil mixture. 5. Arrange the lamb roast in the Ninja Foodi when it displays "Add Food". 6. Roast for 1 hour 20 minutes, flipping once in the middle way. 7. Dish out and serve warm.

Serving Suggestions: Serve with chopped parsley on top.

Variation Tip: You can add cayenne pepper for taste.

Nutritional Information per Serving: Calories: 351 | Fat: 17.9g | Sat Fat: 5.6g | Carbohydrates: 0.6g | Fiber: 0.2g | Sugar: 0g | Protein: 44.3g

Simple Filet Mignon

Prep Time: 10 minutes | Cook Time: 8 minutes | Servings: 4

Ingredients:

4 (6-ounce) filet mignon
2-3 tablespoons olive oil

Salt and ground black pepper, as required

Preparation:

1. Coat both sides of each filet mignon with oil and then rub with steak seasoning and salt. 2. Arrange the lightly greased "Grill Grate" in the crisper basket in the cooking pot of Ninja Foodi Smart XL Grill. 3. Close the Grill with lid and press "Power" button. 4. Select "Grill" and then use the set of arrows to the left of the display to adjust the temperature to "HI". 5. Use the set of arrows to the right of the display to adjust the cook time to 8 minutes. 6. With your hands, gently press down each filet mignon. 7. Press "Start/Stop" to begin preheating. When the display shows "Add Food", open the lid and place the filets onto the "Grill Grate". Close the Grill with lid. 8. After 4 minutes of cooking, flip the filets. 9. When the cooking time is completed, open the lid and transfer the filets onto a platter for about 5 minutes before serving.

Serving Suggestions: Serve with lemon wedges.

Variation Tip: Use filets with no silver skin.

Nutritional Information per Serving: Calories: 425 | Fat: 16.7g | Sat Fat: 6.1g | Carbohydrates: 0.8g | Fiber: 0.6g | Sugar: 0.1g | Protein: 63.9g

Seasoned Fillet Mignon

Prep Time: 10 minutes | Cook Time: 8 minutes | Servings: 2

Ingredients:

2 (1½-2-inch thick) filet mignon
½ tablespoon steak seasoning

Non-stick cooking spray

Preparation:

1. Season the filets with steak seasoning generously. 2. Arrange the lightly greased "Grill Grate" in the crisper basket in the cooking pot of Ninja Foodi Smart XL Grill. 3. Close the Grill with lid and press "Power" button. 4. Select "Grill" and then use the set of arrows to the left of the display to adjust the temperature to "HI". 5. Use the set of arrows to the right of the display to adjust the cook time to 8 minutes. 6. Press "Start/Stop" to begin preheating. 7. When the display shows "Add Food", open the lid and place the filets onto the "Grill Grate". 8. With your hands, gently press down each filet mignon. Close the Grill with lid. 9. After 4 minutes of cooking, flip the filets and spray with cooking spray. 10. When the cooking time is completed, open the lid and serve hot.

Serving Suggestions: Serve alongside the spiced potatoes.

Variation Tip: For more flavors: refrigerate the filets for 2 hours after seasoning.

Nutritional Information per Serving: Calories: 304 | Fat: 11.2g | Sat Fat: 4.3g | Carbohydrates: 0g | Fiber: 0g | Sugar: 0g | Protein: 47.8g

Buttered Strip Steaks

Prep Time: 10 minutes | Cook Time: 8 minutes | Servings: 4

Ingredients:

2 (14-ounce) New York strip steaks
2 tablespoons butter, melted

Salt and ground black pepper, as required

Preparation:

1. Brush each steak with the melted butter and season with salt and black pepper. 2. Arrange the lightly greased "Grill Grate" in the crisper basket in the cooking pot of Ninja Foodi Smart XL Grill. 3. Close the Grill with lid and press "Power" button. 4. Select "Grill" and then use the set of arrows to the left of the display to adjust the temperature to "HI". 5. Use the set of arrows to the right of the display to adjust the cook time to 8 minutes. 6. Press "Start/Stop" to begin preheating. 7. When the display shows "Add Food", open the lid and place the steaks onto the "Grill Grate". 8. With your hands, gently press down each steak. Close the Grill with lid. 9. After 4 minutes of cooking, flip the steaks. 10. When the cooking time is completed, open the lid and transfer the steaks onto a cutting board for about 5 minutes before slicing. 11. Cut each steak into 2 equal-sized portions and serve.

Serving Suggestions: Serve with garlicky green beans.

Variation Tip: D Look for a steak with a nice amount of marbling.

Nutritional Information per Serving: Calories: 296 | Fat: 12.7g | Sat Fat: 6.6g | Carbohydrates: 0g | Fiber: 0g | Sugar: 0g | Protein: 44.5g

Chipotle Strip Steak

Prep Time: 15 minutes | Cook Time: 16 minutes | Servings: 6

Ingredients:

3 canned chipotle peppers with adobo sauce
⅓ cup fresh orange juice
2 tablespoon tomato ketchup
1 tablespoon vegetable oil

1 tablespoon lite soy sauce
1 teaspoon dried oregano
1 garlic clove, minced
4 (10-ounce) strip steaks, trimmed

Preparation:

1. In a food processor, add all ingredients except for steaks and pulse until smooth. 2. Place the mixture in a non-reactive bowl with steaks and mix well. 3. Refrigerate to marinate for about 8 hours. 4. Arrange the lightly greased "Grill Grate" in the crisper basket in the cooking pot of Ninja Foodi Smart XL Grill. 5. Close the Grill with lid and press "Power" button. 6. Select "Grill" and then use the set of arrows to the left of the display to "MED". 7. Use the set of arrows to the right of the display to adjust cook time to 16 minutes. Press "Start/Stop" to begin preheating. 8. When the display shows "Add Food", open the lid and place the steaks onto the "Grill Grate". 9. With your hands, gently press down each steak. Close the Grill with lid. 10. After 8 minutes of cooking, flip the steaks. 11. When the cooking time is completed, open the lid and place the steaks onto a cutting board for about 10 minutes. 12. Cut into desired-sized slices and serve.

Serving Suggestions: Serve alongside the potato mash.

Variation Tip: Use freshly squeezed orange juice.

Nutritional Information per Serving: Calories: 412 | Fat: 16g | Sat Fat: 5.8g | Carbohydrates: 5.4g | Fiber: 0.5g | Sugar: 3.5g | Protein: 58.3g

Simple Rib-Eye Steak

Prep Time: 10 minutes | Cook Time: 8 minutes | Servings: 4

Ingredients:

4 (8-ounce) (1-inch thick) boneless rib-eye steaks

Salt and ground black pepper, as required

Preparation:

1. Season the steaks with salt and black pepper evenly. 2. Arrange the lightly greased "Grill Grate" in the crisper basket in the cooking pot of Ninja Foodi Smart XL Grill. 3. Close the Grill with lid and press "Power" button. 4. Select "Grill" and then use the set of arrows to adjust the temperature to "HI". 5. Use the set of arrows to the right to adjust the cook time to 8 minutes. 6. Press "Start/Stop" to begin preheating. When the display shows "Add Food", open the lid and place the steaks onto the "Grill Grate". 7. With your hands, gently press down each steak. Close the Grill with lid. 8. After 4 minutes of cooking, flip the steaks. 9. When the cooking time is completed, open the lid and serve hot.

Serving Suggestions: Serve with the topping of garlic butter.
Variation Tip: Choose a steak that is uniform in thickness.
Nutritional Information per Serving: Calories: 480 | Fat: 24g | Sat Fat: 8g | Carbohydrates: 0g | Fiber: 0g | Sugar: 0g | Protein: 61.4g

Seasoned Rib-Eye Steak

Prep Time: 10 minutes | Cook Time: 9 minutes | Servings: 4

Ingredients:

2 (10-ounce) rib-eye steaks

1 tablespoon steak seasoning

Preparation:

1. Season steaks with steak seasoning generously. 2. Set aside at room temperature for about 30 minutes. 3. Arrange the lightly greased "Grill Grate" in the crisper basket in the cooking pot of Ninja Foodi Smart XL Grill. 4. Close the Grill with lid and press "Power" button. 5. Select "Grill" and then use the set of arrows to the left of the display to adjust the temperature to "MED". 6. Use the set of arrows to the right of the display to adjust the cook time to 9 minutes. 7. Press "Start/Stop" to begin preheating. When the display shows "Add Food", open the lid and place the steaks onto the "Grill Grate". 8. With your hands, gently press down each steak. Close the Grill with lid. 9. After 5 minutes of cooking, flip the steaks. 10. When the cooking time is completed, open the lid and place the steaks onto a cutting board for about 5 minutes before slicing. 10. Cut each steak into desired-sized slices and serve.

Serving Suggestions: Enjoy with mashed potatoes.
Variation Tip: You can use the seasoning of your choice.
Nutritional Information per Serving: Calories: 300 | Fat: 15g | Sat Fat: 5g | Carbohydrates: 0g | Fiber: 0g | Sugar: 0g | Protein: 38.4g

Lemony Flank Steak

Prep Time: 10 minutes | Cook Time: 12 minutes | Servings: 6

Ingredients:

2 pounds flank steak
3 tablespoons fresh lemon juice
2 tablespoons olive oil
3 garlic cloves, minced

1 teaspoon red chili powder
Salt and ground black pepper, as required

Preparation:

1. In a large-sized bowl, add all the ingredients except for steak and mix well. 2. Add the flank steak and coat with the marinade generously. 3. Refrigerate to marinate for 24 hours, flipping occasionally. 4. Arrange the steak into a greased baking pan. 5. Arrange the lightly greased "Grill Grate" in the crisper basket in the cooking pot of Ninja Foodi Smart XL Grill. 6. Close the Grill with lid and press "Power" button. 7. Select "Grill" and then use the set of arrows to the left of the display to adjust the temperature to "HI". 8. Use the set of arrows to the right of the display to adjust the cook time to 12 minutes. 9. Press "Start/Stop" to begin preheating. 10. When the display shows "Add Food", open the lid and place the steak onto the "Grill Grate". 11. With your hands, gently press down the steak. Close the Grill with lid. 12. After 6 minutes of cooking, flip the steak. 13. When the cooking time is completed, open the lid and place the steak onto a cutting board for about 10 minutes before slicing. 14. Cut the steak into desired-sized slices and serve.

Serving Suggestions: Serve alongside the savory quinoa.
Variation Tip: Trim the steak before cooking.
Nutritional Information per Serving: Calories: 339 | Fat: 17.4g | Sat Fat: 6g | Carbohydrates: 0.9g | Fiber: 0.2g | Sugar: 0.2g | Protein: 42.3g

Spicy & Tangy Flank Steak

Prep Time: 10 minutes | Cook Time: 12 minutes | Servings: 3

Ingredients:

3 garlic cloves, minced
½ teaspoon ground cumin
¼ teaspoon ground coriander
¼ teaspoon cayenne powder

Salt and ground black pepper, as required
2 tablespoons fresh lemon juice
1 (1-pound) flank steak, trimmed

Preparation:

1. In a bowl, blend together garlic, spices, and lemon juice. 2. Add steak and coat with garlic mixture generously. 3. Set aside for about 25-30 minutes. 4. Arrange the lightly greased "Grill Grate" in the crisper basket in the cooking pot of Ninja Foodi Smart XL Grill. 5. Close the Grill with lid and press "Power" button. 6. Select "Grill" and then use the set of arrows to the left of the display to adjust the temperature to "MED". 7. Use the set of arrows to the right of the display to adjust the cook time to 12 minutes. 8. Press "Start/Stop" to begin preheating. 9. When the display shows "Add Food", open the lid and place the steak onto the "Grill Grate". 10. With your hands, gently press down the steak. Close the Grill with lid. After 6 minutes of cooking, flip the steak. 11. When the cooking time is completed, open the lid and place the steak onto a cutting board for about 10 minutes before slicing. 12. Cut the steak into desired-sized slices and serve.
Serving Suggestions: Serve with fresh baby greens.
Variation Tip: Season the steak evenly.
Nutritional Information per Serving: Calories: 302 | Fat: 12.8g | Sat Fat: 5.3g | Carbohydrates: 1.4g | Fiber: 0.2g | Sugar: 0.3g | Protein: 42.4g

Herbed & Spiced Flank Steak

Prep Time: 10 minutes | Cook Time: 20 minutes | Servings: 5

Ingredients:

½ teaspoons dried thyme, crushed
½ teaspoons dried oregano, crushed
1 teaspoon red chili powder
½ teaspoons ground cumin

¼ teaspoons garlic powder
Salt and ground black pepper, as required
1½ pounds flank steak, trimmed

Preparation:

1. In a large bowl, add the dried herbs and spices and mix well. 2. Add the steaks and rub with mixture generously. 3. Set aside for about 15–20 minutes. 4. Arrange the lightly greased "Grill Grate" in the crisper basket in the cooking pot of Ninja Foodi Smart XL Grill. 5. Close the Grill with lid and press "Power" button. 6. Select "Grill" and then use the set of arrows to the left of the display to adjust the temperature to "MED". 7. Use the set of arrows to the right of the display to adjust the cook time to 20 minutes. 8. Press "Start/Stop" to begin preheating. 9. When the display shows "Add Food", open the lid and place the steak onto the "Grill Grate". 10. With your hands, gently press down the steak. Close the Grill with lid. 11. After 10 minutes of cooking, flip the steak. 12. When the cooking time is completed, open the lid and serve hot.
Serving Suggestions: Serve alongside the buttered Brussels sprout.
Variation Tip: Fresh herbs can be used instead of dried herbs.
Nutritional Information per Serving: Calories: 268 | Fat: 11.5g | Sat Fat: 4.7g | Carbohydrates: 0.6g | Fiber: 0.3g | Sugar: 0.1g | Protein: 38g

Honey Flank Steak

Prep Time: 10 minutes | Cook Time: 16 minutes | Servings: 5

Ingredients:

2 garlic cloves, crushed
1 teaspoon fresh ginger, grated
1 tablespoon honey

2 tablespoons olive oil
Ground black pepper, as required
1½ pounds flank steak, trimmed

Preparation:

1. In a large-sized sealable bag, mix together all ingredients except for steak. 2. Add steak and seal the bag. Shake the bag vigorously to coat well. 3. Refrigerate the bag of steak to marinate for about 24 hours. 4. Remove from refrigerator and set aside at room temperature for about 15 minutes. 5. Arrange the lightly greased "Grill Grate" in the crisper basket in the cooking pot of Ninja Foodi Smart XL Grill. 6. Close the Grill with lid and press "Power" button. 7. Select "Grill" and then use the set of arrows to the left of the display to adjust the temperature to "MED". 8. Use the set of arrows to the right of the display to adjust the cook time to 16 minutes. 9. Press "Start/Stop" to begin preheating. 10. When the display shows "Add Food", open the lid and place the steak onto the "Grill Grate". 11. With your hands, gently press down the steak. Close the Grill with lid. 12. After 8 minutes of cooking, flip the steak. 13. When the cooking time is completed, open the lid and place the steak onto a cutting board for about 10 minutes before slicing. 14. Cut the steak into desired-sized slices and serve.
Serving Suggestions: Serve alongside the sautéed leeks.
Variation Tip: Honey can be replaced with maple syrup.
Nutritional Information per Serving: Calories: 328 | Fat: 17g | Sat Fat: 5.5g | Carbohydrates: 4.1g | Fiber: 0.1g | Sugar: 3.5g | Protein: 38g

Garlicky Flank Steak

Prep Time: 10 minutes | Cook Time: 15 minutes | Servings: 6

Ingredients:

3 garlic cloves, minced
2 tablespoons fresh rosemary, chopped

Salt and ground black pepper, as required
2 pounds flank steak, trimmed

Preparation:

1. In a large-sized bowl, add all the ingredients except the steak and mix until well combined. 2. Add the steak and coat with the mixture generously. 3. Set aside for about 10 minutes. 4. Arrange the lightly greased "Grill Grate" in the crisper basket in the cooking pot of Ninja Foodi Smart XL Grill. 5. Close the Grill with lid and press "Power" button. 6. Select "Grill" and then use the set of arrows to the left of the display to adjust the temperature to "MED". 7. Use the set of arrows to the right of the display to adjust the cook time to 15 minutes. 8. Press "Start/Stop" to begin preheating. 9. When the display shows "Add Food", open the lid and place the steak onto the "Grill Grate". 10. With your hands, gently press down the steak. Close the Grill with lid. 11. While cooking, flip the steak after every 4 minutes. 12. When the cooking time is completed, open the lid and place the steak onto a cutting board for about 5 minutes. 13. Cut the steak into desired-sized slices and serve.

Serving Suggestions: Serve with southern-style grits.
Variation Tip: Feel free to use herbs of your choice.
Nutritional Information per Serving: Calories: 299 | Fat: 12.8g | Sat Fat: 5.3g | Carbohydrates: 1.2g | Fiber: 0.5g | Sugar: 0g | Protein: 42.2g

Spiced Tenderloin Steaks

Prep Time: 10 minutes | Cook Time: 10 minutes | Servings: 4

Ingredients:

1 teaspoon onion powder
1 teaspoon garlic powder
1 teaspoon lemon pepper

1 teaspoon paprika
Salt and ground black pepper, as required
4 (6-ounce) beef tenderloin steaks

Preparation:

1. In a small-sized bowl, mix together onion powder, garlic powder, lemon pepper, paprika, salt, and black pepper. 2. Sprinkle the steaks with seasoning mixture evenly. 3. Arrange the lightly greased "Grill Grate" in the crisper basket in the cooking pot of Ninja Foodi Smart XL Grill. 4. Close the Grill with lid and press "Power" button. 5. Select "Grill" and then use the set of arrows to the left of the display to adjust the temperature to "MED". 6. Use the set of arrows to the right of the display to adjust the cook time to 10 minutes. 7. Press "Start/Stop" to begin preheating. 8. When the display shows "Add Food", open the lid and place the steaks onto the "Grill Grate". 9. With your hands, gently press down each steak. Close the Grill with lid. 10. After 5 minutes of cooking, flip the steaks. 11. When the cooking time is completed, open the lid and serve hot.

Serving Suggestions: Serve with the topping of garlic butter.
Variation Tip: Season the steak properly.
Nutritional Information per Serving: Calories: 323 | Fat: 10.7g | Sat Fat: 4g | Carbohydrates: 1.6g | Fiber: 0.4g | Sugar: 0.4g | Protein: 51.9g

Oregano Sirloin Steak

Prep Time: 10 minutes | Cook Time: 17 minutes | Servings: 3

Ingredients:

2 tablespoons fresh oregano, chopped
½ tablespoon garlic, minced
1 tablespoon fresh lemon peel, grated
½ teaspoon red pepper flakes, crushed

Salt and ground black pepper, as required
1 (1-pound) (1-inch thick) boneless beef top sirloin steak

Preparation:

1. In a bowl, add the oregano, garlic, lemon peel, red pepper flakes, salt, and black pepper and mix well. 2. Rub the steak with garlic mixture evenly. 3. Arrange the lightly greased "Grill Grate" in the crisper basket in the cooking pot of Ninja Foodi Smart XL Grill. 4. Close the Grill with lid and press "Power" button. 5. Select "Grill" and then use the set of arrows to the left of the display to adjust the temperature to "MED". 6. Use the set of arrows to the right of the display to adjust the cook time to 17 minutes. 7. Press "Start/Stop" to begin preheating. When the display shows "Add Food", open the lid and place the steak onto the "Grill Grate". 8. With your hands, gently press down the steak. Close the Grill with lid. 9. While cooking, flip the steak occasionally. 10. When the cooking time is completed, open the lid and place the steak onto a cutting board for about 10 minutes. 11. Cut the steak into desired-sized slices and serve.

Serving Suggestions: Serve with cheesy scalloped potatoes.
Variation Tip: Good, fresh meat should be firm, not tough or soft.
Nutritional Information per Serving: Calories: 294 | Fat: 9.8g | Sat Fat: 3.7g | Carbohydrates: 3g | Fiber: 1.5g | Sugar: 0.3g | Protein: 46.4g

Herbed Beef Tenderloin

Prep Time: 10 minutes | Cook Time: 35 minutes | Servings: 12

Ingredients:

1 cup olive oil
4 garlic cloves, peeled
½ cup fresh rosemary, chopped

½ cup fresh thyme, chopped
Salt and ground black pepper, as required
1 (4-pound) center-cut beef tenderloin

Preparation:

1. In a large food processor, add oil, garlic, and herbs and pulse until paste forms. 2. Transfer the paste into a large bowl. 3. Add the tenderloin and coat with mixture generously. 4. Refrigerate the bowl of beef to marinate for at least 2 hours, flipping occasionally. 5. Remove the tenderloin from the refrigerator and set aside at room temperature for at least 30 minutes. 6. Arrange the lightly greased "Grill Grate" in the crisper basket in the cooking pot of Ninja Foodi Smart XL Grill. 7. Close the Grill with lid and press "Power" button. 8. Select "Grill" and then use the set of arrows to the left of the display to adjust the temperature to "MED". 9. Use the set of arrows to the right of the display to adjust the cook time to 30 minutes. 10. Press "Start/Stop" to begin preheating. When the display shows "Add Food", open the lid and place the tenderloin onto the "Grill Grate". 11. With your hands, gently press down the tenderloin. Close the Grill with lid. 12. While cooking, flip the tenderloin after every 10 minutes. 13. When the cooking time is completed, continue cooking for 5 minutes. 14. Open the lid and place the tenderloin onto a cutting board for about 10-15 minutes before slicing. 15. Cut the tenderloin into desired-sized slices and serve.

Serving Suggestions: Serve with buttery mashed potatoes.
Variation Tip: Use a sharp knife to cut the tenderloin into slices.
Nutritional Information per Serving: Calories: 268 | Fat: 31.2g | Sat Fat: 7.9g | Carbohydrates: 3.2g | Fiber: 1.8g | Sugar: 0g | Protein: 44.1g

Vinegar London Broil Steak

Prep Time: 15 minutes | Cook Time: 7 minutes | Servings: 5

Ingredients:

1½ pounds London broil steak, trimmed
¼ cup red wine vinegar
1 tablespoon olive oil
1 tablespoon Worcestershire sauce
2 garlic cloves, minced

1-2 teaspoons fresh rosemary, chopped
1 teaspoon dried thyme
1½ tablespoons spicy mustard
1 teaspoon onion powder
Salt and ground black pepper, as required

Preparation:

1. With a meat mallet, pound each side of steak slightly. 2. In a large-sized plastic, sealable bag, place the remaining ingredients and mix. 3. Place the steak in bag and seal the bag. 4. Shake the bag vigorously to coat well. 5. Refrigerate to marinate for about 2-4 hours. 6. Remove the steak from the bag and set aside at room temperature for about 30 minutes. 7. Arrange the lightly greased "Grill Grate" in the crisper basket in the cooking pot of Ninja Foodi Smart XL Grill. 8. Close the Grill with lid and press "Power" button. 9. Select "Grill" and then use the set of arrows to the left of the display to adjust the temperature to "MAX". 10. Use the set of arrows to the right of the display to adjust the cook time to 7 minutes. 11. Press "Start/Stop" to begin preheating. When the display shows "Add Food", open the lid and place the steak onto the "Grill Grate". 12. With your hands, gently press down the steak. Close the Grill with lid. 13. After 4 minutes of cooking, flip the steak. 14. When the cooking time is completed, open the lid and place the steak onto a cutting board for about 10 minutes before slicing. 15. Cut the steak into desired-sized slices and serve.

Serving Suggestions: Serve alongside the buttered corn.
Variation Tip: The surface of the steak should be moist but not wet or sticky.
Nutritional Information per Serving: Calories: 344 | Fat: 16.9g | Sat Fat: 5.4g | Carbohydrates: 3g | Fiber: 0.7g | Sugar: 1.1g | Protein: 42.1g

Spiced T-Bone Steak

Prep Time: 10 minutes | Cook Time: 8 minutes | Servings: 2

Ingredients:

½ tablespoon paprika
¼ tablespoon red chili powder
¼ tablespoon ground coriander
½ tablespoon garlic powder

½ tablespoon onion powder
Salt and ground black pepper, as required
2 (1-inch) thick T-bone steaks

Preparation:

1. In a small-sized bowl, add all ingredients except for steak and mix until well combined. 2. Coat the steak with spice mixture generously. 3. Arrange the lightly greased "Grill Grate" in the crisper basket in the cooking pot of Ninja Foodi Smart XL Grill. 4. Close the Grill with lid and press "Power" button. 5. Select "Grill" and then use the set of arrows to the left of the display to adjust the temperature to "HI". 6. Use the set of arrows to the right of the display to adjust the cook time to 8 minutes. 7. Press "Start/Stop" to begin preheating. When the display shows "Add Food", open the lid and place the steaks onto the "Grill Grate". 8. With your hands, gently press down each steak. Close the Grill with lid. 9. After 4 minutes of cooking, flip the steaks. 10. When the cooking time is completed, open the lid and serve hot.

Serving Suggestions: Serve with your favorite veggies.
Variation Tip: Adjust the spice level according to your taste.
Nutritional Information per Serving: Calories: 623 | Fat: 34.1g | Sat Fat: 3.7g | Carbohydrates: 4.4g | Fiber: 1.3g | Sugar: 1.4g | Protein: 70.2g

Simple Rump Steak

Prep Time: 10 minutes | Cook Time: 10 minutes | Servings: 5

Ingredients:

1½ pounds aged rump steak, trimmed   2 tablespoons olive oil
Salt and ground black pepper, as required

Preparation:

1. Sprinkle the beef steak with salt and black pepper generously and then, drizzle with oil. 2. Arrange the lightly greased "Grill Grate" in the crisper basket in the cooking pot of Ninja Foodi Smart XL Grill. 3. Close the Grill with lid and press "Power" button. 4. Select "Grill" and then use the set of arrows to the left of the display to adjust the temperature to "MED". 5. Use the set of arrows to the right of the display to adjust the cook time to 10 minutes. 6. Press "Start/Stop" to begin preheating. When the display shows "Add Food", open the lid and place the steak onto the "Grill Grate". 7. With your hands, gently press down the steak. Close the Grill with lid. 8. After 5 minutes of cooking, flip the steak. 9. When the cooking time is completed, open the lid and place the steak onto a cutting board for about 10 minutes before slicing. 10. Cut the steak into desired-sized slices diagonally across the grain and serve.

Serving Suggestions: Serve with tomato salad.
Variation Tip: You can use butter instead of oil.
Nutritional Information per Serving: Calories: 292 | Fat: 13.8g | Sat Fat: 0.8g | Carbohydrates: 0g | Fiber: 0g | Sugar: 0g | Protein: 42.2g

Bacon-Wrapped Beef Tenderloin

Prep Time: 15 minutes | Cook Time: 12 minutes | Servings: 4

Ingredients:

8 bacon strips
4 (8-ounce) center-cut beef tenderloin filets

2 tablespoons olive oil, divided
Salt and ground black pepper, as required

Preparation:

1. Wrap 2 bacon strips around the entire outside of each beef filet. 2. With toothpicks, secure each filet. 3. Coat each wrapped filet with oil and sprinkle with salt and black pepper evenly. 4. Arrange the lightly greased "Grill Grate" in the crisper basket in the cooking pot of Ninja Foodi Smart XL Grill. 5. Close the Grill with lid and press "Power" button. 6. Select "Grill" and then use the set of arrows to the left of the display to adjust the temperature to "HI". 7. Use the set of arrows to the right of the display to adjust the cook time to 12 minutes. 8. Press "Start/Stop" to begin preheating. When the display shows "Add Food", open the lid and place the wrapped filets onto the "Grill Grate". 9. With your hands, gently press down each fillet. Close the Grill with lid. 10. After 6 minutes of cooking, flip the filets. 11. When the cooking time is completed, open the lid and transfer the filets onto a platter for about 10 minutes before slicing.

Serving Suggestions: Serve with lemony herbed couscous.
Variation Tip: Make sure to trim the beef tenderloon before cooking.
Nutritional Information per Serving: Calories: 841 | Fat: 52g | Sat Fat: 16.9g | Carbohydrates: 0.8g | Fiber: 0g | Sugar: 1g | Protein: 87.1g

Herbed Beef Kabobs

Prep Time: 15 minutes | Cook Time: 8 minutes | Servings: 6

Ingredients:

3 garlic cloves, minced
1 tablespoon fresh lemon zest, grated
2 teaspoons fresh rosemary, minced
2 teaspoons fresh parsley, minced
2 teaspoons fresh oregano, minced
2 teaspoons fresh thyme, minced

4 tablespoons olive oil
2 tablespoons fresh lemon juice
Salt and ground black pepper, as required
2 pounds beef sirloin, cut into cubes

Preparation:

1. In a bowl, add all the ingredients except the beef and mix well. 2. Add the beef and coat with the herb mixture generously. 3. Refrigerate to marinate for at least 20-30 minutes. 4. Remove the beef cubes from the marinade and thread onto metal skewers. 5. Arrange the lightly greased "Grill Grate" in the crisper basket in the cooking pot of Ninja Foodi Smart XL Grill. 6. Close the Grill with lid and press "Power" button. 7. Select "Grill" and then use the set of arrows to the left of the display to adjust the temperature to "HI". 8. Use the set of arrows to the right of the display to adjust the cook time to 8 minutes. 9. Press "Start/Stop" to begin preheating. When the display shows "Add Food", open the lid and place the skewers onto the "Grill Grate". 10. With your hands, gently press down each skewer. Close the Grill with lid. 11. After 4 minutes of cooking, flip the skewers. 12. When the cooking time is completed, open the lid and serve hot.

Serving Suggestions: Serve with steamed rice.

Variation Tip: Cut the beef into equal-sized cubes.

Nutritional Information per Serving: Calories: 369 | Fat: 18.9g | Sat Fat: 5g | Carbohydrates: 1.6g | Fiber: 0.6g | Sugar: 0.2g | Protein: 46.2g

Glazed Beef Kabobs

Prep Time: 15 minutes | Cook Time: 14 minutes | Servings: 5

Ingredients:

½ cup BBQ sauce
2 tablespoons Worcestershire sauce
2 tablespoons steak sauce
2 tablespoons vegetable oil
2 tablespoons white vinegar
¼ cup water

2-4 garlic cloves, minced
2 tablespoons dried onion, crushed
2 tablespoons sugar
Salt, as required
1½ pounds beef sirloin steak, cut into 1-inch cubes

Preparation:

1. In a medium non-stick saucepan, mix together all ingredients except for steak over medium heat and bring to a boil. 2. Remove the saucepan of marinade from heat and transfer into a large bowl. Set aside to cool. 3. After cooling, in the bowl of marinade, add steak cubes and coat well. Refrigerate for about 6-8 hours. 4. Remove steak cubes from bowl and discard any excess marinade. 5. Thread steak cubes onto metal skewers. 6. Arrange the lightly greased "Grill Grate" in the crisper basket in the cooking pot of Ninja Foodi Smart XL Grill. 7. Close the Grill with lid and press "Power" button. 8. Select "Grill" and then use the set of arrows to the left of the display to adjust the temperature to "MED". 9. Use the set of arrows to the right of the display to adjust the cook time to 14 minutes. 10. Press "Start/Stop" to begin preheating. When the display shows "Add Food", open the lid and place the skewer onto the "Grill Grate". 11. With your hands, gently press down each skewer. Close the Grill with lid. 12. After 7 minutes of cooking, flip the skewer. 13. When the cooking time is completed, open the lid and serve hot.

Serving Suggestions: Serve alongside the fresh greens.

Variation Tip: Use the BBQ sauce of your choice.

Nutritional Information per Serving: Calories: 469 | Fat: 17.5g | Sat Fat: 5.3g | Carbohydrates: 22.4g | Fiber: 0.3g | Sugar: 17.4g | Protein: 51.8g

Beef & Halloumi Burgers

Prep Time: 15 minutes | Cook Time: 16 minutes | Servings: 5

Ingredients:

1 pound ground beef
4½ ounces halloumi cheese, grated
1 egg
½ tablespoon fresh rosemary, finely
chopped
½ tablespoon fresh parsley, finely
chopped
1 teaspoon ground cumin
Salt and ground black pepper, as required

Preparation:

1. In a large-sized bowl, add all the ingredients and mix until well combined. 2. Make 5 equal-sized patties from the mixture. 3. Arrange the lightly greased "Grill Grate" in the crisper basket in the cooking pot of Ninja Foodi Smart XL Grill. 4. Close the Grill with lid and press "Power" button. 5. Select "Grill" and then use the set of arrows to the left of the display to adjust the temperature to "MED". 6. Use the set of arrows to the right of the display to adjust the cook time to 16 minutes. 7. Press "Start/Stop" to begin preheating. 8. When the display shows "Add Food", open the lid and place the patties onto the "Grill Grate". 9. With your hands, gently press down each patty. Close the Grill with lid. 10. After 8 minutes of cooking, flip the patties. 11. When the cooking time is completed, open the lid and serve hot.

Serving Suggestions: Serve with sweet & sour sauce.

Variation Tip: Strictly follow the ratio of ingredients.

Nutritional Information per Serving: Calories: 277 | Fat: 14.3g | Sat Fat: 7.7g | Carbohydrates: 1.1g | Fiber: 0.2g | Sugar: 0.7g | Protein: 34.2g

Herbed Beef Burgers

Prep Time: 15 minutes | Cook Time: 10 minutes | Servings: 4

Ingredients:

1 pound lean ground beef
¼ cup fresh parsley, chopped
¼ cup fresh cilantro, chopped
1 tablespoon fresh ginger, chopped
1 teaspoon ground cumin
1 teaspoon ground coriander
Salt and ground black pepper, as required

Preparation:

1. In a bowl, add the beef, ¼ cup of parsley, cilantro, ginger, spices, salt, and black pepper and mix until well combined. 2. Make 4 equal-sized patties from the mixture. 3. Arrange the lightly greased "Grill Grate" in the crisper basket in the cooking pot of Ninja Foodi Smart XL Grill. 4. Close the Grill with lid and press "Power" button. 5. Select "Grill" and then use the set of arrows to the left of the display to adjust the temperature to "MED". 6. Use the set of arrows to the right of the display to adjust the cook time to 10 minutes. 7. Press "Start/Stop" to begin preheating. 8. When the display shows "Add Food", open the lid and place the patties onto the "Grill Grate". 9. With your hands, gently press down each patty. Close the Grill with lid. 10. After 5 minutes of cooking, flip the patties. 11. When the cooking time is completed, open the lid and serve hot.

Serving Suggestions: Serve alongside the baby greens.

Variation Tip: Use best quality ground beef.

Nutritional Information per Serving: Calories: 219 | Fat: 7.3g | Sat Fat: 2.7g | Carbohydrates: 1.5g | Fiber: 0.4g | Sugar: 0.1g | Protein: 34.7g

Cheesy Beef & Spinach Burgers

Prep Time: 15 minutes | Cook Time: 14 minutes | Servings: 4

Ingredients:

1½ pounds ground beef

Salt and ground black pepper, as required

2 cups fresh spinach

½ cup mozzarella cheese, shredded

2 tablespoons Parmesan cheese, grated

Preparation:

1. In a bowl, add the beef, salt, and black pepper and mix until well combined. 2. Make 8 equal-sized patties from the mixture. 3. Arrange the patties onto a plate and refrigerate until using. 4. In a frying pan, add the spinach over medium-high heat and cook, covered for about 2 minutes or until wilted. 5. Drain the spinach and set aside to cool. 6. With your hands squeeze the spinach to extract the liquid completely. 7. Place the spinach to a cutting board and then, chop it. 8. In a bowl, add the chopped spinach and both cheese and mix well. 9. Place about ¼ cup of the spinach mixture in the center of 4 patties and top each with the remaining 4 patties. 10. With your fingers, press the edges firmly to seal the filling. 11. Then, press each patty slightly to flatten. 12. Arrange the lightly greased "Grill Grate" in the crisper basket in the cooking pot of Ninja Foodi Smart XL Grill. 13. Close the Grill with lid and press "Power" button. 14. Select "Grill" and then use the set of arrows to the left of the display to adjust the temperature to "MED". 15. Use the set of arrows to the right of the display to adjust the cook time to 12 minutes. 16. Press "Start/Stop" to begin preheating. When the display shows "Add Food", open the lid and place the patties onto the "Grill Grate". 17. With your hands, gently press down each patty. Close the Grill with lid. 18. After 6 minutes of cooking, flip the patties. 19. When the cooking time is completed, open the lid and serve hot.

Serving Suggestions: Serve with corn salad.

Variation Tip: Try to use freshly grated cheese.

Nutritional Information per Serving: Calories: 348 | Fat: 12.4g | Sat Fat: 5.1g | Carbohydrates: 0.7g | Fiber: 0.3g | Sugar: 0.1g | Protein: 54.5g

Beef & Sauerkraut Sandwich

Prep Time: 15 minutes | Cook Time: 5 minutes | Servings: 4

Ingredients:

⅓ cup sauerkraut, rinsed and drained

4 rye bread slices

4 teaspoons unsalted butter, softened

2 tablespoons prepared Thousand Island

dressing, divided

2 ounces Swiss cheese, sliced

4 ounces corned beef, thinly sliced

Preparation:

1. Brush one side of each bread slice with butter. 2. Place 4 bread slices onto a work surface, buttered side down. 3. Now spread dressing over the slices. 4. Place the cheese, corned beef, and sauerkraut over bread slices. 5. Top with the remaining bread, buttered side up. 6. Arrange the lightly greased "Grill Grate" in the crisper basket in the cooking pot of Ninja Foodi Smart XL Grill. 7. Close the Grill with lid and press "Power" button. 8. Select "Grill" and then use the set of arrows to the left of the display to adjust the temperature to "MED". 9. Use the set of arrows to the right of the display to adjust the cook time to 5 minutes. 10. Press "Start/Stop" to begin preheating. When the display shows "Add Food", open the lid and place the sandwiches onto the "Grill Grate". 11. With your hands, gently press down each sandwich. Close the Grill with lid. 12. After 3 minutes of cooking, flip the sandwiches. 13. When the cooking time is completed, open the lid and place the sandwiches onto a platter. 14. Cut 2 halves of each sandwich and serve warm.

Serving Suggestions: Serve with cheese sauce.

Variation Tip: Drain the sauerkraut thoroughly before using.

Nutritional Information per Serving: Calories: 240 | Fat: 15.1g | Sat Fat: 6.9g | Carbohydrates: 16.3g | Fiber: 1.7g | Sugar: 1.6g | Protein: 10.5g

Chipotle Pork Tenderloin

Prep Time: 10 minutes | Cook Time: 15 minutes | Servings: 4

Ingredients:

1 can chipotle chile in adobo sauce plus 1 teaspoon adobo sauce
½ cup fresh orange juice
3 tablespoons fresh lime juice
1 tablespoon red wine vinegar

1 garlic clove, minced
1 teaspoon dried oregano, crushed
½ teaspoon ground cumin
Salt and ground black pepper, as required
2 (8-ounce) pork tenderloins, trimmed

Preparation:

1. In a blender, add chipotle chiles and remaining ingredients except for pork tenderloin and pulse until smooth. 2. In a large re-sealable plastic bag, add chipotle Chile mixture and pork tenderloins. 3. Seal the bag of pork mixture tightly and shake to coat well. 4. Refrigerate to marinate for about 8 hours. 5. Arrange the lightly greased "Grill Grate" in the crisper basket in the cooking pot of Ninja Foodi Smart XL Grill. 6. Close the Grill with lid and press "Power" button. 7. Select "Grill" and then use the set of arrows to the left of the display to adjust the temperature to "HI". 8. Use the set of arrows to the right of the display to adjust the cook time to 15 minutes. 9. Press "Start/Stop" to begin preheating. When the display shows "Add Food", open the lid and place the tenderloins onto the "Grill Grate". 10. With your hands, gently press down each tenderloin. Close the Grill with lid. 11. Flip the tenderloins after every 4 minutes. 12. When the cooking time is completed, open the lid and place both pork tenderloins onto a cutting board for about 5 minutes before slicing. 13. Cut each tenderloin into desired-sized slices and serve.

Serving Suggestions: Serve with buttered asparagus.
Variation Tip: Don't forget to trim the tenderloin.
Nutritional Information per Serving: Calories: 195 | Fat: 5.3g | Sat Fat: 1.4g | Carbohydrates: 5.1g | Fiber: 2.5g | Sugar: 2.7g | Protein: 31.2g

Spiced Pork Tenderloin

Prep Time: 15 minutes | Cook Time: 36 minutes | Servings: 6

Ingredients:

2 teaspoons fennel seeds
2 teaspoons coriander seeds
2 teaspoons caraway seeds
1 teaspoon cumin seeds

½ of bay leaf
Salt and ground black pepper, as required
2 tablespoons fresh dill, chopped
2 (1-pound) pork tenderloins, trimmed

Preparation:

1. In a spice grinder, add fennel seeds, coriander seeds, caraway seeds, cumin seeds, and bay leaf and grind until finely powdered. 2. Add the salt and black pepper and mix well. 3. In a small-sized bowl, place 2 tablespoons of the spice rub. 4. In another small bowl, add remaining rub and dill and mix well. 5. Place 1 tenderloin over a piece of plastic wrap. 6. With a sharp knife, slice through the meat to within ½-inch of the opposite side. 7. Now, open the tenderloin like a book. 8. Cover the tenderloin with another plastic wrap and with a pounder, gently pound into ½-inch thickness. 9. Repeat with the remaining tenderloin. 10. Remove the plastic wrap and spread half of the spice and dill mixture over the center of each tenderloin. 11. Roll the tenderloin like a cylinder. 12. With a kitchen string, tie the roll at several places tightly. 13. Repeat with remaining tenderloin. 14. Rub each roll with spice mixture generously. 15. Cover the rolls with plastic wraps and refrigerate for at least 4-6 hours. 16. Remove the plastic wrap from tenderloins. 17. Arrange the lightly greased "Grill Grate" in the crisper basket in the cooking pot of Ninja Foodi Smart XL Grill. 18. Close the Grill with lid and press "Power" button. 19. Select "Grill" and then use the set of arrows to the left of the display to adjust the temperature to "MED". 20. Use the set of arrows to the right of the display to adjust the cook time to 18 minutes. 21. Press "Start/Stop" to begin preheating. When the display shows "Add Food", open the lid and place the pork rolls onto the "Grill Grate". 22. With your hands, gently press down each pork roll. Close the Grill with lid. 23. While cooking, flip the pork rolls occasionally. When the cooking time is completed, open the lid and place the pork rolls onto a cutting board. 24. With a piece of foil, cover each pork roll for at least 5 minutes before slicing. 25. Cut each pork roll into desired-sized slices and serve.

Serving Suggestions: Serve alongside the roasted Brussels sprout.
Variation Tip: Choose a pork tenderloin with pinkish-red color.
Nutritional Information per Serving: Calories: 313 | Fat: 12.6g | Sat Fat: 4.4g | Carbohydrates: 1.4g | Fiber: 0.7g | Sugar: 0g | Protein: 35.7g

Simple Pork Chops

Prep Time: 10 minutes | Cook Time: 18 minutes | Servings: 2

Ingredients:

2 (6-ounce) (½-inch thick) pork chops
Salt and ground black pepper, as required

Preparation:

1. Season the both sides of the pork chops with salt and black pepper generously. 2. Arrange the lightly greased "Grill Grate" in the crisper basket in the cooking pot of Ninja Foodi Smart XL Grill. 3. Close the Grill with lid and press "Power" button. 4. Select "Grill" and then use the set of arrows to the left of the display to adjust the temperature to "MED". 5. Use the set of arrows to the right of the display to adjust the cook time to 18 minutes. 6. Press "Start/Stop" to begin preheating. When the display shows "Add Food", open the lid and place the pork chops onto the "Grill Grate". 7. With your hands, gently press down each pork chop. Close the Grill with lid. 8. After 12 minutes of cooking, flip the chops. 9. When the cooking time is completed, open the lid and serve hot.
Serving Suggestions: Serve with a garnishing of fresh herbs.
Variation Tip: Season the pork chops evenly.
Nutritional Information per Serving: Calories: 544 | Fat: 42.3g | Sat Fat: 15.8g | Carbohydrates: 0g | Fiber: 0g | Sugar: 0g | Protein: 38.2g

Basil Pork Chops

Prep Time: 10 minutes | Cook Time: 12 minutes | Servings: 4

Ingredients:

¼ cup fresh basil leaves, minced
2 garlic cloves, minced
2 tablespoons butter, melted
2 tablespoons fresh lemon juice
Salt and ground black pepper, as required
4 (6-8-ounce) bone-in pork loin chops

Preparation:

1. In a baking dish, add the basil, garlic, butter, lemon juice, salt, and black pepper and mix well. 2. Add the chops and generously coat with the mixture. 3. Cover the baking dish and refrigerate for about 30-45 minutes. 4. Arrange the lightly greased "Grill Grate" in the crisper basket in the cooking pot of Ninja Foodi Smart XL Grill. 5. Close the Grill with lid and press "Power" button. 6. Select "Grill" and then use the set of arrows to the left of the display to adjust the temperature to "MED". 7. Use the set of arrows to the right of the display to adjust the cook time to 12 minutes. 8. Press "Start/Stop" to begin preheating. When the display shows "Add Food", open the lid and place the pork chops onto the "Grill Grate". 9. With your hands, gently press down each pork chop. Close the Grill with lid. 10. After 6 minutes of cooking, flip the pork chops. 11. When the cooking time is completed, open the lid and serve hot.
Serving Suggestions: Serve with cauliflower mash.
Variation Tip: Use unsalted butter.
Nutritional Information per Serving: Calories: 600 | Fat: 48.1g | Sat Fat: 19.6g | Carbohydrates: 0.7g | Fiber: 0.1g | Sugar: 0.2g | Protein: 38.5g

Marinated Pork Chops

Prep Time: 10 minutes | Cook Time: 13 minutes | Servings: 4

Ingredients:

¾ cup soy sauce
¾ cup brown sugar
1 onion, chopped
2 garlic cloves, minced
4 (6-ounce) boneless pork chops

Preparation:

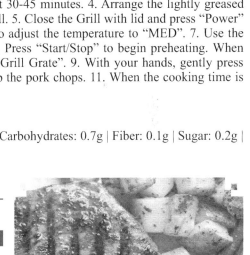
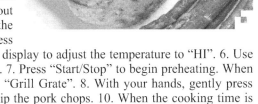

1. In a bowl, place all ingredients and mix well. 2. Refrigerate to marinate for about 4-6 hours. 3. Arrange the lightly greased "Grill Grate" in the crisper basket in the cooking pot of Ninja Foodi Smart XL Grill. 4. Close the Grill with lid and press "Power" button. 5. Select "Grill" and then use the set of arrows to the left of the display to adjust the temperature to "HI". 6. Use the set of arrows to the right of the display to adjust the cook time to 13 minutes. 7. Press "Start/Stop" to begin preheating. When the display shows "Add Food", open the lid and place the pork chops onto the "Grill Grate". 8. With your hands, gently press down each pork chop. Close the Grill with lid. 9. After 8 minutes of cooking, flip the pork chops. 10. When the cooking time is completed, open the lid and serve hot.
Serving Suggestions: Serve alongside the steamed veggies.
Variation Tip: Don't overcook the pork chops.
Nutritional Information per Serving: Calories: 385 | Fat: 6g | Sat Fat: 2g | Carbohydrates: 33.4g | Fiber: 1g | Sugar: 28.4g | Protein: 48.3g

Lemony Pork Chops

Prep Time: 15 minutes | Cook Time: 15 minutes | Servings: 6

Ingredients:

¼ cup fresh lemon juice

2 tablespoons vegetable oil

4 garlic cloves, minced

¼ teaspoon dried oregano

¼ teaspoon dried thyme

Salt and ground black pepper, as required

6 (4-ounce) boneless pork loin chops

Preparation:

1. In a large resealable bag, blend together lemon juice, oil, garlic, salt, dried herbs, salt and black pepper. 2. Place chops in the bag and seal it tightly. 3. Shake the bag to coat well and refrigerate overnight, flipping occasionally. 4. Remove the chops from bag and transfer the remaining marinade into a small saucepan. 5. Place the saucepan of the marinade over medium heat and bring to a boil. 6. Remove the saucepan of marinade from heat, and set aside. 7. Arrange the lightly greased "Grill Grate" in the crisper basket in the cooking pot of Ninja Foodi Smart XL Grill. 8. Close the Grill with lid and press "Power" button. 9. Select "Grill" and then use the set of arrows to the left of the display to adjust the temperature to "MED". 10. Use the set of arrows to the right of the display to adjust the cook time to 10 minutes. 11. Press "Start/Stop" to begin preheating. When the display shows "Add Food", open the lid and place the pork chops onto the "Grill Grate". 12. With your hands, gently press down each pork chop. Close the Grill with lid. 13. After 5 minutes of cooking, flip the chops and baste with cooked marinade. 14. When the cooking time is completed, open the lid and serve hot.

Serving Suggestions: Serve alongside the lettuce.

Variation Tip: You can use the oil of your choice.

Nutritional Information per Serving: Calories: 208 | Fat: 8.6g | Sat Fat: 2.3g | Carbohydrates: 0.9g | Fiber: 0.1g | Sugar: 0.2g | Protein: 29.9g

Spiced Lamb Chops

Prep Time: 15 minutes | Cook Time: 8 minutes | Servings: 4

Ingredients:

1 tablespoon fresh mint leaves, chopped

½ teaspoon garlic paste

½ teaspoon ground allspice

¼ teaspoon ground nutmeg

¼ teaspoon ground green cardamom

¼ teaspoon hot paprika

Salt and ground black pepper, as required

2 tablespoons olive oil

1 tablespoon fresh lemon juice

1 rack of lamb, trimmed and separated into 8 chops

Preparation:

1. In a large bowl, add all the ingredients except for chops and mix until well combined. 2. Add the chops and coat with the mixture generously. 3. Refrigerate to marinate for about 5-6 hours. 4. Arrange the lightly greased "Grill Grate" in the crisper basket in the cooking pot of Ninja Foodi Smart XL Grill. 5. Close the Grill with lid and press "Power" button. 6. Select "Grill" and then use the set of arrows to the left of the display to adjust the temperature to "HI". 7. Use the set of arrows to the right of the display to adjust the cook time to 8 minutes. 8. Press "Start/Stop" to begin preheating. When the display shows "Add Food", open the lid and place the chops onto the "Grill Grate". 9. With your hands, gently press down each chop. Close the Grill with lid. 10. After 4 minutes of cooking, flip the chops. 11. When the cooking time is completed, open the lid and serve hot.

Serving Suggestions: Serve alongside the greens of your choice.

Variation Tip: Separate the rack of lamb into equal-sized chops.

Nutritional Information per Serving: Calories: 368 | Fat: 20.4g | Sat Fat: 0.1g | Carbohydrates: 0.6g | Fiber: 0.2g | Sugar: 0.1g | Protein: 42.7g

Citrus Pork Chops

Prep Time: 10 minutes | Cook Time: 15 minutes | Servings: 6

Ingredients:

¼ cup extra-virgin olive oil
½ cup fresh orange juice
¼ cup fresh lime juice
½ cup fresh cilantro, finely chopped
¼ cup fresh mint leaves, finely chopped
4 garlic cloves, minced
1 tablespoon orange zest, grated

1 teaspoon grated lime zest, grated
1 teaspoon dried oregano
1 teaspoon ground cumin
Salt and ground black pepper, as required
6 thick-cut pork chops

Preparation:

1. In a bowl, add all ingredients and mix well. 2. Cover the bowl and refrigerate to marinate overnight. 3. Remove the pork chops from the bowl of marinade and drip off the excess marinade. 4. Arrange the lightly greased "Grill Grate" in the crisper basket in the cooking pot of Ninja Foodi Smart XL Grill. 5. Close the Grill with lid and press "Power" button. 6. Select "Grill" and then use the set of arrows to the left of the display to adjust the temperature to "MED". 7. Use the set of arrows to the right of the display to adjust the cook time to 15 minutes. Press "Start/Stop" to begin preheating. 8. When the display shows "Add Food", open the lid and place the pork chops onto the "Grill Grate". 9. With your hands, gently press down each pork chop. Close the Grill with lid. 10. After 8 minutes of cooking, flip the pork chops. 11. When the cooking time is completed, open the lid and serve hot.

Serving Suggestions: Serve alongside your favourite veggies.
Variation Tip: Don't cook chops straight from the refrigerator
Nutritional Information per Serving: Calories: 339 | Fat: 22.6g | Sat Fat: 4.2g | Carbohydrates: 4.2g | Fiber: 0.7g | Sugar: 1.8g | Protein: 32.5g

Orange Glazed Pork Chops

Prep Time: 15 minutes | Cook Time: 12 minutes | Servings: 6

Ingredients:

2 tablespoons fresh ginger root, minced
1 teaspoon garlic, minced
2 tablespoons fresh orange zest, grated finely

½ cup fresh orange juice
1 teaspoon chili garlic paste
2 tablespoons soy sauce
6 (½-inch thick) pork loin chops

Preparation:

1. In a bowl, blend all ingredients except for pork chops. 2. Add chops and coat with marinade generously. 3. Cover the bowl of chops and refrigerate to marinate for about 2 hours, tossing occasionally. 4. Arrange the lightly greased "Grill Grate" in the crisper basket in the cooking pot of Ninja Foodi Smart XL Grill. 5. Close the Grill with lid and press "Power" button. 6. Select "Grill" and then use the set of arrows to the left of the display to adjust the temperature to "MED". 7. Use the set of arrows to the right of the display to adjust the cook time to 12 minutes. 8. Press "Start/Stop" to begin preheating. When the display shows "Add Food", open the lid and place the pork chops onto the "Grill Grate". 9. With your hands, gently press down each pork chop. Close the Grill with lid. 10. After 6 minutes of cooking, flip the pork chops. 11. When the cooking time is completed, open the lid and serve hot.

Serving Suggestions: Serve with boiled white rice.
Variation Tip: Use freshly squeezed orange juice.
Nutritional Information per Serving: Calories: 560 | Fat: 42.3g | Sat Fat: 15.9g | Carbohydrates: 3.5g | Fiber: 0.3g | Sugar: 1.9g | Protein: 38.8g

Ketchup Glazed Pork Chops

Prep Time: 10 minutes | Cook Time: 14 minutes | Servings: 6

Ingredients:

2 garlic cloves, crushed
½ cup ketchup
2⅔ tablespoons honey

2 tablespoons low-sodium soy sauce
6 (4-ounce) (1-inch thick) pork chops

Preparation:

1. For glaze: in a bowl, add garlic, ketchup, honey and soy sauce and beat until well combined. 2. Arrange the lightly greased "Grill Grate" in the crisper basket in the cooking pot of Ninja Foodi Smart XL Grill. 3. Close the Grill with lid and press "Power" button. 4. Select "Grill" and then use the set of arrows to the left of the display to adjust the temperature to "MED". 5. Use the set of arrows to the right of the display to adjust the cook time to 14 minutes. 6. Press "Start/Stop" to begin preheating. When the display shows "Add Food", open the lid and place the pork chops onto the "Grill Grate". 7. With your hands, gently press down each pork chop. Close the Grill with lid. 8. After 7 minutes of cooking, flip the pork chops. 9. When the cooking time is completed, open the lid and serve hot.

Serving Suggestions: Serve alongside the potato mash.
Variation Tip: Coat the chops with glaze evenly.
Nutritional Information per Serving: Calories: 414 | Fat: 28.3g | Sat Fat: 10.6g | Carbohydrates: 13.4g | Fiber: 0.1g | Sugar: 12.6g | Protein: 26.3g

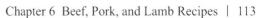

Brined Pork Chops

Prep Time: 15 minutes | Cook Time: 17 minutes | Servings: 4

Ingredients:

2 cups cold water
¼ cup sugar
¼ cup kosher salt
2 cups ice water
4 (8-ounce) (1-inch thick) center-cut pork rib chop
3 tablespoons paprika

½ teaspoon ground chipotle pepper
1 teaspoon garlic powder
1 teaspoon onion powder
1 teaspoon ground cumin
Coarsely ground black pepper, as required
2 tablespoons canola oil

Preparation:

1. For brine: in a large saucepan, add cold water, sugar, and salt over medium heat and cook until salt and sugar are dissolved, dissolved continuously. 2. Remove from the heat and add in 2 cups of ice water. 3. Set aside at room temperature to cool. 4. In a large resealable plastic bag, add the brine and pork chops. 5. Seal the bag and press to coat the chops. 6. Place the bag in a baking dish and refrigerate for about 8-12 hours. 7. Remove chops from brine and rinse under cold running water. 8. With paper towels, pat dry the chops. 9. In a small bowl, mix together the spices. 10. Brush the chops with oil evenly and then coat with spice mixture. 11. Set aside at room temperature for about 30 minutes. 12. Arrange the lightly greased "Grill Grate" in the crisper basket in the cooking pot of Ninja Foodi Smart XL Grill. 13. Close the Grill with lid and press "Power" button. Select "Grill" and then use the set of arrows to the left of the display to adjust the temperature to "MED". 14. Use the set of arrows to the right of the display to adjust the cook time to 12 minutes. Press "Start/Stop" to begin preheating. 15. When the display shows "Add Food", open the lid and place the pork chops onto the "Grill Grate". 16. With your hands, gently press down each pork chop. Close the Grill with lid. 17. After 6 minutes of cooking, flip the pork chops. 18. When the cooking time is completed, open the lid and serve hot.

Serving Suggestions: Serve with buttered rice.

Variation Tip: Rinse the pork chops thoroughly to remove the brine.

Nutritional Information per Serving: Calories: 556 | Fat: 34.1g | Sat Fat: 9.7g | Carbohydrates: 16.9g | Fiber: 2.2g | Sugar: 13.5g | Protein: 47.4g

Glazed Pork Ribs

Prep Time: 15 minutes | Cook Time: 55 minutes | Servings: 8

Ingredients:

2 tablespoons olive oil
1 small onion, minced
1½ cups honey
1 cup Dijon mustard
½ cup cider vinegar

3 tablespoons red pepper flakes, crushed
1 teaspoon Cajun seasoning
Salt and ground black pepper, as required
2 (2-pound) slabs pork baby back ribs

Preparation:

1. In a sauté pan, heat oil over medium heat and sauté onion for about 5 minutes. 2. Add honey, mustard, vinegar, red pepper flakes, Cajun seasoning, salt, and black pepper and stir to combine. 3. Now adjust the heat to low and simmer for about 5 minutes, stirring occasionally. 4. Remove from heat and set aside. 5. Sprinkle ribs with salt and pepper generously. 6. Arrange the lightly greased "Grill Grate" in the crisper basket in the cooking pot of Ninja Foodi Smart XL Grill. 7. Close the Grill with lid and press "Power" button. 8. Select "Grill" and then use the set of arrows to the left of the display to adjust the temperature to "MED". 9. Use the set of arrows to the right of the display to adjust the cook time to 30 minutes. 10. Press "Start/Stop" to begin preheating. When the display shows "Add Food", open the lid and place the ribs onto the "Grill Grate". 11. With your hands, gently press down the ribs. Close the Grill with lid. 12. After 20 minutes of cooking, flip the ribs. 13. When the cook time finished, cook again for 15 minutes. 14. Flip the ribs and coat with sauce once every 5 minutes. Meanwhile, heat the remaining sauce. 15. When the cooking time is completed, open the lid and place the ribs onto a platter. 16. Top with sauce and serve.

Serving Suggestions: Serve alongside the fresh baby greens.

Variation Tip: You can use the spices of your choice.

Nutritional Information per Serving: Calories: 899 | Fat: 59.3g | Sat Fat: 20.7g | Carbohydrates: 55.1g | Fiber: 1.9g | Sugar: 53.1g | Protein: 38g

Spiced Leg of Lamb

Prep Time: 15 minutes | Cook Time: 1 hour 10 minutes | Servings: 10

Ingredients:

6 garlic cloves, minced
Salt and ground black pepper, as required
1 teaspoon ground cumin
1 teaspoon ground cinnamon
1 teaspoon ground cardamom
1 teaspoon paprika
½ teaspoon cayenne powder
2 tablespoons olive oil
1 (4-pound) boneless leg of lamb, butterflied and trimmed

Preparation:

1. In a small bowl, add the garlic cloves, salt and black pepper and with the back of a spoon, mash until a paste forms. 2. Add the spices and stir to combine. 3. Place the leg of lamb onto a smooth surface, cut-side up. 4. Spread ¾ of the mixture in the center, leaving 1-inch border from both sides. 5. Roll the short side to seal the spice mixture and with a kitchen string, tie at many places to form a football like shape. 6. Rub the outer side of roll with remaining spice mixture. 7. With a plastic wrap, cover the roll loosely and refrigerate for at least 2 hours. 8. Arrange the lightly greased "Grill Grate" in the crisper basket in the cooking pot of Ninja Foodi Smart XL Grill. 9. Close the Grill with lid and press "Power" button. 10. Select "Grill" and then use the set of arrows to the left of the display to adjust the temperature to "MED". 11. Use the set of arrows to the right of the display to adjust the cook time to 30 minutes. 12. When the display shows "Add Food", open the lid and place the lamb roll onto the "Grill Grate". 13. With your hands, gently press down the lamb roll. Close the Grill with lid. 14. When the cooking time is completed, flip the lamb and cook again for 30 minutes. 15. Then cook for 10 minutes, halfway through cooking flip once. 16. When the lamb has cooked, open the lid and place the lamb roll onto a cutting board for about 10-20 minutes before slicing. 17. With a sharp knife, cut the roll into desired size slices and serve.

Serving Suggestions: Serve with steamed cauliflower.

Variation Tip: Look for a leg of lamb with light red meat.

Nutritional Information per Serving: Calories: 367 | Fat: 16.2g | Sat Fat: 5.2g | Carbohydrates: 1.2g | Fiber: 0.3g | Sugar: 0.1g | Protein: 51.2g

Spiced Pork Ribs

Prep Time: 10 minutes | Cook Time: 22 minutes | Servings: 8

Ingredients:

2 teaspoons chipotle chile powder
2 teaspoons ancho chile powder
1 teaspoon ground cumin
1 teaspoon garlic powder
Salt, as required
3½ pounds country-style pork ribs

Preparation:

1. In a bowl, mix together all spices. 2. Add ribs and rub with spice mixture generously. 3. Cover and refrigerate to marinate for at least 8 hours. 4. Remove from refrigerator and place the ribs aside at room temperature for about 1 hour. 5. Arrange the lightly greased "Grill Grate" in the crisper basket in the cooking pot of Ninja Foodi Smart XL Grill. 6. Close the Grill with lid and press "Power" button. 7. Select "Grill" and then use the set of arrows to the left of the display to adjust the temperature to "MED". 8. Use the set of arrows to the right of the display to adjust the cook time to 22 minutes. 9. Press "Start/Stop" to begin preheating. When the display shows "Add Food", open the lid and place the ribs onto the "Grill Grate". 10. With your hands, gently press down the ribs. Close the Grill with lid. 11. After 11 minutes of cooking, flip the ribs. 12. When the cooking time is completed, open the lid and serve hot.

Serving Suggestions: Serve alongside the garlicky broccoli.

Variation Tip: Look for the ribs with some marbling in the meat.

Nutritional Information per Serving: Calories: 287 | Fat: 7g | Sat Fat: 2.4g | Carbohydrates: 0.4g | Fiber: 0.1g | Sugar: 0.1g | Protein: 52g

Lemony Pork Kabobs

Prep Time: 15 minutes | Cook Time: 12 minutes | Servings: 5

Ingredients:

¼ cup extra-virgin olive oil
3 tablespoons lemon juice
2 tablespoons red wine vinegar
3 garlic cloves, minced
1 tablespoon fresh thyme, chopped

1 tablespoon fresh oregano, chopped
1 teaspoon lemon zest, grated
Salt and ground black pepper, as required
1½ pounds pork tenderloin, cut into
1-inch cubes

Preparation:

1. In a large bowl, add all the ingredients except for pork cubes and mix until well combined. 2. Add the pork cubes and coat with the mixture generously. 3. Cover the bowl and refrigerate to marinate overnight. 4. Arrange the lightly greased "Grill Grate" in the crisper basket in the cooking pot of Ninja Foodi Smart XL Grill. 5. Close the Grill with lid and press "Power" button. 6. Select "Grill" and then use the set of arrows to the left of the display to adjust the temperature to "MED". 7. Use the set of arrows to the right of the display to adjust the cook time to 12 minutes. 8. Press "Start/Stop" to begin preheating. When the display shows "Add Food", open the lid and place the skewers onto the "Grill Grate". 9. With your hands, gently press down each skewer. Close the Grill with lid. 10. While cooking, flip the skewers after every 3 minutes. 11. When the cooking time is completed, open the lid and serve hot.

Serving Suggestions: Serve with a drizzling of lemon juice.
Variation Tip: Use uniform-size pork cubes.
Nutritional Information per Serving: Calories: 292 | Fat: 15.1g | Sat Fat: 3.2g | Carbohydrates: 1.9g | Fiber: 0.7g | Sugar: 0.3g | Protein: 36g

Pork & Carrot Burgers

Prep Time: 15 minutes | Cook Time: 14 minutes | Servings: 4

Ingredients:

1 pound ground pork
1 small carrot, peeled and finely chopped
1 large onion, finely chopped
1 tablespoon garlic, minced

2 medium eggs
¼ cup breadcrumbs
1 tablespoon Worcestershire sauce

Preparation:

1. In a bowl, blend together all ingredients. 2. Place the mixture in a refrigerator for an hour. 3. Make desired-sized patties from mixture. 4. Arrange the lightly greased "Grill Grate" in the crisper basket in the cooking pot of Ninja Foodi Smart XL Grill. 5. Close the Grill with lid and press "Power" button. 6. Select "Grill" and then use the set of arrows to the left of the display to adjust the temperature to "MED". 7. Use the set of arrows to the right of the display to adjust the cook time to 14 minutes. 8. Press "Start/Stop" to begin preheating. When the display shows "Add Food", open the lid and place the patties onto the "Grill Grate". 9. With your hands, gently press down the patties. Close the Grill with lid. 10. After 7 minutes of cooking, flip the patties. 11. When the cooking time is completed, open the lid and serve hot.

Serving Suggestions: Serve over the hamburger buns.
Variation Tip: Use breadcrumbs of your choice.
Nutritional Information per Serving: Calories: 247 | Fat: 6.6g | Sat Fat: 2.1g | Carbohydrates: 11.2g | Fiber: 1.5g | Sugar: 3.6g | Protein: 34g

Rosemary Lamb Chops

Prep Time: 10 minutes | Cook Time: 8 minutes | Servings: 4

Ingredients:

1 garlic clove, minced
1 tablespoon fresh rosemary leaves, minced

Salt and ground black pepper, as required
4 lamb loin chops

Preparation:

1. In a bowl, add the garlic, rosemary, salt, and black pepper and mix well. 2. Coat the lamb chops with the herb mixture generously. 3. Arrange the lightly greased "Grill Grate" in the crisper basket in the cooking pot of Ninja Foodi Smart XL Grill. 4. Close the Grill with lid and press "Power" button. 5. Select "Grill" and then use the set of arrows to the left of the display to adjust the temperature to "HI". 6. Use the set of arrows to the right of the display to adjust the cook time to 8 minutes. 7. Press "Start/Stop" to begin preheating. When the display shows "Add Food", open the lid and place the lamb chops onto the "Grill Grate". 8. With your hands, gently press down each lamb chop. Close the Grill with lid. 9. After 4 minutes of cooking, flip the lamb chops. 10. When the cooking time is completed, open the lid and serve hot.

Serving Suggestions: Serve the chops with grilled zucchini.
Variation Tip: Lamb chops should contain just the right amount of marbling.
Nutritional Information per Serving: Calories: 295 | Fat: 10.5g | Sat Fat: 3.8g | Carbohydrates: 2.8g | Fiber: 0.4g | Sugar: 0g | Protein: 41.9g

Lemony Lamb Chops

Prep Time: 10 minutes | Cook Time: 9 minutes | Servings: 4

Ingredients:

¼ cup olive oil
2 tablespoons fresh lemon juice
2 tablespoons fresh oregano, chopped
1 teaspoon garlic, minced

Salt and ground black pepper, as required
4 (8-ounce) (½-inch-thick) lamb shoulder blade chops

Preparation:

1. Place all ingredients in a bowl and beat until well combined. 2. Place the chops and marinade into a large-sized sealable plastic bag. 3. Seal the bag and shake vigorously to coat evenly. 4. Set aside at room temperature for about 1 hour. 5. Remove the lamb chops from bag and discard the marinade. 6. With paper towels, pat dry the lamb chops. 7. Season the lamb chops with a little salt. 8. Arrange the lightly greased "Grill Grate" in the crisper basket in the cooking pot of Ninja Foodi Smart XL Grill. 9. Close the Grill with lid and press "Power" button. 10. Select "Grill" and then use the set of arrows to the left of the display to adjust the temperature to "HI". Use the set of arrows to the right of the display to adjust the cook time to 9 minutes. 11. Press "Start/Stop" to begin preheating. When the display shows "Add Food", open the lid and place the lamb chops onto the "Grill Grate". 12. With your hands, gently press down each lamb chop. Close the Grill with lid. 13. After 5 minutes of cooking, flip the lamb chops. 14. When the cooking time is completed, open the lid and serve hot.

Serving Suggestions: Serve with yogurt sauce.
Variation Tip: Allow the lamb chops to reach room temperature before cooking.
Nutritional Information per Serving: Calories: 459 | Fat: 31g | Sat Fat: 7.9g | Carbohydrates: 1.8g | Fiber: 1g | Sugar: 0.3g | Protein: 44.5g

Tangy Lamb Chops

Prep Time: 10 minutes | Cook Time: 8 minutes | Servings: 8

Ingredients:

¼ cup olive oil
¼ cup balsamic vinegar
2 tablespoons fresh lemon juice
3-4 garlic cloves, minced

2 teaspoons dried rosemary, crushed
Salt and ground black pepper, as required
8 (1-inch thick) lamb chops

Preparation:

1. In a bowl, blend together oil, vinegar, lemon juice, garlic, rosemary, salt, and black pepper. 2. Add chops and coat with marinade generously. 3. Cover and refrigerate to marinate for about 4-5 hours. 4. Remove the bowl of chops from refrigerator and set aside at room temperature for at least 30 minutes. 5. Arrange the lightly greased "Grill Grate" in the crisper basket in the cooking pot of Ninja Foodi Smart XL Grill. 6. Close the Grill with lid and press "Power" button. 7. Select "Grill" and then use the set of arrows to the left of the display to adjust the temperature to "MED". 8. Use the set of arrows to the right of the display to adjust the cook time to 8 minutes. 9. Press "Start/Stop" to begin preheating. When the display shows "Add Food", open the lid and place the chops onto the "Grill Grate". 10. With your hands, gently press down each chop. Close the Grill with lid. 11. After 4 minutes of cooking, flip the chops. 12. When the cooking time is completed, open the lid and serve hot.

Serving Suggestions: Serve alongside the beans salad.
Variation Tip: Don't forget to grease the grill grate.
Nutritional Information per Serving: Calories: 375 | Fat: 18.8g | Sat Fat: 5.4g | Carbohydrates: 0.5g | Fiber: 0g | Sugar: 0.1g | Protein: 47.9g

Minty Lamb Chops

Prep Time: 10 minutes | Cook Time: 20 minutes | Servings: 4

Ingredients:

1½ pounds lamb loin chops, trimmed
1 tablespoon fresh lemon juice
¼ cup fresh parsley, chopped
2 tablespoons fresh mint leaves, chopped

1 tablespoon olive oil
Salt and ground black pepper, as required

Preparation:

1. In a bowl, add lamb loin chops, lemon juice, parsley, mint, oil, salt, and black pepper and mix well. 2. Arrange the lightly greased "Grill Grate" in the crisper basket in the cooking pot of Ninja Foodi Smart XL Grill. 3. Close the Grill with lid and press "Power" button. 4. Select "Grill" and then use the set of arrows to the left of the display to adjust the temperature to "MED". 5. Use the set of arrows to the right of the display to adjust the cook time to 20 minutes. 6. Press "Start/Stop" to begin preheating. When the display shows "Add Food", open the lid and place the lamb chops onto the "Grill Grate". 7. With your hands, gently press down each lamb chop. Close the Grill with lid. 8. After 10 minutes of cooking, flip the lamb chops. 9. When the cooking time is completed, open the lid and serve hot.

Serving Suggestions: Mashed potatoes make a classic pairing with lamb chops.
Variation Tip: Lamb chops that have dried edges and do not smell fresh should not be purchased.
Nutritional Information per Serving: Calories: 268 | Fat: 16.1g | Sat Fat: 5g | Carbohydrates: 0.6g | Fiber: 0.3g | Sugar: 0.1g | Protein: 48g

Garlicky Lamb Chops

Prep Time: 10 minutes | Cook Time: 6 minutes | Servings: 6

Ingredients:

4 garlic cloves, minced

1 Serrano pepper, chopped

2 tablespoons fresh rosemary, chopped

¼ teaspoon cayenne powder

Salt and ground black pepper, as required

1 tablespoon fresh lemon juice

2 tablespoons olive oil

6 (6-ounce) (¾-inch thick) lamb chops

Preparation:

1. In a food processor, add garlic and remaining ingredients except chops and pulse until paste forms. 2. Transfer the paste into a large bowl. 3. Add chops and coat with paste generously. 4. Cover the bowl of chops and refrigerate for at least 1-2 hours. 5. Remove the bowl of chops from a refrigerator and set aside at room temperature for at least 20 minutes before cooking. 6. Arrange the lightly greased "Grill Grate" in the crisper basket in the cooking pot of Ninja Foodi Smart XL Grill. 7. Close the Grill with lid and press "Power" button. 8. Select "Grill" and then use the set of arrows to the left of the display to adjust the temperature to "HI". 9. Use the set of arrows to the right of the display to adjust the cook time 6 minutes. 10. Press "Start/Stop" to begin preheating. When the display shows "Add Food", open the lid and place the chops onto the "Grill Grate". 11. With your hands, gently press down each chop. Close the Grill with lid. 12. After 3 minutes of cooking, flip the chops. 13. When the cooking time is completed, open the lid and serve hot.

Serving Suggestions: Serve alongside the yogurt dip.

Variation Tip: Lamb chops with dried-out edges should not be purchased.

Nutritional Information per Serving: Calories: 363 | Fat: 17.4g | Sat Fat: 5.2g | Carbohydrates: 1.4g | Fiber: 0.6g | Sugar: 0.1g | Protein: 48g

Herbed Rack of Lamb

Prep Time: 15 minutes | Cook Time: 25 minutes | Servings: 8

Ingredients:

2 (2½-pounds) racks of lamb, chine bones removed and trimmed

Salt and ground black pepper, as required

2 tablespoons Dijon mustard

2 teaspoons fresh rosemary, chopped

2 teaspoons fresh parsley, chopped

2 teaspoons fresh thyme, chopped

Preparation:

1. Season the rack of lamb evenly with salt and black pepper. 2. Coat the meaty sides of racks with mustard, followed by fresh herbs, pressing gently. 3. Arrange the lightly greased "Grill Grate" in the crisper basket in the cooking pot of Ninja Foodi Smart XL Grill. 4. Close the Grill with lid and press "Power" button. 5. Select "Grill" and then use the set of arrows to the left of the display to adjust the temperature to "HI". 6. Use the set of arrows to the right of the display to adjust the cook time to 25 minutes. 7. Press "Start/Stop" to begin preheating. When the display shows "Add Food", open the lid and place the racks of lamb onto the "Grill Grate". 8. With your hands, gently press down each rack of lamb. Close the Grill with lid. 9. While cooking, flip the racks of lamb after every 9 minutes. 10. When the cooking time is completed, open the lid and place racks of lamb onto a cutting board for about 10 minutes. 11. Carve the racks of lamb into chops and serve.

Serving Suggestions: Serve longside the lemon wedges.

Variation Tip: Make sure to remove the silver skin from the rack of lamb.

Nutritional Information per Serving: Calories: 532 | Fat: 21g | Sat Fat: 7.5g | Carbohydrates: 0.6g | Fiber: 0.4g | Sugar: 0g | Protein: 79.8g

Lamb Burgers

Prep Time: 15 minutes | Cook Time: 8 minutes | Servings: 6

Ingredients:

2 pounds lean ground lamb
1 large onion, finely chopped
2 garlic cloves, minced
1 green chili pepper, seeded and chopped
1 tablespoon fresh cilantro, chopped
2 eggs, beaten

2 teaspoons prepared mustard
1 tablespoon garam masala powder
1 tablespoon dry fenugreek leaves, crushed
Salt, as required

Preparation:

1. In a bowl, blend together all ingredients. 2. Place the mixture in refrigerator for an hour. 3. Make 12 equal-sized sized patties from mixture. 4. Arrange the lightly greased "Grill Grate" in the crisper basket in the cooking pot of Ninja Foodi Smart XL Grill. 5. Close the Grill with lid and press "Power" button. 6. Select "Grill" and then use the set of arrows to the left of the display to adjust the temperature to "MED". 7. Use the set of arrows to the right of the display to adjust the cook time to 8 minutes. 8. Press "Start/Stop" to begin preheating. When the display shows "Add Food", open the lid and place the patties onto the "Grill Grate". 9. With your hands, gently press down the patties. Close the Grill with lid. 10. After 4 minutes of cooking, flip the patties. 11. When the cooking time is completed, open the lid and serve hot.

Serving Suggestions: Serve with tzatziki sauce.
Variation Tip: For the best result, grind your meat at home.
Nutritional Information per Serving: Calories: 334 | Fat: 32.2g | Sat Fat: 9.9g | Carbohydrates: 4g | Fiber: 1.1g | Sugar: 1.2g | Protein: 2.7g

Simple Sirloin Steak

Prep Time: 5 minutes | Cook Time: 7 minutes | Servings: 4

Ingredients:

2 (5-ounce) sirloin steaks, trimmed   Salt and ground black pepper, as required

Preparation:

1. Season the steak with salt and black pepper evenly. 2. Arrange the lightly greased "Grill Grate" in the crisper basket in the cooking pot of Ninja Foodi Smart XL Grill. 3. Close the Grill with lid and press "Power" button. 4. Select "Grill" and then use the set of arrows to the left of the display to adjust the temperature to "HI". 5. Use the set of arrows to the right of the display to adjust the cook time to 7 minutes. 6. Press "Start/Stop" to begin preheating. 7. When the display shows "Add Food", open the lid and place the steaks onto the "Grill Grate". 8. With your hands, gently press down each steak. Close the Grill with lid. 9. After 4 minutes of cooking, flip the steaks. 10. When the cooking time is completed, open the lid and serve hot.

Serving Suggestions: Serve alongside the glazed carrots.
Variation Tip: Add herbs as you like.
Nutritional Information per Serving: Calories: 263 | Fat: 8.8g | Sat Fat: 3.3g | Carbohydrates: 0g | Fiber: 0g | Sugar: 0g | Protein: 43g

Lamb Chops with Apple Sauce

Prep Time: 15 minutes | Cook Time: 12 minutes | Servings: 8

Ingredients:

Apple Sauce:
3 sprigs parsley leaves
½ cup mint leaves
1 apple, sliced and cored
Lamb Chops:
¼ cup olive oil
1 rack of lamb
3 cloves garlic, minced

1 tablespoon lemon juice
⅓ cup olive oil

Salt and black pepper, to taste
2 teaspoons rosemary, chopped

Preparation:

1. Select the "Grill" button on Ninja Foodi Smart XL Grill and regulate the settings at MED for 12 minutes. 2. Merge all the ingredients of apple sauce into a blender and blend well. 3. Pour the apple sauce in a jar and refrigerate. 4. In a large bowl, put all the lamb marinade ingredients and mix thoroughly. 5. Slice rack of lambs into chops and rub the marinade over the chops. 6. Marinate for about 30 minutes and keep aside. 7. Arrange the lamb chops in the Ninja Foodi when it displays "Add Food". 8. Grill for about 12 minutes, flipping once in between. 9. Dole out in a platter and serve warm.

Serving Suggestions: You can also serve it with apple sauce.
Variation Tip: To add taste variation, you could add dried basil leave.
Nutritional Information per Serving: Calories: 271 | Fat: 20.3g | Sat Fat: 4.5g | Carbohydrates: 5g | Fiber: 1.2g | Sugar: 3g | Protein: 17.6g

Marinated Rib-Eye Steak

Prep Time: 15 minutes | Cook Time: 11 minutes | Servings: 3

Ingredients:

3 tablespoons balsamic vinegar
3 tablespoons soy sauce
1 tablespoon honey
1 tablespoon olive oil

¼ teaspoon Worcestershire sauce
1 tablespoon garlic, minced
Freshly ground black pepper, as required
2 (8-ounce) rib-eye steaks

Preparation:

1. In a bowl, place all ingredients except for steaks and mix well. 2. Add the steaks and coat with marinade generously. 3. Refrigerate to marinate for 4-8 hours. 4. Arrange the lightly greased "Grill Grate" in the crisper basket in the cooking pot of Ninja Foodi Smart XL Grill. 5. Close the Grill with lid and press "Power" button. 6. Select "Grill" and then use the set of arrows to the left of the display to adjust the temperature to "HI". 7. Use the set of arrows to the right of the display to adjust the cook time to 11 minutes. 8. Press "Start/Stop" to begin preheating. 9. When the display shows "Add Food", open the lid and place the steaks onto the "Grill Grate". 10. With your hands, gently press down each steak. Close the Grill with lid. 11. After 6 minutes of cooking, flip the steaks. 12. When the cooking time is completed, open the lid and transfer the steaks onto a cutting board for about 5 minutes before slicing. 13. Cut each steak into 2 equal-sized portions and serve.

Serving Suggestions: Serve with lemony herbed couscous.
Variation Tip: You can use tamari instead of soy sauce.
Nutritional Information per Serving: Calories: 398 | Fat: 20.7g | Sat Fat: 6g | Carbohydrates: 8.2g | Fiber: 0.2g | Sugar: 6.2g | Protein: 42.1g

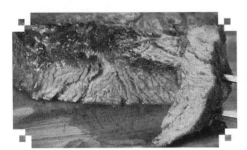

Spiced Rib-Eye Steak

Prep Time: 15 minutes | Cook Time: 12 minutes | Servings: 8

Ingredients:

2 (1½-pound) rib-eye steaks
1 teaspoon ground cumin
1 teaspoon ground coriander
1 teaspoon smoked paprika

1 teaspoon cayenne powder
1 teaspoon garlic powder
Salt and ground black pepper, as required

Preparation:

1. In a small-sized bowl, blend together the spices, salt, and black pepper. 2. Rub the steaks with spice mixture generously. 3. Arrange the lightly greased "Grill Grate" in the crisper basket in the cooking pot of Ninja Foodi Smart XL Grill. 4. Close the Grill with lid and press "Power" button. 5. Select "Grill" and then use the set of arrows to the left of the display to adjust the temperature to "HI". 6. Use the set of arrows to the right of the display to adjust the cook time to 12 minutes. 7. Press "Start/Stop" to begin preheating. 8. When the display shows "Add Food", open the lid and place the steaks onto the "Grill Grate". 9. With your hands, gently press down each steak. Close the Grill with lid. 10. After 6 minutes of cooking, flip the steaks. 11. When cooking time is completed, open the lid and place the steaks onto a cutting board for about 5 minutes befire slicing. 12. Cut each steak into desired-sized slices and serve.

Serving Suggestions: Serve with a topping of herb butter.
Variation Tip: Don't overcook your steak.
Nutritional Information per Serving: Calories: 467 | Fat: 37.6g | Sat Fat: 15.1g | Carbohydrates: 0g | Fiber: 0g | Sugar: 0g | Protein: 30.1g

Pork Spare Ribs

Prep Time: 15 minutes | Cook Time: 18 minutes | Servings: 6

Ingredients:

½ cup rice vinegar
6 garlic cloves, minced
2 tablespoons soy sauce
12 (1-inch) pork spare ribs

2 tablespoons olive oil
Salt and black pepper, to taste
½ cup cornstarch

Preparation:

1. Select the "Grill" button on Ninja Foodi Smart XL Grill and regulate the settings at MED for 18 minutes. 2. In a large bowl, mingle the garlic, vinegar, soy sauce, salt, and black pepper. 3. Add the pork ribs and generously coat with the garlic mixture.
4. Refrigerate to marinate overnight and then dredge with the cornstarch. 5. Drizzle with oil and place in the Ninja Foodi when it displays "Add Food". 6. Grill for about 18 minutes, tossing once in the middle way. 7. Dole out in a platter and serve warm.

Serving Suggestions: Serve with lemon juice on top.
Variation Tip: You can also use white vinegar instead of rice vinegar.
Nutritional Information per Serving: Calories: 681 | Fat: 52.7g | Sat Fat: 18.7g | Carbohydrates: 11.2g | Fiber: 0.2g | Sugar: 0.1g | Protein: 34.6g

BBQ Pork Ribs

Prep Time: 10 minutes | Cook Time: 12 minutes | Servings: 6

Ingredients:

2 pounds boneless country-style pork ribs   ½ cup BBQ sauce
Salt and ground black pepper, as required

Preparation:

1. Season the ribs with salt and black pepper evenly. 2. Coat the ribs with about ¼ cup of sauce. 3. Arrange the lightly greased "Grill Grate" in the crisper basket in the cooking pot of Ninja Foodi Smart XL Grill. 4. Close the Grill with lid and press "Power" button. 5. Select "Grill" and then use the set of arrows to the left of the display to adjust the temperature to "HI". 6. Use the set of arrows to the right of the display to adjust the cook time to 12 minutes. 7. Press "Start/Stop" to begin preheating. When the display shows "Add Food", open the lid and place the ribs onto the "Grill Grate". 8. With your hands, gently press down the ribs. Close the Grill with lid. 9. After 9 minutes of cooking, flip the ribs and coat with remaining sauce. 10. When the cooking time is completed, open the lid and serve hot.

Serving Suggestions: Serve alongside fresh greens.
Variation Tip: Use your favorite BBQ sauce.
Nutritional Information per Serving: Calories: 247 | Fat: 5.4g | Sat Fat: 1.8g | Carbohydrates: 7.6g | Fiber: 0.1g | Sugar: 5.4g | Protein: 39.6g

Beef & Feta Burgers

Prep Time: 15 minutes | Cook Time: 14 minutes | Servings: 4

Ingredients:

1 ⅓ pounds ground beef   Salt and ground black pepper, as required
1 tablespoon plain yogurt   4 ounces feta cheese, cut into 4 slices
2 teaspoons dried thyme

Preparation:

1. In a large bowl, add all the ingredients except for feta and mix until well combined. 2. Make 8 patties from the mixture. 3. Place 1 cheese slice between two patties, and press slightly to seal the edges. 4. Repeat with remaining beef patties and cheese slices. 5. Arrange the lightly greased "Grill Grate" in the crisper basket in the cooking pot of Ninja Foodi Smart XL Grill. 6. Close the Grill with lid and press "Power" button. 7. Select "Grill" and then use the set of arrows to the left of the display to adjust the temperature to "MED". 8. Use the set of arrows to the right of the display to adjust the cook time to 14 minutes. 9. When the display shows "Add Food", open the lid and place the patties onto the "Grill Grate". 10. With your hands, gently press down each patty. Close the Grill with lid. 11. After 7 minutes of cooking, flip the patties. 12. When the cooking time is completed, open the lid and serve hot.

Serving Suggestions: Serve with the topping of sour cream.
Variation Tip: Use best quality ground beef.
Nutritional Information per Serving: Calories: 295 | Fat: 16.9g | Sat Fat: 8.3g | Carbohydrates: 1.8g | Fiber: 0.2g | Sugar: 1.4g | Protein: 34g

Chapter 7 Dessert Recipes

Lava Cake

Prep Time: 15 minutes | Cook Time: 12½ minutes | Servings: 4

Ingredients:

⅔ cup chocolate chips
½ cup unsalted butter, softened
2 large eggs
2 large egg yolks
1 cup confectioners' sugar

1 teaspoon peppermint extract
⅓ cup all-purpose flour plus more for dusting
2 tablespoons powdered sugar
⅓ cup fresh raspberries

Preparation:

1. Microwave chocolate chips and butter on high heat for about 30 seconds. Stir the mixture well. 2. Whisk the eggs, powdered sugar, confectioners' sugar, peppermint extract. and egg yolks until well combined. 3. Add the flour and fold gently, stirring to combine. 4. Select "Bake" mode on Ninja Foodi smart XL grill and regulate the temperature to 375°F. Let it preheat for 10 minutes. 5. Grease 4 ramekins with butter and dust each with a bit of flour. 6. Place the mixture evenly into the prepared ramekins. 7. When Ninja Foodi displays "Add Food," arrange the ramekins into the tray. Bake for about 10-12 minutes. 8. When they are done, place the ramekins on a wire rack for about 5 minutes. 9. Loosen the cake by running a spatulla or knife around the sides of the ramekins. 10. Finally, invert each cake onto a dessert plate and dust it with powdered sugar. 11. Garnish with fresh raspberries. Serve warm immediately.
Serving Suggestions: Serve with vanilla ice cream and cherry sauce.
Variation Tip: You can also use fresh fruits with the lava cake.
Nutritional Information per Serving: Calories: 424 | Fat: 24.1g | Sat Fat: 14.7g | Carbohydrates: 47.5g | Fiber: 1.1g | Sugar: 12.9g | Protein: 4.8g

Brownies

Prep Time: 10 minutes | Cook Time: 18 minutes | Servings: 12

Ingredients:

1 packet Ghiradelli Brownie Mix
1 egg

⅓ cup vegetable oil
2 teaspoons water

Preparation:

1. Take a bowl and add all ingredients to it. Mix well. 2. Place the mixture in the brownie mold. 3. Select "Bake" mode in the Ninja Foodi Smart XL Grill. Regulate the temperature at 325°F for 18 minutes; when it displays "Add Food," place the brownie mould in the Ninja Foodi. 4. Bake for 18 minutes and place a toothpick in the brownie. If it comes clean, they are baked. 5. Dish out and serve.
Serving Suggestions: Serve hot with coffee.
Variation Tip: You can add in some walnuts.
Nutritional Information per Serving: Calories: 279 | Fat: 14g | Sat Fat: 2.6g | Carbohydrates: 39g | Fiber: 1.1g | Sugar: 14g | Protein: 2.5g

Brownies Muffins

Prep Time: 10 minutes | Cook Time: 20 minutes | Servings: 12

Ingredients:

1 package Betty Crocker fudge brownie mix
¼ cup walnuts, chopped

1 egg
⅓ cup vegetable oil
2 teaspoons water

Preparation:

1. In a bowl, mix well all the ingredients. 2. Select "Bake" on the Ninja Foodi Smart XL Grill and set the temperature to 300°F and the cook time to 20 minutes. 3. Grease 12 muffin molds with oil. 4. Place the mixture evenly into the prepared muffin molds. 5. Arrange the molds into the Ninja Foodi cooking pot. 6. Bake for 20 minutes at 300°F. Insert a toothpick in the middle. If it comes out clean, then the muffins are ready. 7. Remove the muffin molds from the grill for about 10 minutes. 8. Finally, invert the muffins onto a wire rack to completely cool before serving. 9. Serve and enjoy!
Serving Suggestions: Serve with hot coffee.
Variation Tip: You can also add in some milk chocolate chunks.
Nutritional Information per Serving: Calories: 235 | Fat: 9.6g | Sat Fat: 1.4g | Carbohydrates: 35.6g | Fiber: 1.8g | Sugar: 24.1g | Protein: 2.7g

Milky Donuts

Prep Time: 15 minutes | Cook Time: 24 minutes | Servings: 12

Ingredients:

For Doughnuts

1 cup all-purpose flour
1 cup whole wheat flour
2 teaspoons baking powder
Salt, to taste
¾ cup sugar

1 egg
1 tablespoon butter, softened
½ cup milk
2 teaspoons vanilla extract

For Glaze

2 tablespoons icing sugar
1 tablespoon cocoa powder

2 tablespoons condensed milk

Preparation:

1. Select "Air Crisp" mode on the Ninja Foodi Smart XL Grill and Set the temperature to 390°F. Set the cook time to 7 minutes. 2. Mix dry ingredients in a large bowl, including flours, salt, and baking powder. 3. In another bowl, whisk sugar and egg until fluffy and light. 4. Add the flour mixture and stir until well combined. 5. Add the butter, milk, and vanilla extract and mix until a soft dough forms. 6. Refrigerate the dough for at least 1 hour. 7. Now, roll the dough to ½-inch thickness. 8. Cut 24 small doughnuts from the rolled dough with a small doughnut cutter. 9. Grease the cooking pot. Place doughnuts in a single layer on the tray and air fry for about 6-8 minutes. 10. Remove from the air fryer and transfer the doughnuts onto a platter to cool completely. 11. Mix the condensed milk, cocoa powder, and icing sugar in a small bowl. 12. Spread the glaze over the doughnuts. Serve.

Serving Suggestions: Sprinkle with sugar sprinkles and serve with coffee.

Variation Tip: You can use vanilla frosting.

Nutritional Information per Serving: Calories: 134 | Fat: 2.1g | Sat Fat: 1.1g | Carbohydrates: 26.9g | Fiber: 0.8g | Sugar: 16.2g | Protein: 2.6g

Raisin Bread Pudding

Prep Time: 15 minutes | Cook Time: 12 minutes | Servings: 4

Ingredients:

1 cup milk
1 egg
1 tablespoon brown sugar
½ teaspoon ground cinnamon
¼ teaspoon vanilla extract

2 tablespoons raisins, soaked in hot water for about 15 minutes
2 bread slices, cut into small cubes
1 tablespoon chocolate chips
1 tablespoon sugar

Preparation:

1. Mix well milk, egg, cinnamon, brown sugar, and vanilla extract in a mixing bowl and stir in the raisins. 2. In a baking dish, spread the bread cubes and top evenly with the milk mixture. 3. Refrigerate for about 15-20 minutes. 4. Select "Broil" mode on Ninja Foodi Smart XL Grill and regulate the temperature to 375°F. Set the cook time to 12 minutes. 5. Remove from refrigerator and sprinkle with chocolate chips and sugar on top. 6. Arrange the dish in Ninja Foodi once it displays "Add Food," and broil for about 12 minutes. 7. Remove from the Ninja Foodi and serve warm.

Serving Suggestions: Serve with whipped cream or cream cheese frosting.

Variation Tip: You can add walnuts as well.

Nutritional Information per Serving: Calories: 119 | Fat: 3.4g | Sat Fat: 1.7g | Carbohydrates: 18.3g | Fiber: 0.6g | Sugar: 12.4g | Protein: 4.4g

Grilled Pineapple Dessert

Prep Time: 2 minutes | Cook Time: 10 minutes | Servings: 2

Ingredients:

8 slices of fresh pineapple
1 teaspoon ground cinnamon

2 teaspoons brown sugar

Preparation:

1. Select "Grill" on Ninja Foodi Smart XL Grill on HI for 10 minutes. 2. Sprinkle some sugar and cinnamon on the pineapple slices on both sides. 3. In a single layer, place pineapple slices on the grill once it displays "Add Food ." Grill at LO for 7 minutes, flipping them halfway through the cooking time. 4. Serve warm, and enjoy!

Serving Suggestions: You can serve it with some maple syrup, honey, and ice cream.

Variation Tip: You can add chopped nuts.

Nutritional Information per Serving: Calories: 199 | Fat: 1.1g | Sat Fat: 0g | Carbohydrates: 49.6g | Fiber: 7.2g | Sugar: 40.4g | Protein: 2.9g

Pumpkin Streusel Pie Bars

Prep Time: 15 minutes | Cook Time: 45 minutes | Servings: 16

Ingredients:

1¾ cups all-purpose flour
⅔ cup quick-cooking oats
⅔ cup light brown sugar, firmly packed
1 cup cold butter, diced
1 (16-ounce) can of pumpkin
1 (14-ounce) can condensed milk,

sweetened
1½ teaspoons pumpkin pie spice
1 teaspoon salt, divided
1 teaspoon lemon zest
2 large eggs

Preparation:

1. Select "Bake" mode on Ninja Foodi Smart XL Grill and regulate the temperature to 350°F. Set the cook time to 10 minutes. 2. Prepare the pan with baking spray and flour, line it with parchment paper extending the sides. Set aside. 3. In a large mixing bowl, combine flour, oats, brown sugar, and ½ teaspoon salt. Mix butter until the mixture appears crumbly. Gently press the mixture into the bottom of the pan. 4. When Ninja Foodi displays "Add Food", place the pan in Ninja Foodi and bake for 10 minutes. Once done, let it cool for 30 minutes. 5. Whisk pumpkin, condensed milk, eggs, pumpkin pie spice, lemon zest, and remaining ½ teaspoon salt in a large mixing bowl. Pour over the cooled crust. 6. Place the pan in Ninja Foodi and bake until the filling is set, about 45 minutes. 7. Let it cool completely. Refrigerate for about 4 hours. 8. Using the edges of the foil, lift from the pan. Cut into squares using a serrated knife.
Serving Suggestions: Serve with whipped cream or mascarpone cheese.
Variation Tip: You can use cinnamon powder as well.
Nutritional Information per Serving: Calories: 337 | Fat: 14.9g | Sat Fat: 9g | Carbohydrates: 46g | Fiber: 2g | Sugar: 22.7g | Protein: 6.3g

Air Fryer S'mores

Prep Time: 1 minute | Cook Time: 4 minutes | Servings: 4

Ingredients:

8 Graham crackers
4 marshmallows

4 Hershey's chocolate bar

Preparation:

1. Select "Air Crisp" mode on Ninja Foodi Smart XL Grill and regulate the temperature to 390°F. Set the cook time to 4 minutes. 2. Using a graham cracker, place half on the cooking pot with one marshmallow on top. 3. Air crisp at 390°F for 4 minutes. 4. Once done, carefully remove with tongs and add the chocolate and other graham crackers on top. Serve.
Serving Suggestions: Serve with whipped cream or peanut butter.
Variation Tip: You can use gluten-free graham crackers for a healthier option.
Nutritional Information per Serving: Calories: 93 | Fat: 4g | Sat Fat: 2g | Carbohydrates: 14g | Fiber: 1g | Sugar: 9g | Protein: 1g

Chocolate Mug cake

Prep Time: 15 minutes | Cook Time: 13minutes | Servings: 1

Ingredients:

¼ cup self-rising flour
5 tablespoons caster sugar
1 tablespoon cocoa powder

3 tablespoons coconut oil
3 tablespoons whole milk

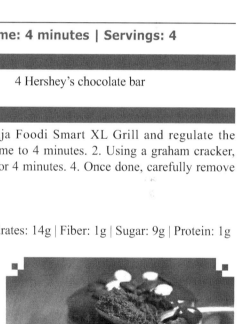

Preparation:

1. In a shallow mug, add all the ingredients and mix until well combined. 2. Select "Bake" mode on Ninja Foodi smart XL grill and set the temperature to 390°F. Set the cook time to 13 minutes. 3. Arrange the mug into the Ninja Foodi once it displays "Add Food." 4. Bake for about 13 minutes. 5. Remove from Ninja Foodi and serve warm.
Serving Suggestions: Top with chocolate ganache and mini marshmallows
Variation Tip: You can substitute chocolate for cocoa powder
Nutritional Information per Serving: Calories: 536 | Fat: 43.3g | Sat Fat: 36.6g | Carbohydrates: 37.2g | Fiber: 2.5g | Sugar: 11g | Protein: 5.7g

Stuffed Apples

Prep Time: 15 minutes | Cook Time: 13 minutes | Servings: 4

Ingredients:

For Stuffed Apples:
4 small firm apples, cored
½ cup golden raisins

2 tablespoons sugar
½ cup blanched almonds

For Vanilla Sauce:
½ cup whipped cream
2 tablespoons sugar

½ teaspoon vanilla extract

Preparation:

1. In a food processor, add raisins, almonds, and sugar and pulse until chopped. 2. Carefully stuff each apple with a raisin mixture. 3. Select "Air Crisp" mode on the Ninja Foodi Smart XL Grill. Set the temperature to 355°F. Set the cook time to 10 minutes. 4. Line Ninja Foodi cooking pot with parchment paper. Place apples into the prepared pot once Ninja Foodi displays "Add Food." 5. Air crisp for about 10 minutes. 6. For the vanilla sauce: in a pan, add the cream, sugar, and vanilla extract and cook until the sugar is dissolved, stirring continuously. 7. Once the apples are done, remove the pot from Ninja Foodi and transfer the apples onto plates to cool slightly. 8. Top with the vanilla sauce and serve.

Serving Suggestions: Top with cream cheese frosting.

Variation Tip: You can use cinnamon and brown sugar.

Nutritional Information per Serving: Calories: 329 | Fat: 11.1g | Sat Fat: 3.4g | Carbohydrates: 60.2g | Fiber: 7.6g | Sugar: 46.5g | Protein: 4g

Peach Cobbler

Prep Time: 5 minutes | Cook Time: 10 minutes | Servings: 1

Ingredients:

For the Peaches:
1 peach ripe
½ tablespoon brown sugar

½ tablespoon butter, melted
1 pinch cinnamon

For the Topping:
1 tablespoon all-purpose flour
1 tablespoon rolled oats
1 tablespoon melted butter

½ tablespoon brown sugar
1 pinch cinnamon

Preparation:

1. Select "Broil" mode on Ninja Foodi Smart XL Grill and regulate it at 375°F for 3 to 5 minutes. 2. Grease a ramekin with oil or butter. Remove the pit from the peach and cut it into ½-inch slices. 3. In a small bowl. Melt butter in the microwave. Then, add brown sugar, cinnamon, and sliced peaches. Gently toss until peaches are well-coated in a cinnamon-sugar mixture. Layer peach slices in the bottom of the ramekin. 4. Mix flour, oats, brown sugar, and cinnamon in a separate bowl. Mix well. Cut cold butter into small pieces and then press it into the dry mixture using a fork. Mix until the crumbly topping forms. Sprinkle the topping over the peaches evenly. 5. Place ramekin in preheated Ninja Foodi Smart XL Grill when it says 'Add Food' and broil for 10 minutes. Remove when the topping is golden brown, and the peaches are tender. 6. Serve hot!

Serving Suggestions: Serve with ice cream or whipped cream.

Variation Tip: You can top it up with salted caramel as well. You can use any other fruit.

Nutritional Information per Serving: Calories: 171 | Fat: 2g | Sat Fat: 1g | Carbohydrates: 38g | Fiber: 3g | Sugar: 26g | Protein: 4g

Air Fried Oreos

Prep Time: 2 minutes | Cook Time: 6 minutes | Servings: 12

Ingredients:

12 oreos
1 cup pancake mix

1 cup milk
¼ cup water

Preparation:

1. Select "Air Crisp" mode in the Ninja Foodi Smart XL Grill. Regulate temperature at 360°F andset the cook time to 6 minutes. 2. Combine pancake mix with milk and water. 3. Once the Ninja Foodi Smart XL Grill displays "Add Food," dip each oreo into the mix and place it in the preheated cooking pot. 4. Be sure to coat the cookie thoroughly; you may need to use your fingers to work the batter around it. 5. Cook for 6 minutes, flipping halfway through the cooking time.

Serving Suggestions: Garnish with powdered sugar.

Variation Tip: You can serve it with whipping cream.

Nutritional Information per Serving: Calories: 344 | Fat: 23g | Sat Fat: 5.3g | Carbohydrates: 19g | Fiber: 8g | Sugar: 6g | Protein: 17g

Vanilla Donuts

Prep Time: 20 minutes | Cook Time: 6 minutes | Servings: 8

Ingredients:

2 cups powdered sugar
¼ cup whole milk
1 teaspoon vanilla extract

1 (16-ounce) tube prepared biscuit dough
Non-stick cooking spray
½ teaspoon ground cinnamon

Preparation:

1. For glaze: in a medium-sized bowl, place the powdered sugar, milk, and vanilla extract and beat well. Set aside. 2. Arrange the biscuit dough onto a smooth surface. 3. With a 1-inch ring mold, cut a hole in the center of each round of dough. 4. Place dough rounds onto a plate and refrigerate for about 5 minutes. 5. Coat each dough round with cooking spray evenly. 6. Arrange the lightly greased "Grill Grate" in the crisper basket in the cooking pot of Ninja Foodi Smart XL Grill. 7. Close the Grill with lid and press "Power" button. 8. Select "Grill" and then use the set of arrows to the left of the display to adjust the temperature to "MED" 9. Use the set of arrows to the right of the display to adjust the cook time to 3 minutes. 10. Press "Start/Stop" to begin preheating. When the display shows "Add Food", open the lid and place 4 donut rounds onto the "Grill Grate". 11. With your hands, gently press down each donut. Close the Grill with lid. 12. When the cooking time is completed, open the lid and transfer the donuts onto a platter. 13. Repeat with the remaining donuts. 14. Coat the warm donuts with glaze and sprinkle with cinnamon. 15. Serve immediately.

Serving Suggestions: Serve with the sprinkling of sprinkles.

Variation Tip: Use pure vanilla extract.

Nutritional Information per Serving: Calories: 303 | Fat: 8.1g | Sat Fat: 3.1g | Carbohydrates: 53g | Fiber: 0.8g | Sugar: 33g | Protein: 4.2g

Mini Apple Pies

Prep Time: 20 minutes | Cook Time: 30 minutes | Servings: 6

Ingredients:

For Crust:
1½ cups flour
1 teaspoon sugar
½ cup unsalted butter

¼ cup chilled water
Salt, to taste

For Filling:
4 Granny Smith apples, peeled and finely chopped
1 teaspoon fresh lemon zest, finely grated
1 teaspoon ground cinnamon
¼ teaspoon ground nutmeg

2½ tablespoons sugar
2 tablespoons flour
Salt, to taste
2 tablespoons fresh lemon juice
2 tablespoons butter

For Topping:
1 egg, beaten
1 teaspoon ground cinnamon

3 tablespoons sugar

Preparation:

1. For Crust: Mix flour, sugar, butter, and salt well in a bowl. Add chilled water and mix until a dough forms. With plastic wrap, cover the bowl and refrigerate for about 30 minutes. 2. For filling: In a large bowl, mix well all the ingredients. Set aside. 3. For topping: In a separate bowl, combine the beaten egg, cinnamon, and sugar. 4. Assemble: Roll the dough to ½-inch thickness. 5. With a ramekin, cut 12 circles from the dough. 6. Place 6 circles in the bottom of 6 ramekins and press slightly. 7. Add the filling mixture to the ramekins and top with the remaining circles. 8. Pinch the edges to seal the pies. 9. Carefully cut 3 slits in each pastry and coat evenly with the beaten egg. 10. Sprinkle each pie with cinnamon-sugar mixture. 11. Select "Bake" mode on Ninja Foodi Smart XL Grill and set the temperature to 350°F. Set the cook time to 30 minutes. 12. Once the grill is preheated and displays "Add Food," arrange the ramekins into the cooking pot. 13. Bake for about 30 minutes. 14. Once done, remove the ramekins and leave to cool for about 10-15 minutes before serving. 15. Serve warm.

Serving Suggestions: Drizzle salted caramel sauce.

Variation Tip: You can skip the lemon zest.

Nutritional Information per Serving: Calories: 442 | Fat: 22.6g | Sat Fat: 2.1g | Carbohydrates: 58.2g | Fiber: 9g | Sugar: 29.2g | Protein: 5.2g

Strawberry Cupcakes

Prep Time: 20 minutes | Cook Time: 12 minutes | Servings: 12

Ingredients:

For Cupcakes
2 cups refined flour
¾ cup icing sugar
2 teaspoons beet powder
For Frosting:
1 cup butter
1 (8-ounces) package of cream cheese, softened
2 teaspoons vanilla extract

1 teaspoon cocoa powder
¾ cup peanut butter
3 eggs

¼ teaspoon salt
4½ cups powdered sugar
Few drops of pink food color

Preparation:

1. For cupcakes: In a bowl, put all the ingredients, and with an electric whisker, whisk until well combined. 2. Place the mixture into silicon cups. 3. Select "Bake" mode on Ninja Foodi Smart XL Grill and regulate the temperature to 340°F. Set the cook time to 10 minutes. 4. Once it displays "Add Food," place the silicon cups into the Ninja Foodi cooking pot. 5. Bake for about 10-12 minutes 6. Remove the silicon cups from the grill and let the cupcakes cool on a wire rack for a couple of minutes. 7. For frosting: Mix butter, cream cheese, vanilla extract, and salt in a large bowl. Add the powdered sugar (slowly and gradually), whisking well after each addition. Add a few drops of pinkfood color. 8. Pipe frosting over each cupcake. 9. Garnish with fresh strawberries and serve.

Serving Suggestions: Sprinkle some wafers.

Variation Tip: You can use cream cheese frosting as well.

Nutritional Information per Serving: Calories: 599 | Fat: 31.5g | Sat Fat: 4.1g | Carbohydrates: 73.2g | Fiber: 8g | Sugar: 53.4g | Protein: 9.3g

Fruity Crumble

Prep Time: 15 minutes | Cook Time: 20 minutes | Servings: 6

Ingredients:

1 cup all-purpose flour
½ cup fresh blackberries
⅓ cup sugar, divided
1 tablespoon fresh lemon juice

1 fresh apricot, pitted and cubed
Pinch of salt
1 tablespoon cold water
¼ cup chilled butter, cubed

Preparation:

1. Select "Broil" mode on the Ninja Foodi Smart XL Grill. Set the temperature to 390°F. Set the cook time to 10 minutes. Grease a baking pan. 2. Toss apricots, blackberries, 2 tablespoons of sugar, and lemon juice in a large bowl. 3. Spread the fruit mixture into the prepared baking pan. 4. Mix the flour with the remaining sugar, salt, water, and butter in another bowl. Mix until the mixture becomes crumbly. 5. Spread the flour mixture evenly over the fruit mixture. 6. When the Ninja Foodi Smart XL Grill displays " Add Food," place the pan on the cooking pot. Broil for about 20 minutes. 7. Remove the baking pan and serve warm.

Serving Suggestions: Serve with fresh whipped cream and raspberries.

Variation Tip: You can use brown sugar.

Nutritional Information per Serving: Calories: 291 | Fat: 12g | Sat Fat: 7.4g | Carbohydrates: 43.3g | Fiber: 2g | Sugar: 18.5g | Protein: 3.7g

Lemon Bars

Prep Time: 15 minutes | Cook Time: 25 minutes | Servings: 12

Ingredients:

For the crust:
1½ cups packed almond flour, fine-blanched
2 tablespoons coconut flour
¼ teaspoon almond extract

¼ teaspoon salt
¼ cup butter, melted and cooled
¼ cup pure maple syrup

For the filling:
Zest from 1 lemon
½ cup pure maple syrup
4 large eggs

⅔ cup lemon juice, freshly squeezed
1 tablespoon coconut flour, sifted

Preparation:

1. Select "Bake" mode on Ninja Foodi Smart XL Grill. Set the temperature to 350°Fahrenheit and the cook time to 10 minutes. 2. Grease the cooking pot with butter. 3. To prepare the crust, combine the almond flour, salt, and coconut flour in a mixing bowl. Add butter, pure maple syrup, and almond extract in dry ingredients. Combine to form the dough with your hands; press the dough evenly into the prepared cooking pot. 4. Place the pot in the Ninja Foodi grill once it displays "Add Food," and bake for 15 minutes. 5. While the crust bakes, make the filling by whisking together the lemon zest, lemon juice, eggs, pure maple syrup, and sifted coconut flour in a mixing bowl. 6. When the crust is baked, pour the filling into it slowly and steadily. 7. Reduce temperature to 325°F, place the bars in the Ninja Foodi immediately, and bake for 20-25 minutes until the filling is set and no longer jiggles. 8. Cool on a wire rack before refrigerating for at least 4 hours to firm up the bars. Cut out 12 bars with a sharp knife. 9. Serve and enjoy!

Serving Suggestions: Garnish with lemon zest.

Variation Tip: You can also use arrowroot starch instead of coconut flour.

Nutritional Information per Serving: Calories: 84 | Fat: 4.4g | Sat Fat: 1.3g | Carbohydrates: 8g | Fiber: 1g | Sugar: 5.7g | Protein: 3.1g

Apple Bread Pudding

Prep Time: 15 minutes | Cook Time: 44 minutes | Servings: 8

Ingredients:

For Bread Pudding
10½ ounces bread, cubed
½ cup apple, peeled, cored, and chopped
½ cup raisins
¼ cup walnuts, chopped
1½ cups milk

¾ cup water
5 tablespoons honey
2 teaspoons ground cinnamon
2 teaspoons cornstarch
1 teaspoon vanilla extract

For Topping
1⅓ cups plain flour
½ cup brown sugar

7 tablespoons butter

Preparation:

1. Mix bread, apples, raisins, and walnuts in a large bowl. 2. Add the remaining pudding ingredients in the milk in another bowl and pour in the bread mixture. Mix until well combined. 3. Refrigerate for about 15 minutes, tossing occasionally. 4. For the topping: In a bowl, mix the flour and sugar. Add cold butter cubes until a crumbly mixture forms. 5. Select " Air Crisp" mode on the Ninja Foodi Smart XL Grill. Regulate the temperature to 355°F. Set the cook time to 22 minutes. 6. Place the mixture evenly into 2 baking pans and spread the topping mixture on top of each. 7. Place the pans into the crisper basket once Ninja Foodi displays "Add Food." Air crisp for about 22 minutes. 8. Remove from Ninja Foodi and serve warm.

Serving Suggestions: Sprinkle powdered sugar and serve with caramel sauce.

Variation Tip: You can add a pinch of nutmeg for taste variation.

Nutritional Information per Serving: Calories: 432 | Fat: 14.8g | Sat Fat: 2.1g | Carbohydrates: 69.1g | Fiber: 4.7g | Sugar: 32g | Protein: 7.9g

Vanilla Soufflé

Prep Time: 15 minutes | Cook Time: 39 minutes | Servings: 6

Ingredients:

¼ cup butter, softened
¼ cup all-purpose flour
½ cup plus 2 tablespoons sugar, divided
1 cup milk
3 teaspoons vanilla extract, divided

4 egg yolks
5 egg whites
1 teaspoon cream of tartar
2 tablespoons confectioners' sugar plus extra for dusting

Preparation:

1. In a mixing bowl, mix butter and flour until smooth paste forms. 2. Mix ½ cup of sugar and milk in a pan over low heat and cook, stirring continuously. Soon the sugar will be dissolved. 3. Add the flour mixture, whisking continuously, and simmer for about 3-4 minutes or until the mixture becomes thick. 4. Stir in 1 teaspoon of vanilla extract. Set aside for 10 minutes to cool. 5. In a bowl, mix egg yolks and 1 teaspoon of vanilla extract. 6. Add the egg yolk mixture into the milk mixture and mix until well combined. 7. Add the egg whites, cream of tartar, remaining sugar, and vanilla extract in another bowl and whisk until stiff peaks form. 8. Gently fold the egg whites mixture into the milk mixture. 9. Select "Bake" mode in Ninja Foodi Smart XL Grill and set the temperature to 330°F. Set the cook time to 15 minutes. 10. Grease 6 ramekins and sprinkle each with a pinch of sugar. Place the mixture evenly into the prepared ramekins, and smooth the top surface with the back of a spoon. 11. Arrange the ramekins into the Ninja Foodi in 2 batches. 12. Bake souffle for about 14-16 minutes when Ninja Foodi displays "Add Food." When done, remove from Ninja Foodi and cool slightly. 13. Sprinkle with the powdered sugar and serve warm.

Serving Suggestions: Serve with vanilla cookies.

Variation Tip: You can also use gluten-free flour or almond flour

Nutritional Information per Serving: Calories: 238 | Fat: 11.6g | Sat Fat: 6.5g | Carbohydrates: 26.5g | Fiber: 0.1g | Sugar: 21.7g | Protein: 6.8g

Chocolate Souffle

Prep Time: 15 minutes | Cook Time: 16 minutes | Servings: 2

Ingredients:

3 ounces semi-sweet chocolate, chopped
½ teaspoon pure vanilla extract
2 tablespoons all-purpose flour
¼ cup butter

2 eggs, egg yolks, and whites separated
3 tablespoons sugar
1 teaspoon powdered sugar plus extra for dusting

Preparation:

1. In a microwave-safe bowl, put the butter and chocolate. Microwave on high heat for about 2 minutes or until melted completely, stirring after every 30 seconds. 2. Remove from microwave and stir the mixture until smooth. 3. In another bowl, whisk egg yolk with sugar and vanilla extract. 4. Add the chocolate mixture and mix until well combined. 5. Gently fold the flour in the mixture and mix well. 6. Whisk egg whites in a separate bowl and whisk until soft peaks form. 7. Fold the whipped egg whites in 3 portions into the chocolate mixture. 8. Select "Air Crisp" mode on the Ninja Foodi smart XL grill and set the temperature to 330°F. Preheat on high for 10 min. 9. Grease 2 ramekins and sprinkle each with a pinch of sugar. 10. Place the mixture evenly into the prepared ramekins, and smooth the top surface with the back of a spoon. 11. Arrange the ramekins in the Ninja Foodi once it displays "Add Food". Air fry for about 14 minutes. 12. Remove from the air fryer and set aside to cool slightly. 13. Sprinkle with the powdered sugar and serve warm with ice cream on the side.

Serving Suggestions: Top with some chocolate ganache.

Variation Tip: You can use dark chocolate instead of semi-sweet chocolate.

Nutritional Information per Serving: Calories: 569 | Fat: 38.8g | Sat Fat: 23g | Carbohydrates: 54.1g | Fiber: 0.5g | Sugar: 42.4g | Protein: 6.9g

Shortbread Fingers

Prep Time: 15 minutes | Cook Time: 12 minutes | Servings: 10

Ingredients:

⅓ cup caster sugar
1⅔ cups plain flour

¾ cup butter

Preparation:

1. In a bowl, mix sugar, flour, and butter. Mix until a smooth dough forms. 2. Cut the dough into 10 equal-sized fingers. 3. With a fork, lightly prick the fingers. 4. Select "Bake" mode on Ninja Foodi Smart XL Grill and Set the temperature to 355°F. Set the cook time to 12 minutes. 5. Lightly grease the cooking pot and arrange fingers in a single layer. 6. Place the pot into the Ninja Foodi Smart XL Grill once it displays "Add Food," and bake for about 12 minutes. 7. Remove the shortbreads and let them cool for about 5-10 minutes. Serve.
Serving Suggestions: Serve with tea.
Variation Tip: You can use gluten-free flour.
Nutritional Information per Serving: Calories: 223 | Fat: 14g | Sat Fat: 8.8g | Carbohydrates: 22.6g | Fiber: 0.6g | Sugar: 6.7g | Protein: 2.3g

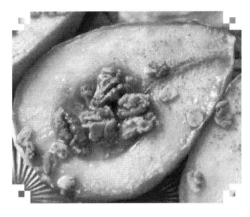

Maple Baked Pears

Prep Time: 10 minutes | Cook Time: 25 minutes | Servings: 4

Ingredients:

4 pears, cut into halves and cored
1 teaspoon pure vanilla extract

½ cup pure maple syrup
¼ teaspoon ground cinnamon

Preparation:

1. Select "Bake" mode in Ninja Foodi Smart XL Grill and preheat for 10 minutes at 375°Fahrenheit. 2. Take out the cooking pot and line it with parchment paper. 3. Mix pears with vanilla extract and maple syrup. Sprinkle cinnamon in and toss the pears. 4. When Ninja Foodi displays "Add Food," place the pears on the cooking pot and bake for 25 minutes. 5. Dish out and enjoy!
Serving Suggestions: You can serve it with honey and mascarpone cheese.
Variation Tip: You can add some nutmeg if you want.
Nutritional Information per Serving: Calories: 227 | Fat: 0.4g | Sat Fat: 0g | Carbohydrates: 58.5g | Fiber: 6.6g | Sugar: 44g | Protein: 0.8g

Sweet Plantains

Prep Time: 10 minutes | Cook Time: 8 minutes | Servings: 3

Ingredients:

2 plantains, cut in half and sliced horizontally
1 tablespoon butter, melted

1 tablespoon brown sugar
⅛ teaspoon ground cinnamon

Preparation:

1. Coat the plantain slices with melted butter evenly. 2. Arrange the lightly greased "Grill Grate" in the crisper basket in the cooking pot of Ninja Foodi Smart XL Grill. 3. Close the Grill with lid and press "Power" button. 4. Select "Grill" and then use the set of arrows to the left of the display to adjust the temperature to "MAX". 5. Use the set of arrows to the right of the display to adjust the cook time to 8 minutes. 6. Press "Start/Stop" to begin preheating. When the display shows "Add Food", open the lid and place the plantain slices onto the "Grill Grate". 7. With your hands, gently press down each plantain slice. Close the Grill with lid. 8. After 4 minutes, flip the plantain slices. 9. When the cooking time is completed, open the lid and transfer the plantain slices onto a plate. 10. Sprinkle with the brown sugar and cinnamon and serve.
Serving Suggestions: Serve with the topping of whipped cream.
Variation Tip: Plantain is best with a slightly firm texture.
Nutritional Information per Serving: Calories: 191 | Fat: 4.3g | Sat Fat: 2.6g | Carbohydrates: 41g | Fiber: 2.7g | Sugar: 20.7g | Protein: 1.6g

Apple Crisp

Prep Time: 10 minutes | Cook Time: 40 minutes | Servings: 12

Ingredients:

Filling
2½ pounds honeycrisp apples, thinly sliced
½ cup white sugar
½ tablespoon all purpose flour
1 teaspoon ground cinnamon
1 teaspoon ground nutmeg
½ cup water

Topping
1 cup old fashioned oats
1 cup all purpose flour
1 cup brown sugar packed
¼ teaspoon baking powder
¼ teaspoon baking soda
½ cup butter, softened

Preparation:

1. Select "Bake" mode in Ninja Foodi Smart XL Grill and regulate the temperature at 350°F for 40 minutes. 2. Place the sliced apples evenly in the Ninja Foodi Smart XL Grill cooking pot. 3. Mix the sugar, flour, cinnamon, and nutmeg in a bowl. 4. Evenly pour this over the apples. Then pour the water over the apples. Finally, mix apples to coat with sugar evenly. 5. Combine the oats, flour, brown sugar, baking powder, and baking soda in another bowl. Mix in the softened butter, which should be a crumbly mixture. 6. Evenly spread this mixture on top of the apples. 7. When Ninja Foodi Smart XL Grill displays "Add Food," place the cooking pot and let it bake for 40 minutes. Do check in between. 8. Serve warm and enjoy!

Serving Suggestions: Serve with Vanilla Ice Cream

Variation Tip: Add some nuts and top it with salted caramel for taste variation.

Nutritional Information per Serving: Calories: 444 | Fat: 14g | Sat Fat: 9g | Carbohydrates: 78g | Fiber: 5g | Sugar: 53g | Protein: 4g

Strawberry & Pineapple Skewers

Prep Time: 15 minutes | Cook Time: 10 minutes | Servings: 8

Ingredients:

2 cups pineapple, cut into 1-inch pieces
2 cups fresh strawberries, hulled

Olive oil cooking spray
2 tablespoons maple syrup

Preparation:

1. Thread the fruit pieces onto the pre-soaked wooden skewer. 2. Spray the skewers with cooking spray and then drizzle with maple syrup. 3. Arrange the lightly greased "Grill Grate" in the crisper basket in the cooking pot of Ninja Foodi Smart XL Grill. 4. Close the Grill with lid and press "Power" button. 5. Select "Grill" and then use the set of arrows to the left of the display to adjust the temperature to "MED". 6. Use the set of arrows to the right of the display to adjust the cook time to 10 minutes. 7. Press "Start/Stop" to begin preheating. When the display shows "Add Food", open the lid and place the skewers onto the "Grill Grate". 8. With your hands, gently press down each skewer. Close the Grill with lid. 9. While cooking, flip the skewers after every 3 minutes. 10. When the cooking time is completed, open the lid and serve warm.

Serving Suggestions: Serve with sweet yogurt dip.

Variation Tip: Use fresh fruit.

Nutritional Information per Serving: Calories: 45 | Fat: 0.2g | Sat Fat: 0g | Carbohydrates: 11.5g | Fiber: 1.3g | Sugar: 8.8g | Protein: 0.5g

Conclusion

This cookbook is packed with delicious recipes that are perfect for grilling. From burgers and chicken to seafood and vegetables, there's something for everyone in this cookbook. If you're like me, you love to grill. And if you're like me, you also love your Ninja Foodi. So when I saw that Ninja now has a Smart XL Grill, I was intrigued. And when I saw that it comes with six stainless steel kebab skewers, a roasting rack, and a recipe book, I was sold. I've only had it for a few days, but I've already used it to make grilled chicken, grilled vegetables, and kebabs. It's so easy to use and the results are amazing. The chicken was juicy and flavorful and the vegetables were perfectly cooked. The kebabs were my favorite – they were so juicy and had great flavor. I'm looking forward to trying more recipes from the included recipe book and I'm sure I'll be coming up with some of my own as well. If you love to grill, I highly recommend it!

Appendix 1 Measurement Conversion Chart

WEIGHT EQUIVALENTS

US STANDARD	METRIC (APPROXINATE)
1 ounce	28 g
2 ounces	57 g
5 ounces	142 g
10 ounces	284 g
15 ounces	425 g
16 ounces (1 pound)	455 g
1.5pounds	680 g
2pounds	907 g

VOLUME EQUIVALENTS (DRY)

US STANDARD	METRIC (APPROXIMATE)
⅛ teaspoon	0.5 mL
¼ teaspoon	1 mL
½ teaspoon	2 mL
¾ teaspoon	4 mL
1 teaspoon	5 mL
1 tablespoon	15 mL
¼ cup	59 mL
½ cup	118 mL
¾ cup	177 mL
1 cup	235 mL
2 cups	475 mL
3 cups	700 mL
4 cups	1 L

TEMPERATURES EQUIVALENTS

FAHRENHEIT(F)	CELSIUS (C) (APPROXIMATE)
225 °F	107 °C
250 °F	120 °C
275 °F	135 °C
300 °F	150 °C
325 °F	160 °C
350 °F	180 °C
375 °F	190 °C
400 °F	205 °C
425 °F	220 °C
450 °F	235 °C
475 °F	245 °C
500 °F	260 °C

VOLUME EQUIVALENTS (LIQUID)

US STANDARD	US STANDARD (OUNCES)	METRIC (APPROXIMATE)
2 tablespoons	1 fl.oz	30 mL
¼ cup	2 fl.oz	60 mL
½ cup	4 fl.oz	120 mL
1 cup	8 fl.oz	240 mL
1½ cup	12 fl.oz	355 mL
2 cups or 1 pint	16 fl.oz	475 mL
4 cups or 1 quart	32 fl.oz	1 L
1 gallon	128 fl.oz	4 L

Appendix 2 Air Fryer Cooking Chart

Meat and Seafood	Temp	Time (min)
Bacon	400°F	5 to 10
Beef Eye Round Roast (4 lbs.)	390°F	45 to 55
Bone to in Pork Chops	400°F	4 to 5 per side
Brats	400°F	8 to 10
Burgers	350°F	8 to 10
Chicken Breast	375°F	22 to 23
Chicken Tender	400°F	14 to 16
Chicken Thigh	400°F	25
Chicken Wings (2 lbs.)	400°F	10 to 12
Cod	370°F	8 to 10
Fillet Mignon (8 oz.)	400°F	14 to 18
Fish Fillet (0.5 lb., 1-inch)	400°F	10
Flank Steak (1.5 lbs.)	400°F	10 to 14
Lobster Tails (4 oz.)	380°F	5 to 7
Meatballs	400°F	7 to 10
Meat Loaf	325°F	35 to 45
Pork Chops	375°F	12 to 15
Salmon	400°F	5 to 7
Salmon Fillet (6 oz.)	380°F	12
Sausage Patties	400°F	8 to 10
Shrimp	375°F	8
Steak	400°F	7 to 14
Tilapia	400°F	8 to 12
Turkey Breast (3 lbs.)	360°F	40 to 50
Whole Chicken (6.5 lbs.)	360°F	75

Desserts	Temp	Time (min)
Apple Pie	320°F	30
Brownies	350°F	17
Churros	360°F	13
Cookies	350°F	5
Cupcakes	330°F	11
Doughnuts	360°F	5
Roasted Bananas	375°F	8
Peaches	350°F	5

Frozen Foods	Temp	Time (min)
Breaded Shrimp	400°F	9
Chicken Burger	360°F	11
Chicken Nudgets	400°F	10
Corn Dogs	400°F	7
Curly Fries (1 to 2 lbs.)	400°F	11 to 14
Fish Sticks (10 oz.)	400°F	10
French Fries	380°F	15 to 20
Hash Brown	360°F	15 to 18
Meatballs	380°F	6 to 8
Mozzarella Sticks	400°F	8
Onion Rings (8 oz.)	400°F	8
Pizza	390°F	5 to 10
Pot Pie	360°F	25
Pot Sticks (10 oz.)	400°F	8
Sausage Rolls	400°F	15
Spring Rolls	400°F	15 to 20

Vegetables	Temp	Time (min)
Asparagus	375°F	4 to 6
Baked Potatoes	400°F	35 to 45
Broccoli	400°F	8 to 10
Brussels Sprouts	350°F	15 to 18
Butternut Squash (cubed)	375°F	20 to 25
Carrots	375°F	15 to 25
Cauliflower	400°F	10 to 12
Corn on the Cob	390°F	6
Eggplant	400°F	15
Green Beans	375°F	16 to 20
Kale	250°F	12
Mushrooms	400°F	5
Peppers	375°F	8 to 10
Sweet Potatoes (whole)	380°F	30 to 35
Tomatoes (halved, sliced)	350°F	10
Zucchini (½-inch sticks)	400°F	12

Appendix 3 Recipes Index

Made in the USA
Middletown, DE
28 November 2022

16238659R00085